You Gotta Have Wa

Also by Robert Whiting

The Chrysanthemum and the Bat

You Gotta Have Wa

Robert Whiting

Macmillan Publishing Company

New York

Collier Macmillan Publishers

London

Portions of *You Gotta Have Wa* were previously
published in *Smithsonian, Sports Illustrated, Reader's
Digest,* and *Winds.*

Macmillan Publishing Company
866 Third Avenue, New York, NY 10022
Collier Macmillan Canada, Inc.

Library of Congress Cataloging-in-Publication Data
Whiting, Robert
  You gotta have Wa/Robert Whiting.
    p. cm.

  1. Baseball—Japan.   I. Title
GV863.77.A1W47   1989   88-38408   CIP
796.357'0952—dc19

Printed in the United States of America

BOMC offers recordings and compact discs, cassettes
and records. For information and catalog write to
BOMR, Camp Hill, PA 17012.

To my wife Machiko, one of the few living Japanese who doesn't like baseball, but who still found it in her heart to help me with this book.

Contents

CONTENTS

Acknowledgments

I'd like to thank the following people who all helped me with this book in one way or another: Corky Alexander, editor-in-chief, *Tokyo Weekender;* Koichiro Ando, *Esquire Japan* editor; Michiko Araki, journalist; Randy Bass; Bob Brown, public relations director of the Baltimore Orioles; Connie Bond, associate editor, *Smithsonian;* Pete Carrie and Robert Creamer, *Sports Illustrated;* Warren Cromartie, outfielder, Tokyo Giants; Mrs. Roland A. Crowe; Neil Gross, *Business Week;* Masao Kikuchi, editor, *Playboy Japan;* Noriko Kobayashi, interpreter; Leron Lee and Leon Lee, S.K. Asahi Shimbun, Robert Klaverkamp, publisher, *AsiaWeek;* Brian McKenna; Midori Matsui, translator; Masayuki Matsumoto, writer; Anton Merkin; Kiyoshi Nagasawa, editor-in-chief *Esquire,* Japan; Mitsuyoshi Okazaki, Bungei Shinju; Jiro Oishii, *Daily Sports;* Gil Rogin, *Time-Life;* Morie Saito, Mainichi *Daily News;* Eduardo Sanchez, McCann-Erickson; Julia Scully, Fraser Steele, Paul Solman, McNeil-Lehrer; Takashi Shimada, Boston Consulting Group; Howard Smith, BBC; Shoichi Suzuki, *Shukan Gendai;* Yukiko Shimahara, interpreter; Dwight Spenser, Shunji Terada, *Nikkan Gendai;* Toshiyuki Ueda, *Gekan Gendai;* Alice Volpe, Robert Wargo, editor-in-chief, *Intersect;* Masahiko Watase, editor, *Shukan Gendai;* Junji Yamagiwa. Also a tip of the cap to the Carmel Oendan, Sheldon, Jo, Ned, Joseph, Margo, Buck, Debbie, Peggy, and also to Pat and Barbara Connor in New York.

Special thanks to Miwako Atarashi and the staff at the

Japanese Baseball Hall of Fame and Museum, for their ongoing kindness and cooperation; to Tom Chapman, editor of *Winds,* who published earlier versions of the Oendan and Koshien Tournament material and who provided much encouragement over the years; and to Greg Starr, associate editor at *Winds,* for his continuing support and for the title, "The Schoolboys of Summer."

Also a special note of gratitude to Bill Suzukawa of the *Daily Sports;* Kozo Abe of the *Yukan Fuji;* Hidesuke Matsuo, former chief editor of *Number;* and Atsushi Imamura of the *Weekly Bunshun,* for advice, assistance, and friendship offered—and gratefully accepted.

I am particularly grateful to Masayuki Tamaki, who helped me in so many ways. Tamaki-san gave me a guided tour of the wonders of Koshien High School ball, including a delightful trip to Rakusei Koko in Kyoto. He opened up the world of Meiji Era baseball to me and provided materials from his own private library. He also read the completed manuscript, ferreted out a number of errors, and offered thoughtful suggestions. To him—and to his wife Kyoko—I owe a special debt of gratitude.

In addition, I want to thank Greg Davis and Tim Porter for listening while I read parts of the manuscript to them, Elmer Luke, who read it all and suggested certain revisions, and, most of all, Tom Scully, in Tokyo, who edited the first finished draft and offered invaluable comments and insights in the process.

Finally, I wish to thank Betsy Rapoport, who started this project in the spring of 1987, and Rick Wolff, my astute and encouraging editor, who engineered it to a safe conclusion. To him, his associate Jeanine Bucek, and copy editor Paul Heacock, a big *"arigato."*

I researched this book over a period of years beginning in 1976 and ending in 1988. Much of that time, I lived in Tokyo writing for various Japanese and American publications. A previous book, *The Chrysanthemum and the*

Bat, was quite successful in Japan and many doors opened up to me as a result. The genesis of this book was an article I wrote for *Sports Illustrated,* entitled "You Gotta Have Wa." A subsequent piece I did for the *Smithsonian,* "East Meets West in the Japanese Game of Besuboru," brought MacMillan into the project.

I interviewed most of the people mentioned in this book, although Yoshiaki Tsutsumi and a couple of others could not make themselves available. I also relied on secondary sources—books, accounts in Japanese newspapers and magazines, and television reports—and many of the incidents described in the book. The Baseball Hall of Fame and Museum in the Tokyo Dome, with its library of 28,000 books and magazine articles was a particularly useful source of historical materials. Also informative were many of the museum's exhibits. The *Yokohama Kaiko Shiryo-Kan* provided Meiji Era newspapers, both in English and Japanese.

The list of interviewees includes the following: Joji Abe, Kozo Abe, Chris Arnold, Bruce Anderson, Toshiro Ashiki, Osamu Arai, Doug Ault, Roberto Barbon, Linda Bass, Randy Bass, Johnny Bench, Don Blasingame, Sara Blasingame, Clete Boyer, Hal Breeden, Dan Briggs, Rod Carew, Gary Carter, Bob Castillo, Mike Clark, Keith Comstock, Warren Cromartie, Hector Cruz, Tommy Cruz, Dick Davis, Takenori Emoto, Yutaka Enatsu, Fumio Furuya, Rich Gale, Clyde Haberman, David Halberstam, Isao Harimoto, Tatsunori Hara, Orel Hershisher, Whitey Herzog, Dave Hilton, Patti Hilton, Tsuneo Horiuchi, Bob Horner, Dick Howser, Prof. Masaru Ikei, Kazuo Ito, Atsushi Imamura, Naoki Inose, Tim Ireland, Kennichi Ishida, Dr. Frank Jobe, Dave Johnson, Toru Kawasaki, Dr. Robert Kerlan, Harvey Kurland, Sachio Kinugasa, Willy Kirkland, Nicola Koizumi, Bowie Kuhn, Toyo Kunimitsu, Pete LaCock, Rich Lancellotti, Leon Lee, Leron Lee, Pamela Lee, Vicquie Lee, Jim Lefebvre, Brad Leslie, Mike Lum,

ACKNOWLEDGMENTS

Ramona Lum, Jim Lyttle, Carolyn Macha, Ken Macha, Ted McAneely, Bill Madlock, Charlie Manuel, Beverly Marshall, Jim Marshall, Bobby Marcano, Gene Martin, Felix Millan, Don Money, Sharon Money, Masaaki Mori, Choji Murata, Yoshiko Murata, Shigeo Nagashima, Luigi Nakajima, Hiromichi Nakamura, Jumbo Nakane, Jim Nettles, Fumio Nishino, Katsuya Nomura, Hiromitsu Ochiai, Ben Oglivie, Kunikazu Ogawa, Sadaharu Oh, Masayaru Okada, Steve Ontiveros, Pat Ontiveros, Keiji Osawa, Carlos Ponce, Dave Roberts, Frank Robinson, Pete Rose, Mike Reinbach, Luis Sanchez, John Scott, Barney Schulz, Toshi Shimada, Takezo Shimoda, John Sipin, Reggie Smith, Faga Soluita, Tony Solaita, Daryl Spencer, Don Sutton, Bill Suzukawa, Ryuji Suzuki, Shoichi Suzuki, Naoki Takahashi, Kennichi Takemura, Masayuki Tamaki, Ichiro Tanuma, Okichi Terauchi, Gary Thomasson, Jim Tracy, Jim Tyrone, Toshiyuki Ueda, Tadahiro Ushigome, Masahiko Watase, Gregory Wells, Linda White, Roy White, Terry Whitfield, Bump Wills, Bucky Woy, Ichiro Yagi, Koji Yamamoto, Kazuhiro Yamauchi, Wally Yonamine, Jane Yonamine.

This book was written between September 1987 and August 1988 in Tokyo, Seoul, New York, Mogadishu, and Kamakura, using a Toshiba T1100PLUS battery-operated laptop computer.

Robert Whiting
Kamakura, Japan
November 1988

Introduction/Ground Rules

This is a book about the frequently unsuccessful attempts of Americans and Japanese to get along with each other— as seen through a sport they share in common. The following will help prepare you for entry into the strange and fascinating world of *besuboru*.

- The Japanese have been playing baseball for over one hundred years, professionally since 1935.
- There are two pro leagues, the Central and the Pacific, with six teams each. The pennant winners meet in late October in the Japan Series.
- Most teams are owned by major corporations for public relations purposes. For example, the Hanshin Tigers and the Kintetsu Buffaloes are owned by private railway companies. The Yomiuri Giants, Japan's most popular team, and the Chunichi Dragons belong to newspapers, while the Yakult Swallows and the Taiyo Whales are the property of a health food firm and a fish company, respectively. The Hiroshima Carp are jointly owned by the citizens of Hiroshima and Toyo Kogyo, a leading car manufacturer. The Nippon Ham Fighters are owned by a pork producer and the Seibu Lions by a leading land developer. In the fall of 1988, two long-standing Osaka-based franchises owned by railroad companies were sold. The Orient Leasing Company, a financial firm that leases computer office equipment, bought the Hankyu Braves,

while the Daiei Corporation, a supermarket chain operator, purchased the Nankai Hawks, and moved them to Fukuoka in Kyushu.

- The twelve teams play a 130-game schedule that begins in early April and ends in late September. However, the rainy season in mid-June through mid-July and the September typhoons collectively cause quite a few postponements; these games are made up in October each year before the Series.
- Ties are allowed and count in the official standings, the result of a rule which says no extra-inning may begin after four hours or twelve innings of play in the Pacific League and 12 innings in the Central League. This causes some unusual pennant race finishes. The Kintetsu Buffaloes lost the 1988 pennant to the Seibu Lions by a margin of .002 percentage points. The Buffaloes fell short in the final game of the season when the Lotte Orions held them to a 4–4 ten-inning tie that was called after four hours and twelve minutes of play.
- The Pacific League employs the designated hitter while the Central League does not.
- The teams fill their rosters with high school, college, and semipro stars in an annual player draft. Each franchise has a farm team which plays an eighty-game season. There are two minor leagues, the Eastern and the Western, with six teams each.
- The Japanese use bats manufactured from domestic wood, and their baseballs (marginally smaller than those used in the U.S. major leagues) are made from imported cowhide.
- They also use the same rulebook, in translation, although the Japanese strike zone is wider on each side of the plate by the width of one baseball.
- Most of the ballparks are somewhat smaller than

those in the U.S., although some like the Tokyo Dome have major league dimensions.

- The biggest star the Japanese game of baseball has ever produced is Sadaharu Oh, who hit 868 home runs in a twenty-two-year career for the Tokyo Giants (1959–80). Oh managed the Giants to one pennant in five years (1984–88) before he was asked to retire at the end of the 1988 season.

- Total attendance is estimated at 20 million annually, although there are no completely accurate attendance records kept. Whenever the Tokyo Giants play to a capacity crowd in their stadium (the Tokyo Dome), front-office executives announce the attendance as 56,000. Yet according to the local fire department, seating capacity in the Dome is 46,314 with room for maybe 3,000 more to stand. That the Japanese newspapers continue to print the Giant PR chief's figure instead of the fire chief's statistic is one of the many mystifying peculiarities of Japan's national sport.

1

The Visitation

I don't know whether the Japanese system is good or not. I just don't understand it.

Bob Horner

He walked off the plane at Narita Airport, wearied by his long flight, blinking in confusion at the waiting crush of cameras, lights, and microphones. Reporters on the scene that warm April afternoon remarked that no foreign visitor to Japan had ever received such a tremendous welcome—not Ronald Reagan, not Princess Diana, not even Michael Jackson.

The visitor was not a head of state or a movie star. He was only an American baseball player. Nevertheless, to many Japanese, his appearance in their country was an event of national proportions and historical significance.

Japan was at the height of its economic muscle. Japanese interests owned 54 percent of all the cash in the world's banks, 65 percent of all Manhattan real estate, and 3 per cent of the entire U.S. national debt. A staid Japanese insurance company had paid 39 million dollars for Van Gogh's painting *Sunflower*.

And now, in what one TV commentator had called the pièce de résistance, a Japanese baseball team had outbid the American major leagues for a prime American player: James Robert Horner.

Bēsubōru was unquestionably the country's national sport. It was the most talked about subject amongst Japanese after the weather, the yen-dollar rate, and sex. And while imported sluggers were by no means new to Japan—name players like Frank Howard, Dick Stuart, and Reggie Smith had all emigrated to the Land of the Rising Sun after their own suns set in the West—no one in Horner's class had ever deigned to come over.

Horner had hit 215 home runs in nine seasons with the Atlanta Braves. A player of All-Star proportions, at twenty-nine, he was at his peak. After decades of bench-warmers and faded stars, here, finally, was an American product worth paying for.

Horner had snob appeal among people who were notoriously finicky about buying foreign goods. The Japanese preferred only brand-name imports and did not care how much they cost. A bottle of Napoleon brandy sold for two hundred dollars after going through Japan's infamous, complex distribution system. A BMW cost a hundred thousand dollars, and a packet of glacial ice cubes went for twenty bucks. Yet there was never any lack of buyers because possessing such items brought one prestige.

To the Japanese, this bona fide major leaguer from Atlanta was the ultimate status symbol, for he gave their game a credibility it lacked and, at two million dollars a year, was also by far the most expensive player they had ever acquired.

That Horner had come to Japan was a simple matter of economics. After a reasonably good season with the Braves in 1986, in which he had hit .273, with 27 home runs and 87 RBIs, Horner tested his worth in the free-agent market.

When no club met his asking price of two million dollars, Horner turned to the Yakult Swallows of Japan's Central League, who did—at least for one season. It was the fattest single-year contract in the history of Japanese professional baseball, more than twice what the highest-paid Japanese star was getting. His signing was such gigantic news that the pilot of the JAL flight that carried him to Japan had personally requested his autograph.

The Swallows were based in Tokyo, a city of tremendous energy and enthusiasm for baseball. However, nearly all of its 12 million residents were fans of Yakult's crosstown neighbor, the Yomiuri Giants, Japan's oldest professional team, winner of thirty-three CL pennants, sixteen Japan Series titles, and something of a national institution.

The Swallows, with but one championship in their thirty-seven-year history, drew around twenty-seven thousand fans a game, far behind the Giants' nightly average of nearly fifty thousand.

Their owner, Hisami Matsuzono, was a flamboyant entrepreneur who had acquired a massive fortune purveying a yogurt health drink called Yakult. In 1965, he had bought the team from the Sankei Corporation, a major multimedia group, as a means of promoting his company. His ideas about running a baseball team, however, were somewhat unorthodox. He was an unabashed Giants fan and was frequently quoted as saying the ideal situation would be for the Giants to finish first and the Swallows runner-up.

In the spring following the Swallows' lone victorious year of 1978, he called a team meeting to tell his players that he did not expect them to win again. Second place would be just fine. Said one outfielder, "He sort of implied that it was the Giants' turn to win."

There were, it appeared, practical reasons for Matsuzono's sentiments. Statistics showed that whenever the Swallows defeated the Giants, sales of Yakult products dropped. It was true with other teams as well. If the Swallows swept a series, say, from the Hiroshima Carp, sales would fall temporarily in the Hiroshima region. Beating the Giants, however, meant a business nosedive all over the land. Giants fans were everywhere.

The Swallows had finished last in 1986, which was, not

coincidentally, a profitable year for the parent company. Thus when Matsuzono signed Horner and proclaimed he wanted nothing less than another flag, fans and reporters were not sure what to believe. "It's a PR stunt," said one writer, "That's all."

None of this was yet known to Horner, who, frazzled and nearly blinded by camera flashes, submitted to an impromptu press conference—facing nearly two hundred print and TV journalists. When it was over, a convoy of press cars followed his limousine the hour-and-a-half drive to his hotel in Tokyo, where they camped outside for the duration of the evening.

That first day was only a hint of what was to come. Horner later told a friend that if he had known what he was in for, he might never have signed.

Horner was not the only *gaijin* (foreigner, outsider) to play in Japan that year. There were a total of twenty-one others under contract to the twelve teams of the Central and Pacific leagues (two per varsity team was the limit). Many of them greeted the arrival of their illustrious colleague with skepticism. Said Warren Cromartie, a former Montreal Expo who had hit .363 for the Tokyo Giants the previous year:

"Guys like Horner don't know what adversity is. He never played in the minor leagues. He's used to chartered airplanes, big locker rooms, and at least one day off a week. It will take him five months to get over the shock."

It took a special kind of person to play in Japan. A man had to deal with a different type of pitching, a wider strike zone, and unpredictable umpires. The life of a ballplayer was so regimented by club rules that many Americans compared it to being in the army . . . or worse.

It required a certain emotional adjustment that many found difficult to make—as Ben Oglivie would attest. A former American League home run champion who was no longer wanted by the Milwaukee Brewers, he had

signed on as a free agent with the Kintetsu Buffaloes in
1987. But Oglivie, thirty-eight, was traumatized by the
move. One day in late March after he returned to his new
apartment in Osaka from a long preseason road trip, he
packed his bags and, without a word to anyone, boarded
a plane for his home in Phoenix.

Oglivie, a serious, introspective man who read Thoreau
and Kierkegaard, told a writer that he was just not "mentally ready" for it all.

> It was a terrible time. My whole life had been a com-
> mitment to the major leagues and I had no other ambi-
> tion than to stay there. I would have played for Mil-
> waukee or any other big-league team for half of the
> money I had been making. But the Brewers wouldn't
> even talk to me. The owners were clamping down and
> they didn't want to pay my salary of $500,000 when
> they could get ten younger guys for the same money.
> I kept waiting for some kind of offer. Then the Kintetsu
> Buffaloes approached me in January.
>
> I really didn't want to be in Japan. It was totally off
> the wall. I went through a period when I couldn't figure
> out what was going on. It was just so different.
>
> Everything built up and it all hit me that day. I was
> super-tired, more mentally fatigued than physically
> from being in such an alien environment. I'd been
> training since early February. And I just said to myself,
> "I don't belong here." So I left and I wasn't planning to
> come back.

Harried Kintetsu officials flew to Arizona and enticed
Oglivie to return. Just exactly how, no one would say, but
speculation had it that a significant increase in Oglivie's
half-million-dollar salary helped make a difference.

Although most Japanese put Horner's arrival in the
same category as the Second Coming of Christ, and assumed there would be no Oglivie-like problems, there

was peevish opposition in some quarters, especially when it was discovered that Horner had not practiced in seven months.

It did not take long for reporters to dredge up Horner's reputation for weight problems, for chronic injuries, and for being something of a swillpot. One TV morning talk show host pounced on him: "He says he's six feet one inch, ninety-seven kilograms. Hmmmm. He looks a lot heavier to me. He looks like a pro wrestler if you want to know the truth. He also looks like he likes to drink. We hear he's been hurt a lot, that he has a bad elbow, that he has broken his wrist twice. It makes me ask the question, Why is he here? It must be because he's not wanted in the United States."

Owner Matsuzono ignored such criticism and made it clear he expected Horner to hit fifty home runs, even though a month of the season had already gone by, and issued him a uniform with the number 50 on the back, lest Horner forget his assignment.

Tokyo's Jingu Stadium, home of the Swallows, is located in Meiji Shrine Park, a grove of trees that forms one of the rare havens of green in an overcrowded, polluted city. Once a decaying prewar relic redolent of fried squid, the stadium was renovated in 1982. New seating was installed, along with artificial grass and a giant million-dollar electronic marvel of a scoreboard that lit up with "Guts Baseball" and other inspiring slogans.

The dimensions of Jingu, however, stayed the same. Like other stadiums in Japan, it seemed designed for *Homu ran* hitters like Horner—298 down the foul lines and 394 to center. Thus it was that forty-eight thousand expectant fans had filled the stands on the brisk evening of May 6, for the debut of Yakult's chunky, blond-haired American.

In right field, the Swallows' long-time cheerleader, a bespectacled sign painter in his fifties named Masayasu

Okada, had passed out his usual assortment of colorfully painted frying pans, drumsticks, and other noisemakers to fans in the stands. Several thousand strong, they stood, swaying and chanting cheers as the game began. Each of them carried a transparent pastel-colored umbrella to be waved in unison in the event of a Yakult home run.

They didn't have to wait long. In the fifth inning, Horner belted a homer into the right field cheering section. *"Fure! Fure!"* (Hooray! Hooray!) screamed the fans, their jubilant cries reverberating around the stadium. His blast propelled the Swallows to a 5–3 win over the Hanshin Tigers and the next night, he smacked three more home runs, two over the left field fence and one off the wall in center, in yet another Yakult victory, 6–3.

By this time, Okada had composed a special Horner cheer for his followers to yell: *"Go-go* Ho-nah. *Rettsu-go* Ho-nah!"* And Tiger left fielder Noriyoshi Sano had devised a special plan to rescue the battered Tiger pitching staff. "I'll put springs on my spikes," he said, "and leap up and catch the ball before it goes out."

By the end of his first week, Horner had two more home runs, he was hitting .533, and the Swallows had climbed to .500, two-and-a-half games out of first. More important, the team was drawing capacity crowds every night.

"He can hit a pitch in any location," exclaimed former star Tetsuharu Kawakami, Japan's equivalent of Ted Williams. "He's got perfect form," gushed Shigeo Nagashima, Japan's equivalent of Joe DiMaggio. Swallows manager Junzo Sekine, a warm-faced, kindly man with a lifetime losing record, could only keep repeating, *"Sugoi,"* a Japanese word that means both "terrible" and "wonderful."

Swallows fans were even more emphatic. "I'm so happy I could die," one said. "I've never seen a foreigner like this before. He'll hit fifty home runs and we'll win the pennant." Banners appeared at the park which read, "Don't ever go back to America!"

It seemed as if the entire Japanese archipelago had suddenly stopped to watch Bob Horner. His face graced the front pages of every sports daily for a solid week. Three different networks interrupted telecasts of other games for video updates on Horner's latest at-bat. Horner Corner features became a regular part of the evening news and one TV station ran an hour-long Bob Horner special on a Sunday night in prime time—all this before he had even played ten games.

Moreover, on Tokyo's bustling stock exchange, Yakult stock shot up several points, while noodle sales at the colorful stalls underneath the Jingu grandstand plummeted. No one wanted to leave his seat and miss seeing Horner in action.

The newspapers gave Horner a nickname: *Akaoni* (the Red Devil), after a mythical creature from Buddhist lore—a red-skinned, horned ogre, capable of awful and awesome deeds. It was high praise. And although his bat cooled in his second week, as the opposition began pitching him more cautiously, Honah *kokka* (the Horner Effect) became the latest addition to the Japanese baseball lexicon. It was in reference to a vigorous new mood of confidence on the Swallows team. "With Honah-*san* in the lineup," said one player, "we can beat anyone."

A story appearing in the *Nikkan Sports,* a leading daily, completed the canonization of St. Horner.

> There is no need to worry about Horner going home suddenly or causing trouble like the other gaijin. He won't be like Oglivie. He is trying to get as accustomed to the team as fast as possible, assimilating the Japanese culture and trying his hardest to be like a Japanese. In the short time he has been here, Horner has taken on the "challenge" of Japanese food. He has mastered the use of chopsticks.
>
> The other day at dinner with a correspondent from the *Atlanta Constitution,* Horner assumed the role of

teacher of Japanese table manners. "Never pour your own glass until you fill that of others," he told his fellow American.

In pregame practice, he calls out to his teammates by name—Watanabe, Hirosawa, Sugiura. He pats them on the shoulder.

When the Atlanta reporter made reference to "your Braves," Horner quickly corrected him: "I'm a Yakult Swallow," he said, thereby emphasizing that he has forgotten his major league pride and is thinking only of the team.

Almost immediately, he had begun doing TV commercials, which would bring him nearly half a million dollars. He appeared in overalls, suspenders, and a straw hat, with a popular young movie actress, drinking Suntory Beer. *"Mo ippon"* (Give me another one), said Country Bob, crushing an empty beer can in his hands. Within days, there were life-size cardboard cutouts of him in liquor shops all over the land.

At first Horner was euphoric over his success. He would meet fellow American players for drinks at the Tokyo Hard Rock Cafe, a popular watering hole in the frenetic neon-lit entertainment district of Roppongi, and tell them how much he loved Japan: "This place is great," he would say.

"Of course you love it," said American Rick Lancelotti, a wise-cracking outfielder who played for the Carp. "You're making a zillion dollars. They wipe your ass for you when you take a shit. I'd think it was great too. Wait until you've been here for a while and things start to get a little rough. Wait until they put the squeeze on you."

"Ransu" (Lance) as the Japanese called him, had hit eight home runs in April. He had not seen a fastball since.

Veteran foreigners knew it could not last. Nearly every *gaijin* went through a period of adjustment in his first year in Japan. Horner would be no different. Of that, they were all certain.

Horner, however, had other, more immediate problems. Privacy is not a familiar concept in a country where millions of people are packed together like sushi in a box lunch. Now that Horner was a star in Japan, he was beginning to make that painful realization.

The hyperactive Japanese media had locked on to him like a heat-seeking missile. Great numbers of them waited outside his Tokyo apartment every morning. They followed him to the ballpark in cabs, and when he came home at night, there they were again.

He couldn't get rid of them, even when the team went on the road. At Tokyo Station, they would surround him on the platform. They boarded the train with him and stood in the aisles by his seat to snap him looking out the window, "admiring the Japanese countryside," and they packed the lobby of every hotel he checked into.

They were like Lilliputians inspecting Gulliver. In Sasebo, when he went to see the movie *Platoon*, several reporters went right along with him and interviewed him about the film afterward. In Sapporo, he got a haircut and the sports dailies reported such edifying details as how many centimeters of blond hair were removed from his head, how he felt after it was all over, and what effect it might have on his batting.

The capacity of the public for absorbing useless detail about him was infinite. They wanted to know his opinions on the trade gap between the U.S. and Japan, Irangate, the Seoul Olympics, the rising yen, the falling dollar, and the baby panda in the Ueno Zoo.

There was no end to it. The only way for Horner to escape the clawing mass of reporters was to stay in his boxlike apartment, watching Clint Eastwood movies on video, or in the trainer's room at the ballpark.

It got so that he would refuse to talk to people on the field before a game. If a writer popped the standard Japanese reporter's question, "How's your condition?" he would not answer. He would stand there at the batting cage, pretending not to hear, staring at the field, the pack of the press gathered behind him like hungry vultures.

One night, after a game in Yokohama with the Taiyo Whales, a friend saw Horner sitting in the darkened stadium parking lot waiting for Lee to finish a meeting and give him a ride home. The doors were locked, the windows were rolled up and Horner was slouched down in his seat. Said the friend, "He seemed so intimidated by it all. It was as if he was afraid to venture out by himself."

It was not long before Lancelotti's prediction came true. The Central League pitchers stopped throwing strikes to the Red Devil and Horner stopped hitting home runs. He had only three in the month following his opening binge and his average sank all the way to .300. Opposing moundsmen would only deal him breaking pitches on the outer fringes of the strike zone—an off-speed curve here, a forkball there, a *shooto* (screwball) when he least expected it—and he would walk or he would swing in frustration at a bad pitch. "I need a boat oar to hit the ball," he moaned.

Horner's petulance began to show. In one game, the Swallows were losing 17–5 when he came to bat in the eighth inning. There were two outs and the bases were empty. Still he walked. When the inning ended, he went back to the bench and slammed his bat in anger, scattering his teammates.

His game, like that of most major leaguers, was one of challenge. "You throw me your best stuff," he would say, "I'll see if I can hit it. That's big-league baseball." But the Japanese version of the game was not played that way, as Horner began to discover.

The Japanese game was a cautious one, not one of assertive strategy and tactics, but one of walks, of sacrifice bunts in the first inning—a step-by-step approach that seemed to reflect the conservative bent of Japanese society as a whole. There were more 3–2 counts and a three-pitch strikeout was almost nonexistent.

It was designed to avoid unpleasant confrontations and embarrassing mistakes. Nobody wanted to look bad. Nobody wanted to be the one that fouled up and threw a home run pitch—especially to a *gaijin*.

Their style also suited their physical limitations. Because the average Japanese player was about five feet nine inches tall and 170 pounds, they had to play a more tactical game when going against foreigners.

There were people like Giants star Suguru Egawa, a big man with a ninety-three-mile-per-hour fastball, who would challenge Horner and who once struck him out three times in a row. But the Egawas were the exception.

Furthermore, not all the fans were sympathetic to Horner's predicament. To some, his ursine frame conjured up unpleasant images from the past of the physically overbearing *gaijin*. On the cover of one popular adult comic book was a drawing of a hippopotamus in a Yakult Swallows uniform, wielding a bat at home plate. The hippo had yellow hair sticking out from under a baseball cap and the number 50 was clearly visible on his jersey.

Horner, known for his sharp batting eye in the U.S., began to gripe more and more about the umpires. One sunny afternoon in Morioka, a city in northern Honshu, he took a low curveball that broke in on his shins and pushed him back.

"Strike!" intoned the umpire. Horner stared at him with such disgust that the TV cameras zoomed in for a lingering, close-up look. He was still steaming when the next pitch came over the outside corner for a called strike three. He looked at the umpire once more, muttered something the TV mikes could not pick up, and strode back to the bench.

Horner denied saying "fuck you," as a helpful newspaper had reported the next morning for the elucidation of its readers, and the umpires in turn denied they were picking on the new American player. And they let it be known that if he kept on complaining they would not hesitate to remove him from the field.

In late June, shortly after a TV announcer had proclaimed to his audience that "Horner had after all proved to be only an ordinary human being," Horner met again with Lancelotti and the others. He had 11 home runs, 25 strikeouts and 21 walks in 29 games.

"I've got to get out of here," he was quoted as saying, "I can't believe this shit."

They sat there and laughed and Lancelotti said, "Welcome to Japan. Now you are one of us."

Horner had, in fact, thought about leaving more than once as he confessed in his autobiography, *Eureka! Different Baseball across the Globe,* published in Japanese the following year. "If it hadn't been for Leon Lee," he said, "I don't know what I might have done. I think I set a world record for having dinner with a teammate."

Lee was a strapping first baseman from the St. Louis Cardinal chain who had been in Japan for ten years during which he had averaged .308 and hit 246 home runs. The other American players liked to say he deserved a Purple Heart for putting up with Japanese baseball so long.

Lee was affable and astute and he doubled as Horner's guide, chauffeur, and part-time interpreter. After games, Horner and Lee would go drinking at the Hard Rock Cafe, or other American-style places with names like Tony Roma's, Nicola's Pizza House, Maggie's Revenge, and Chaps.

Horner would bemoan the latest injustice he had been subjected to in Japan and Leon would listen patiently and explain the facts of life:

> These are the most face-conscious people I've ever seen. It's a big loss of face for a pitcher here to give up a home run to a *gaijin.* The umpires feel they have to

equalize things because *gaijin* are bigger. An umpire once told me that since my arms were longer than those of the Japanese batters, I had to have a wider strike zone, if you can believe that. Another one informed me that my strike zone should always be a certain distance from my body, so it didn't matter whether I stood close to the plate or far away from it. The strike zone moved with me, so to speak.

You can't turn around and fuss at the umpires and kick your helmet thinking you're going to intimidate these guys. Every time you bitch, they are going to squeeze you that much harder. You just have to adjust, and try to get a hit before you get two strikes. You have to learn to hit bad balls.

After the liquid therapy and the lecture, Horner's angst would be eased—at least until the next day. At the end of the season, the other American ballplayers would joke that Leon deserved a second Purple Heart for listening to Horner's complaints every night.

Another part of the problem was that the Japan to which Horner had emigrated, however temporarily, was still a feudalistic society in many respects. Company presidents were like feudal lords and Yakult's Matsuzono was certainly no exception.

There were strict rules of behavior in the Matsuzono shogunate. The players were not allowed to drive foreign cars (when Lee joined the team from the Taiyo Whales, he had to sell his Mercedes-Benz and buy a Toyota), they were forbidden to grow facial hair, there was to be no special treatment for any individual, and there were never to be any contract squabbles. When a players' union was officially formed in 1985, the Swallows joined but then withdrew from it en masse, when it became apparent their boss was displeased with their behavior.

For Horner, however, Matsuzono was willing to make exceptions. On the road, he installed Horner in the most luxurious western-style hotel that could be found, while the rest of the team stayed in cheaper accommodations—often communal-style Japanese inns. He was also given carte blanche in regard to training. Lee, who normally did things the Japanese way, was given the same special dispensation so Horner could have company.

Swallows manager Sekine did not object. Perhaps he recalled the year Yakult had three different managers, two of whom resigned in midseason.

While his teammates assiduously went through their daily exhausting grind of pregame drills lasting two-and-a-half hours, the Red Devil would shoot the breeze with Leon in the outfield, or go into the trainer's room for a snooze on the massage table.

Horner assured reporters that this was normal for him. In fact, he told them, in Atlanta, when the weather had turned brutally hot, he would frequently not take any practice at all—not even one swing of his bat, or one ground ball, or one sprint in the outfield. He would just go to the park, put on his uniform, and wait for the game to begin. Better to save your energy for the game, he explained.

Many Japanese were horrified to hear this. To them, pregame practice was as much a part of playing baseball as the game itself. To some people, it was more important. A good hard workout every day was considered imperative in order to show the fans, the press, and the opposition that the team was full of fight and ready to play ball. Besides, constant practice was a must if you really wanted to become good. The more you worked the better you got. Everyone knew that.

The Japanese were perfectionists and it was their belief that with constant work and an indefatigable will, one could accomplish anything: overcome injury and pain, defeat a more powerful foe in battle, win the batting title, or whatever. Indeed, the emphasis on "making the effort" was so strong in Japan that how hard a man tried was considered by many to be the ultimate measure of his worth. Results were almost secondary.

That Horner could expect to succeed without even working up a sweat before a game was somehow sacrilegious. It went against the whole Japanese philosophy on sports and life. A *Tokyo Shimbun* reporter lamented, "What will happen to our traditional style of baseball with its emphasis on group harmony and hard training? If Americans like Horner don't care about things like that, we will gradually lose our game, and that would be terrible."

Now that Horner, with his laissez-faire philosophy of baseball, was faltering, the Japanese press was ready to cut him down to size. When Sekine and the Yakult coaches cajoled Horner into an extra practice session, it was widely reported in the media.

Most Americans who knew Horner described him as a nice enough guy, a good family man who donated money to charity and who had suffered greatly when his younger brother Scott died the year before. Horner was a good hitter, they said, but a so-so fielder, a player who was injury prone and, as a result, spent too much time on the sidelines.

Japanese fans, however, began to wonder if they had an Ugly American on their hands. When the rainy season began in June—a month of rain or drizzle and fluctuating temperatures—Horner missed several games due to a bad cold.

He left in the middle of one contest with a fever and went to nearby Keio Hospital—followed by a mob of photographers. The next morning, a sports daily ran the headline: *"Shokuba Hoki!"* (Horner Deserts Post!)

When he sat out the next day and the next and the one after that, a writer cracked, "He's sick all right, he's sick of Japan."

By July 11, Horner had played in enough games to have 16 home runs, with a batting average of .322, but when he strained his back swinging at a pitch and went on the disabled list many Japanese were sure they had been sold a bill of goods.

Earlier in the year, the Swallows had begun calling him *sensei*, a term of respect that means teacher, master, or doctor. It was a tribute to Horner's knowledge of batting—which he was always willing to pass on to a teammate.

"Is the *sensei* playing today," the players would ask of manager Sekine and Sekine would tilt his head, suck wind, and say, "Well, gee, I don't know. We'll have to wait and see how he feels."

But when nearly a month had passed and he continued to come to the stadium every day to get a massage and say he was not yet quite well enough to play, there were people who began to use the word sarcastically, like the Yakult coach who remarked, "If we wait for the *sensei* to tell us he's ready to play, the season will be over."

In early August, he made an attempt to return. In one tightly fought contest with the Giants, his back stiffened and he had to come out. Later that evening, on a late news program, an angry sportscaster, a former star shortstop named Yukinobu Kuroe let Horner have it: "People paid money to see him play. He had an obligation to stay in the game. What he did was really rude to the fans."

The Horner drama had unfolded against a background of increasing friction between the U.S. and Japan over trade, with Americans complaining that Japanese markets were closed and Japanese retorting that Americans made nothing worth buying.

On August 19, the out-of-action Horner was interviewed for a segment of the MacNeil-Lehrer show, taped in Tokyo. "People in Japan say you're a typical American product," said correspondent Paul Solman as the cameras rolled, "powerful but unreliable. What is your response to this?"

Horner sat in his windbreaker and street clothes at a table in the Swallows' gleaming, air-conditioned clubhouse, and stared at his interrogator. It was almost six o'clock and outside, in steamy oppressive heat, forty-five thousand fans were waiting impatiently for the game to begin, hoping that Horner would play.

He shifted in his seat and answered, "I heard all that talk at Atlanta too. People don't realize that ballplayers are human. Even stars get sick."

The interview ended and Solman watched bemusedly as Horner hopped in a cab and sped off into the night. Said a Japanese member of the camera crew, "If this keeps up I'll have to sell my shares of Yakult stock."

Then, somehow, it all started to click again. His back healed completely, he returned to the lineup full-time, and he started to hit once more with authority. As Leon had suggested, he made certain adjustments to counter the erratic umpiring. He hit 6 home runs in his first seven games back, 15 in his next thirty-four, to finish with 31 in a total of 303 at-bats. He also had 51 walks in ninety games, a normal full season's complement in the U.S. It was projected that if Horner had played in every game of the 130-game season, he would have hit 51 homers. (The home run crown went to Lancelotti who had 39, and no commercials. In the Pacific League, Oglivie had pulled himself together to hit .300 with 24 home runs.)

Yakult ended the season in fourth place, nineteen-and-a-half games behind the pennant-winning Giants, but still a considerable improvement over their usual last-place finish. The club also set an all-time attendance record, averaging thirty-four thousand per game. At twelve dollars a ticket, it did not require mathematical genius to figure out how much Horner was worth. At season's end, the Swallows offered him a reported ten million dollars to put his chop on a new three-year contract.

But Horner said he needed time to think.

      Ⓢ   Ⓢ   Ⓢ

Horner could not understand Japan. It was a strange, complex place. He had begun thinking that ever since his boss told him he was a Giants fan. The daily routine tended to grate on his nerves and he did not know if he could handle another year there.

Many other American players felt the same way. There were the incessant meetings, for example: daily pregame preparatory meetings, impromptu midgame strategy sessions in which the players would huddle around their manager in front of the dugout, and nightly postgame conferences to review the team's mistakes.

In the U.S. major leagues, meetings were a sometime thing. Most players knew what they were supposed to do. But in Japan, they had to be told constantly. If the team lost, well, fault had to be found and blame had to be laid. If the team won, mistakes in the evening's game had to be pointed out. One could never be too careful.

The Japanese team was an extremely delicate mechanism, the coaches believed, and the slightest little tic could throw it out of whack. It needed constant tuning and the people in charge simply could not stop tinkering with it. They were baseball hypochondriacs—always looking for something wrong. After the Giants' batting coach had studied Horner's form for a month, he noted ten different flaws that needed to be rectified.

Horner and the other Americans had respect for the Japanese system. The Japanese had come a long way with their philosophy of hard work and quality control, but, in the final analysis, they were just too much. They didn't know when to stop, be it at the office or on the ball field.

Burdened by all its strictures and excesses, there was no joy in the Japanese game. Its participants approached their task as if it were an assembly-line job at Toyota. They were at the park ten hours a day. It was "work ball," as one player had said, and Horner thought that was as good a description as one could make of the Japanese game. Americans *played* ball. Japanese worked at it.

There was nothing at all mellow or laid back about his hosts. They were unremittingly formal, disciplined, cerebral, and incredibly uptight (at least when they were sober). The standard look was Military Grim. Only in Japan, he discovered, did both company workers and kindergarten students alike take medicine for stress.

In baseball, they were always talking about mood, proper team mood. In Japan surrendering the first run in a game was thought so psychologically damaging to team mood that defeat was almost inevitable. Going 0-for-4 was a serious slump. A two-game losing streak was cause for absolute panic.

They talked about pressure as if it were a disease: the pressure of falling behind; the pressure of a one-run lead. The pressure of being in first place. The pressure of a winning streak. *Taihen* was the word they used. It meant "dreadful, serious." It was almost a tangible, palpable thing. They played each game as if there were no tomorrow, using starting pitchers in relief, pinch-hitting in early innings, and sacrifice bunting, at every conceivable opportunity.

Leon's brother Leron, who played for the Lotte Orions, was part of a play he once described as the strangest he had ever seen:

It was in the eighth inning of a one-run game with the Nankai Hawks. I was on third base. There was one out, the bases loaded, a 3–2 count on the batter. Our manager was afraid of a double play, so he put the squeeze

sign on. The Nankai manager read the sign and ordered
a pitchout. Think about that for a minute. The pitcher
pitched out and our batter tried to bunt it anyway. Now
think about that for a minute. The batter missed and
the catcher threw me out coming down from third.
Double play, end of inning. I talked about that play with
my brother for hours. We didn't know what to make of
it—whether it was the stupidest play we'd ever seen. Or
the smartest.

Horner was a nervous guy, but the Japanese, especially
the coaches, were the most nervous group of people he
had ever seen. They were positively neurotic.[1]

To him the rigidity of the Japanese system bordered at
times on the ridiculous. If a team couldn't have pregame
practice, playing the game was unthinkable. It might rain
and clear up by game time, but if there had been no
practice, then everyone would go home.

"I grew to hate rain in Japan," said Horner. "In the U.S.,
it could rain all day and we'd still play the game, practice
or no. We'd sit there and wait until nine in the evening,
if necessary, and if it stopped raining then we'd play ball.
Not in Japan. No way."

In his one season, Horner had discovered that Japanese
baseball was a totally different world with its own set of
assumptions and values. Better men than he had been
driven to distraction by it.

⚾   ⚾   ⚾

And so, in the end, he decided he did not want to
endure another season in Japan, no matter how much
money Yakult paid him. He wanted to go back to the U.S.

---

1. Many American players said that tied games were ideal for Japan
because they took some of the pressure off. Shinsuke Hori, president
of the Pacific League, confessed that ties "suited the Japanese character. That way," he said, "nobody loses."

where real baseball was played, where his young children could get an American education, where he had a chance to get 1,000 major league hits, 1,000 major league RBIs, and 250, perhaps 500, major league home runs—statistics that mattered to people.

Back in the U.S., his agent talked to the St. Louis Cardinals, who were interested in Horner as a replacement for Jack Clark, but were not interested in paying the kind of money Yakult was offering.

Horner said he didn't care.

He vehemently disavowed a *Sporting News* report that had him telling Dal Maxvill, the Cardinals' general manager, "Please do something. Please give me enough money to get me out of Japan. I don't want to go back there."

But when St. Louis offered him a one-year contract for $950,000 with half a million more in bonus clauses for games played, he signed, much to Matsuzono's dismay—and thus ended the Saga of the Red Devil.

2

A History

Baseball is more than just a game. It has eternal value. Through it, one learns the beautiful and noble spirit of Japan.

Suishu Tobita (1886–1965)
Japan's original "God of Baseball"

This country has got its national flag all wrong. Instead of a rising sun in the center, there should be a baseball.

British tourist

Baseball in Japan can be traced back to the early days of the Meiji Era (1867–1912), when a young American named Horace Wilson, teaching history and English at Tokyo's Kaisei Gakko, handed his students a ball and a bat and introduced them to the fundamentals of America's new national pastime.

Albert Bates, another American teacher at Kaitaku University in Tokyo, is said to have organized the first formal game in 1873, while Hiroshi Hiraoka, a railway engineer who had become an ardent Red Sox fan as a student in Boston, established Japan's first team, the Shimbashi Athletic Club Athletics, in 1883. His players were railway engineers, station workers, and foreign technicians who used makeshift gloves and ran the bases wearing *geta* (wooden sandals).

Before the Meiji restoration, the western concept of sport had been virtually unknown in Japan. There was sumo wrestling, which had developed out of fourth-century Shinto rites, and horseback riding, swimming, and kendo, among others, which were done for military training purposes. The idea of athletics for fun, however, was an alien one. There was, in fact, no Japanese equivalent for the word *sport*. Since no one knew quite how to translate it, it became *supōttsu*.

As Japan opened its doors to the world, however, ending nearly three hundred years of feudal isolation, it began an all-out modernization effort to catch up with the West and imported many facets of Western civilization.

The transformation of Japan into a modern state was indeed remarkable. When the shogun—Japan's then military ruler—relinquished power, he was clad in formal samurai robes and a traditional topknot hairstyle. A scant two years later, the Emperor Meiji was holding court in a three-piece suit and top hat.

Western sports quickly became the rage and a particular passion developed for baseball. The Japanese found the one-on-one battle between pitcher and batter similar in psychology to sumo and the martial arts. It involved split-second timing and a special harmony of mental and physical strength. As such, the Ministry of Education deemed it good for the national character.

Baseball, or *yokyu* (field ball) as it was also known, became the sport of the upper class and soon there were several high school and college teams in the Tokyo area. It was so well received that even British professors found themselves having to teach it to their students. In fact, an Englishman named F. William Strange, who lectured at Tokyo University, became the first person to write down the rules of the game for the Japanese, in a book entitled *Outdoor Games* (1878).

From the beginning, Japanese who coached baseball

regarded it as a moral discipline, like kendo—a tool of education for developing purity and self-discipline. They applied to it the martial art philosophy of endless training, self-denial, and emphasis on spirit. (In some schools, a batter who tried to avoid being hit by a pitch was penalized by not being allowed to take first base. It was reasoned that he had failed to demonstrate the proper courage.)

Nowhere was baseball more of a martial art than at the First Higher School of Tokyo, Japan's most elite prep school. Ichiko, as it was called, was a training ground for those on their way to the prestigious Imperial University, and ultimately, to positions of leadership in the nation.

Ichiko students lived in school dormitories, isolated from the public. It was a way of keeping them pure and of preserving Japanese traditions in the flood of foreign culture washing over Japan. The Ichiko baseball team had an ascetic routine which included Zen meditation and year-round practice.

That philosophy made Ichiko diametrically opposed to baseball rival Meiji Gakuin, which was the most Americanized of Japanese educational institutions. Meiji was founded by Christian missionaries from the United States. Most of the professors were American. So were the baseball coaches and their approach to practice was comparatively casual and carefree.

Thus, whenever the two schools played each other there was more at stake than simple victory or defeat. It was a test of cultural systems. One Ichiko-Meiji encounter, in fact, turned so violent it threatened to disrupt diplomatic relations between the U.S. and Japan.

By the sixth inning of that game—played in 1891—Meiji had a 6–0 lead and the several-thousand-strong Ichiko cheering section, including a large contingent from the school's judo club, was bitterly disappointed.

They sat there in their judo outfits jeering the opposition when suddenly a solitary figure—a foreigner—clambered over the bamboo fence on the Ichiko side of the field and dropped down to the ground.

His name was William Imbrie, an American professor at Meiji. He had come late to the game only to find the main and rear gates closed. So he had used his Yankee ingenuity and climbed over the fence.

This, however, was no ordinary fence. To Ichiko students it was sacred, in the arcane way that a judo or kendo *dōjō* (practice hall) was sacred. One did not climb in through the window of a *dōjō,* a repository of spirit thought to be purer than the world outside. A *dōjō* deserved special deference, a bow of respect at the front door.

The Ichiko fence, known as the "Fence of Soul," symbolically separated the secular world—as represented by Meiji Gakuin—from the inner, more traditional world which Ichiko embodied. It was strictly forbidden for anyone to climb over it. That a Meiji man had defiled the fence—a *gaijin* at that—only compounded what was already a grievous sin.

The members of the judo club, already annoyed at losing the game, were livid at this latest outrage. They began screaming insults at Imbrie and rushed down from the stands to attack him. As Imbrie fled to the Meiji side, someone struck him in the face with a bat, opening a gash under his eye and sending blood spurting down his face.

Imbrie was a kindly, religious man who loved Japan and when he discovered the nature of his transgression he was deeply embarrassed. When he went home, after receiving medical treatment, he didn't even tell his wife what had happened.

If Imbrie was willing to drop the matter, however, other foreigners in Japan were not. Local English newspapers played up the incident as an example of the xenophobic, uncivilized ways of the Japanese. The American embassy lodged a formal complaint with the Japanese foreign ministry and foreigners living in Japan began to fear for their safety.

At the time of the incident, the Japanese government had been preparing to renegotiate various foreign treaties, including one with the United States. The treaties Japan had signed with the U.S. in the time since Commodore Matthew Perry and his Black Ships had forced open the country in 1853 had not been advantageous and the government was hoping to secure more favorable terms.

However, with the American embassy angry over the Imbrie affair, Japanese leaders feared their cause would be severely compromised. They worried that the U.S. would seize upon the issue of security for foreign nationals and delay negotiating any new pact. They also worried that the political opposition within Japan would use the opportunity to attack the ruling party.

The foreign ministry quickly took the matter up with the ministry of education, which promptly called in the Ichiko authorities and ordered them to somehow resolve the problem. Within days, Ichiko had formally acknowledged all blame in the matter. An emissary was dispatched to Meiji Gakuin to officially convey the school's regrets and the American embassy was notified through the proper Japanese government channels that Ichiko would make appropriate rectification.

Then foreign ministry officials, ranking Ichiko representatives, and several of the students involved paid a visit to Professor Imbrie's residence to beg his forgiveness, which the good professor granted.

One account of the meeting, however, described the students as openly hostile, sitting on Imbrie's Western-style furniture in Japanese fashion, legs crossed, defiant expressions on their faces—even as they apologized.

Imbrie stayed in Japan for a total of forty-eight years. He spoke out on behalf of his adopted country during the

Russo-Japanese War and was eventually decorated for his efforts by the Japanese government. But he would always be remembered most for his role as the central figure in what went down in history as the infamous *Imuburi Jiken*—the Imbrie Incident.

It was indeed a black time for Ichiko. What mattered most to the school, however, was not the humiliating apology it had been forced to make, but rather the galling defeat it suffered at the hands of the "American Meiji" nine.

Ichiko's baseball team returned to the practice field to redouble their efforts. The new Ichiko regimen was nicknamed Bloody Urine, for it was said that the players practiced so hard they urinated blood at the end of the day.

In one drill, a pitcher stood a mere 20 feet away from home plate and fired fastballs at the catcher with all his might. By the end of the exercise, the pitcher was exhausted and the catcher's body black-and-blue.

Ichiko players were forbidden to use the word *ouch!*—no matter how much a ball stung their hands on a frozen winter's day or how badly they bruised their bodies during sliding practice. Those who could not suppress the pain were allowed to use the word *kayui* (it itches). It was their way of demonstrating spirit, the sine qua non of any good Japanese athlete.

Ichiko's pitchers each threw several hundred pitches a day in practice. Their pitching arms frequently became badly bent from throwing too many curveballs. To straighten them out, they would hang from the branches of the cherry trees that bordered the field—presumably screaming *kayui* as they did.

With this fierce resolve, Ichiko became the most powerful team in Japan—defeating Meiji and all other schools and going on to accomplish a feat that made the popularity of baseball soar to even greater heights.

One sunlit afternoon in 1898, they traveled by train to Yokohama to take on a team of Americans, the Yokohama

Country Athletic Club nine. It was the first encounter ever between the two countries on a baseball field and, incredibly, to the Japanese, Ichiko won—by the fantastic score of 29–4.

Granted, the Americans were only part-time players. They were merchants, traders, and missionaries who played for fun. But they were still a team from the *honke* (main house) of baseball and the Japanese had beaten them.

Their great triumph made newspaper headlines across the land. It electrified the nation and gave it a tremendous boost of confidence. As one Japanese historian has written, "Foreigners could not hope to understand the emotional impact of this victory, but it helped Japan, struggling toward modernization after centuries of isolation, overcome a tremendous inferiority complex it felt toward the more industrially advanced West." What made the victory even sweeter was that heretofore Japanese had not been allowed inside the Yokohama club compound.

The Yokohama Americans were naturally mortified. They had taken their foes lightly—so lightly they almost had not agreed to play the game in the first place. They called for a rematch, which they got, and which they lost 35–9. They strengthened their team with sailors from U.S. Navy ships anchored in Yokohama harbor, and lost a third time, 22–6, this time at Ichiko's park, in front of several thousand spectators and a mob of reporters.

After each game, there had been tea and cakes served, congratulations by the losers and attempts at modesty by the victors. It was, of course, all in the name of good will and international friendship, but the Japanese could not hide their jubilation. The Ichiko squad was younger, faster, stronger, better trained, and superior in every facet of the game.[1]

---

1. The Americans finally beat Ichiko in Game 4, 14–12, after adding a professional ballplayer who was serving on a visiting U.S. Navy ship.

The First Higher School went on to beat the Yokohama team many more times. Pitcher Kotaro Moriyama, who later threw a shutout against the Americans (or *sukonku Gému*—skunk game—as the Japanese said), became a hero of such proportions that he inspired a popular saying: "To be hit by Moriyama's fastball is an honor exceeded only by being crushed under the wheels of the imperial carriage."

In the wake of Ichiko's stunning victories, schools all over Japan began forming baseball clubs. Ichiko players became national heroes and upon graduating, they fanned out to educational institutions throughout the nation to teach students the finer points of this foreign game they had so obviously mastered.

By the early twentieth century, intercollegiate baseball was the country's major sport. It had become a symbol of the nation's progress in its efforts to catch the West. Leading universities like Keio, Waseda, and Meiji were playing overseas competition, starting with a tour of the U.S. West Coast in 1905 by Waseda, in which it compiled a 7–19 record against schools like Stanford, USC, and Washington.

At home, the twice-annual Keio-Waseda three-game series had become the country's biggest baseball rivalry, drawing crowds of over sixty thousand. Warring student cheer groups were such a problem—their ranks often swelled by judo club members—that play was suspended on more than one occasion. The Keio-Waseda games were banned for twenty years starting in 1905.

Not everyone was overjoyed with the popularity of this alien sport. In 1911, the influential conservative daily *Asahi Shimbun* ran an editorial series entitled "The Evil of Baseball," quoting several leading educators who opposed the game. A University of Tokyo physician claimed that it was bad for the development of the personality because of "mental pressure" placed on ballplayers to win for the honor of their school. A colleague of his added that throwing a baseball all the time caused lopsided body development and that the shock of catching a fastball caused the brain to vibrate.

General Maresuke Nogi, a hero in Japan's victory over the Russians in 1905, feared that players spent too much time getting drunk in Western-style restaurants after practice, while the chief of the high schools bureau in the ministry of education said flatly, "Baseball doesn't fit the Japanese school system." He insisted that only "pure" Japanese athletics like kendo and judo were suitable for the Japanese.

Noted educator Inazo Nitobe, later to become Japan's ambassador to the League of Nations, summed up the general tone of the polemics in a famous essay in which he called baseball a "pickpocket's sport" where players tried to swindle their opponents and to steal bases. It was therefore suited to Americans, he said, but not Englishmen or Germans. Sticking the knife in deeper, he added, "It is impossible for the Americans to play a brave game like rugby, the national sport of the British, in which the players hang on to the ball even though their nose is being crushed and their skull dented."

Perhaps the most emotional attack came from a writer who said, "Those who like baseball are those who think prostitution is good."

Baseball survived the assault, however, thanks in part to support by rival papers, led by the *Yomiuri Shimbun*. Editorialists argued forcefully the game's value in teaching spirit. Yukichi Fukazawa, the founder of Keio University, said, "Sports is education too," and suggested that students who traveled abroad to play baseball learned much from their exposure to different cultures.

Supporters also claimed that baseball was good because it taught the Japanese the value of sacrificing oneself for the good of the group and was therefore ideally suited to the people as a whole. They pointed out that many notables in Japanese industry and government had played baseball in their youth without incurring great damage to their health, character, or subsequent careers.

The list included such luminaries as cabinet minister Jutaro Komura who negotiated the Treaty of Portsmouth that settled the Russo-Japanese War, and Jigoro Kano, the man who fused the knowledge of the old jujitsu schools of the Japanese samurai into a form called judo. Kano had been absolutely crazy about baseball in his youth. He quit playing only because he believed judo required total commitment.

If nothing else, the spirited debate helped to increase the circulations of the newspapers involved and when it was all over, baseball was more popular than ever. In fact, the *Asahi Shimbun*, in one of the great turnabouts of newspaper history, went on to sponsor the annual National High School Baseball Summer Tournament, which today is one of the biggest amateur sporting events in the world.

Although the pro game was years away from taking hold in Japan, a figure emerged whose philosophy would influence the way his countrymen played baseball for the rest of the twentieth century. His name was Suishu Tobita, and by the time he died in 1965 he had become known as the god of Japanese baseball. He was the prototypical Japanese manager, compared by many to Connie Mack.

Tobita was born in 1886 in the conservative prefecture of Ibaragi, which had strongly supported the Tokugawa shogunate against the Meiji restoration. His father, a village head man, was a traditionalist who valued samurai beliefs greatly and who was as violently opposed to foreign sports as he was to the opening up of Japan to the West.

Perhaps because his father was so conservative, young Suishu was attracted to baseball. It was fashionable, like

Western-style clothing, shoes, and pocket watches. He played it secretly while attending middle school and later, at Waseda University, he became captain of the baseball team.

Tobita, a second baseman, was not a great player. He was small—five feet three inches—and slight, but he was also smart and speedy and had a passionate desire to win. He was attracted to the view of Waseda manager Iso Abe that sport was a modern replacement for war.

When Waseda lost several games in a row to a visiting University of Chicago team in 1910, by humiliating scores of 9–2, 15–4, and 20–0, Tobita was crushed. He quit baseball to assume responsibility for the losses and vowed someday, somehow, to take revenge. "I'll beat Chicago if I have to die to do it," he said.

Nine years later, he was offered the chance to manage Waseda. Although it meant a big drop in pay from his post at the *Yomiuri Shimbun,* Tobita did not care. He said he would take the job even if his family had to eat rice gruel.

By this time, Tobita had crystallized his theories of managing. He believed that players should love their teams in the way that one loved one's hometown or one's country, that they should show total allegiance and obedience to their manager and that they should never, ever complain. He compared baseball to Bushido, the way of the samurai,[2] in which only morally correct athletes could excel, and saw Zen ramifications in the sport. As he once wrote:

---

2. *Bushido:* a combination of various religious and other elements that emphasized the martial arts in the training of the samurai warrior class. The Bushido code demanded of samurai: loyalty, self-control, discipline, piety, ceremonial propriety, selflessness, and learning, as well as military skill.

Bushido reflected the traditional principles of the morality of the Japanese. Bushido and Zen were integrated into the modern-day philosophy of the Japanese martial arts.

The purpose of training is not health but the forging of the soul, and a strong soul is only born from strong practice.

To hit like a shooting star, to catch a ball beyond one's capabilities . . . such beautiful plays are not the result of technique but the result of good deeds. For all these are made possible by a strong spiritual power.

Student baseball must be the baseball of self discipline, or trying to attain the truth, just as in Zen Buddhism. It must be much more than just a hobby. In many cases it must be a baseball of pain and a baseball practice of savage treatment. Only with the constant cultivation of tears, sweat and bleeding can a player secure his position as such.

Tobita likened practice to the religious penance found in Buddhism—a kind of asceticism—and he worked his players even harder than players on the Ichiko team had been worked. He would make his players field ground balls until they dropped, or as Tobita himself described it, "until they were half dead, motionless, and froth was coming out of their mouths." His system came to be known as *shi no renshu* (death training).

"A manager has to love his players," he wrote, "but on the practice field he must treat them as cruelly as possible, even though he may be crying about it inside. That is the key to winning baseball. If the players do not try so hard as to vomit blood in practice, then they can not hope to win games. One must suffer to be good."

Tobita's personal motto was "Perfect Baseball." A pitcher was expected to throw every pitch with all his might. A batter was expected to hit line drives every time up. Slow curves and fly balls were unacceptable, as was anything less than total concentration on every play. "Players who lose and don't cry," he would say, "don't care enough."

Tobita's system worked. He guided Waseda to several

titles and its greatest season ever, a perfect 36–0 record in 1925 which included three wins and a tie against the visiting University of Chicago (the scores were 1–0, 1–0, 3–3, and 1–0).

Having fulfilled his pledge, Tobita retired and went on to a different kind of fame as a baseball columnist for the *Asahi Shimbun*. A talented and perceptive writer, he won many literary awards and in 1965 was honored by the emperor for his cultural achievements and contributions to sport.

There were some college managers of Tobita's time who tried the easier, more "rational" American approach to baseball, but Tobita's method was so successful—and so dramatic—that most others chose to follow it.

The grip that amateur baseball, with its focus on purity, had on the country was so strong that the first professional baseball league was not formed until 1936. The idea of playing for money struck many Japanese as somehow profane.

Still, the professional brand of ball was not entirely unknown. In the fall of 1908, a team of major league reserves and Pacific Coast League players called the Reach All-Americans became the first pro team to play in Japan. They were sponsored by the Reach Sporting Goods Company, which had taken an interest in the growing Japanese market. The Americans easily won all of the seventeen games they played against Japanese college competition.

In 1910, an infielder named Art Schaeffer who played minor league ball, and a pitcher named Tommy Thompson, who played briefly for the New York Giants under John McGraw, coached at Keio University in the winter of 1910. And in 1913, the Giants and the Chicago White Sox played three games in Japan on the first leg of a world tour before crowds of several thousand, many of whom sat tailor-fashion on mats in the bleachers. The White Sox beat the Giants twice and a combined Giants–White Sox team defeated the Keio University nine, 12–3.

The Japanese found the Americans' behavior strange. The honorable *gaijin* put on pregame demonstrations of warming up without using a bat or a ball, and they did not doff their caps and bow when they came up to bat as the Japanese did. Moreover Bill Klem was the loudest umpire they had ever heard.

Still, the *Jiji Shimpo* newspaper pointed out that New York manager John McGraw, known in his own country as a harsh autocrat, was a "real gentleman." (In the meantime, a sharp-eyed observer in the American group noted in the official diary of the tour that "Japanese girls age rapidly after their tenth year.")

In 1920, another mixed bag of PCL players and part-time big leaguers called the Hunter All-Americans played several games in Japan, comfortably winning all. They were organized by Herb Hunter, an infielder with major league experience, who returned to Japan in 1922 with a second team.

This version of the All-Americans included Waite Hoyt, Herb Pennock, and an outfielder named Stengel. It gained the distinction of being the first American professional team to lose a game to the Japanese when a slim left-handed pitcher named Ono, playing for the Mainichi industrial-league team of Osaka, set them and Hoyt down, 9–3.[3]

Hunter later took Ty Cobb to Japan one winter for a brief stint of coaching and in 1931, arranged a tour of major league All-Stars, featuring Lou Gehrig, Lefty Grove, Mickey Cochrane, Frankie Frisch, Rabbit Maranville, Lefty O'Doul, and Al Simmons. (Babe Ruth was busy

---

3. A team of players from the old Negro League, called the Royal Giants, visited Japan in 1927 and 1932, compiling records of 23–0 and 23–1, respectively.

making a movie.) This trip was sponsored by the *Yomiuri Shimbun* as part of a circulation-boosting campaign.

Gehrig and company won all seventeen games they played against college all-stars performing before large, enthusiastic crowds who marveled at the speed and power of the Americans. Losing by such scores as 20–3, 22–4, and 19–1, the Japanese admitted their embarrassment at being on the same field as the big leaguers. (A representative of the Japanese side even asked for a twenty-run handicap.) Their attitude disturbed Gehrig, who told his hosts at the end of the tour, "I had heard about *yamato damashi* (Japanese fighting spirit) and I thought I could learn something from it. But unfortunately, all I saw were players jogging to first on ordinary grounders. When I saw a runner coming down the line at me, grinning, I felt like punching him."

There were those on the Japanese side who did not find the American style of spirit very admirable either. "They have power and ability," said Suishu Tobita, "but they weren't serious."

Although Tobita had admired Ty Cobb for his no-nonsense attitude, he thought many of the American professionals generally inferior in character, incapable of understanding the spirit of Bushido. He particularly disliked Lefty Grove. In one game with the bases empty and none out, Grove had picked up a ground ball hit back to the pitcher's mound and, laughing, threw the ball to the third baseman, who then relayed it to first base just in time to nip the runner.

It was Grove's idea of a joke, but to Tobita that was a terrible insult. The incident helped color his view of American big leaguers for years to come.

During their trip, the Americans reached other lows in manners. On the voyage over, Rabbit Maranville had made the acquaintance of a Japanese admiral returning from Washington, D.C., whom he promptly nicknamed

Icky. When Icky fell asleep in a deck chair one day, Rabbit inked a face on his bald head.

During a visit to the prime minister's residence, the Japanese head of state was suddenly called out of the room and several members of the American group took the opportunity to purloin vases, fountain pens, and Havana cigars as souvenirs.

Yomiuri sponsored another tour in 1934, using Lefty O'Doul as point man after a money dispute with Hunter. This time the roster included Babe Ruth, Charlie Gehringer, and Jimmie Foxx, as well as Gehrig. Ruth had originally refused to go. He had just been released by the Yankees and was not in the best of spirits. But when a Tokyo businessman and baseball enthusiast named Sotaro Suzuki, who was helping O'Doul set up the games, showed him a Japanese poster printed up for the tour on which Ruth was the only player featured, the Babe's ego got the better of him and he agreed to make the trip.

Ruth was a big hit. An enormous crowd lined the streets for his motorcade from Tokyo Station down the Ginza to the Imperial Hotel. Sixty-five thousand people squeezed into Jingu Stadium for his first game. They bowed reverentially to the empty Emperor's Box at the start of the contest, and then screamed *banzai rusu* for the rest of the afternoon.

Seventy-five thousand came to see him at Osaka's Koshien Stadium. To commemorate that event, a bust of Ruth was erected outside the main gate—where it still stands today.

Ruth hit 14 homers as the All-Stars won all seventeen games against a team of amateur Japanese stars. The only bright spot for the Japanese was an eighteen-year-old right-hander from Kyoto named Eiji Sawamura. Sawamura took the mound against the Americans in Shizuoka and, perhaps inspired by Mount Fuji, the sacred Japanese mountain visible in the background, held the Americans hitless until the fifth inning. He used a blinding

fastball and a wide-breaking curve to strike out Gehringer, Ruth, Gehrig, and Foxx in succession. The only run
he surrendered was a seventh-inning homer by Gehrig,
losing 1–0.

The games took place amidst increasing tensions between the U.S. and Japan over the latter's advances into
Manchuria. During his stay, substitute catcher Moe Berg,
a Princeton linguist who spoke Japanese and who later did
high-level espionage for the U.S. during World War II,
slipped away in disguise to take rooftop photos of Tokyo
with a small camera. His pictures were later used to plan
American bombing raids.

Other members of the group felt certain they were
being spied upon in return, that their hotel phones were
bugged. Said Mack, "You just didn't know what was behind the smile of the Japanese."

Ruth was so popular, however, that for a time the problems between the U.S. and Japan were largely forgotten.
In fact, Ruth later wrote in his autobiography:

> Despite the treacherous attack that Japan made on us
> seven years later, I cannot help but feel that the recep-
> tion which millions of Japanese gave us was genuine.
> They lined the streets of the Ginza, the Broadway of
> Tokyo, for miles and greeted us as if we were real
> heroes. Everywhere we went, they feted us and tried to
> make our stay pleasant. No doubt there were plenty of
> stinkers among them, but looking back at that visit, I
> feel it is another example of how a crackpot govern-
> ment can lead a friendly people into war.
> They couldn't hit a lick, but I was surprised at their
> high class fielding, and the ability of some of their pitch-
> ers.

Japan, of course, was already on its inexorable path to
militarism and the seeds of war had been planted. After
the Americans went home, *Yomiuri Shimbun* owner Mat-

sutaro Shoriki was stabbed by a member of a rightist group. The group charged, among other things, that he had conspired to defile a sacred area by allowing the American professionals to play baseball in Jingu Stadium, the Mecca of college baseball.

Shoriki was unfazed. Encouraged by the response of the fans to Ruth, he established Japan's first professional baseball team, the Dai Nippon Tokyo Yakyu Kurabu (the Great Japan Tokyo Baseball Club), in December 1934, quickly signing up Sawamura and other top Japanese stars.

Dai Nippon toured the U.S. in 1935, playing 102 various PCL and semipro teams and winning 93 games. Wearing uniforms with numbers written in Chinese characters, they confused Americans trying to keep score. Their lengthy name was also so difficult for their hosts to master that Shoriki changed it to the Tokyo Giants, after the National League team from New York.

The Americans were impressed with Sawamura and one team actually tried to sign him, albeit by nefarious means. A Pittsburgh Pirates scout sought out Japan's top pitcher before a night game in Milwaukee with the Milwaukee Red Sox. He produced a piece of paper from his vest pocket and requested Sawamura's autograph. Sawamura was suspicious of all the small print above the area he was asked to sign and showed it to Sotaro Suzuki, who had accompanied the Giants on their tour and who was fluent in English. Suzuki accurately identified the document as a standard major league contract, handed it back to the scout, and suggested politely what he might do with it.

Although Sawamura was intrigued by the idea of pitching a season in the U.S. major leagues, he thought there were too many obstacles for him to overcome to actually do it, as he once confessed in a magazine article:

> My problem is I hate America and I can not make myself like Americans. I'm not good at the language, I

can't eat as much rice as I wish when I'm there and the women are too haughty. In America, you can not even tie your shoestrings if there is a woman around. People like myself can not possibly survive in an environment where such uncomfortable customs exist.

By 1936, Hanshin Railways and six other firms had followed Yomiuri and the Japanese Professional League was formed. Its charter stressed the lofty ideals of fair play and the improvement of the national spirit. Shoriki himself decreed his players must "always be gentlemen."

Many Japanese remained skeptical, however, that the pros could supplant the amateurs in the hearts and minds of the fans. Sawamura himself had wanted passionately to remain an amateur and to play for Waseda University. It was only after his debt-ridden father had committed him to a Yomiuri Giants contract without his knowledge, securing a hefty loan in the process, that he reluctantly agreed to turn pro.

Pro baseball struggled in its early years, with average crowds of fewer than five thousand. One stadium, built on the least expensive real estate that could be found, was so close to Tokyo Bay that incoming tides often flooded the field.

Still, the Giants drew well and the new league produced its share of stars, almost all of them under contract to Yomiuri. Sawamura, for example, won 33 games one season, and Victor Starfin, a Russian-born pitcher who had been raised in Japan (his parents were refugees from the Russian Revolution) went on to register 300 wins in a long career. There was also Shigeru Mizuhara, a charismatic third baseman from Keio University who once started a riot by picking up an apple that had been thrown on the field during a Waseda-Keio game and tossing it into the Waseda cheering section. And then there was Tetsuharu Kawakami, who went on to win several batting titles and star in a movie about his life.

During the war, the game took a back seat to more pressing matters. American baseball terminology was banned (*bēsubōru* became *yakyu* or "field ball"), as was the hidden-ball trick, a symbol of American chicanery believed unworthy of the Japanese. Players were referred to as "soldiers" or "warriors" and games were often preceded by grenade-throwing contests. Eventually, play was suspended altogether, as every able-bodied man was enlisted in the futile effort to fend off the advancing enemy.

Although Imperial Army soldiers were heard to scream "To hell with Babe Ruth" in the jungles of the South Pacific, Ruth was still deemed to have a high enough standing with the Japanese that he was almost called upon to act as a peace negotiator in the fading months of the war. A U.S. government plan called for the Babe to be flown to Guam to make a series of radio broadcasts to the people of Japan. As Ruth put it, he was to appeal to their sporting instincts to give up, and to tell them what the U.S. had in store for them if they did not surrender. In the end, however, the plan was scrapped as the U.S. high command opted for a more forceful approach—the A-bomb.

By the time the war was over, seventy-two professional Japanese players had lost their lives, including Sawamura, whose ship was torpedoed in the East China Sea, and a former twenty-game winner for the Nagoya team named Shinichi Ishimaru, who flew to his death in a kamikaze attack on a U.S. ship in 1944. Masaru Ikei wrote this touching account of Ishimaru's last hours in his fine book, *White Ball over the Pacific:*

Ishimaru completed a final letter to a naval attaché. Its contents were as follows:
"I'm very happy to have chosen baseball as my profession. There have been many hardships, but also great

joy. I'm twenty-four and I have nothing to regret. I'm finishing my career as a ballplayer and it is my destiny to die as a navy officer. My life will end with the word of *chuko* (fidelity to Emperor and one's parents).

Prior to his departure at ten o'clock in the morning, he played a game of catch with a fellow navy man Koichi Hondo, who had been a first baseman at Hosei Daigaku.

Sohachi Yamaoka, a navy reporter, served as the umpire.

"I'll get in the plane after I throw ten strikes," said Ishimaru in a voice choked with emotion.

With grave sorrow, Yamaoka began calling the balls and strikes.

Ishimaru pitched his last strike, then threw the ball on the ground, tied a *hachimaki* (cloth) around his head and put on his flying gloves.

Then he got in his plane and started the engine. The plane began to move down the runway and the nose lifted skyward, with a great sound. It disappeared into the southern sky. And it never returned.

His glove and ball were later returned to the Ishimaru family in Saga.

Some of Japan's stars survived. Mizuhara wound up in a Siberian POW camp, where he introduced baseball to his Russian captors. Kawakami spent three years in the infantry in Kumamoto. Starfin, legally a *gaijin*, was forced to stay in Tokyo under police surveillance. (He was killed in 1956 when the car he was driving collided with a Tokyo streetcar.)

Defeat in WWII had devastated Japan. By the war's end, many baseball parks, or what was left of them, were being used as barley fields to fight against widespread starvation. The area beneath the grandstands housed repatriated soldiers.

But as the nation began to rise from the ashes of defeat,

Allied High Command officials recognized baseball's potential for boosting morale and allowed it to resume. Sports fans in peacetime Japan began to ease up somewhat on their insistence that players be simon-pure. One of their new heroes was a pro named Hiroshi Oshita, a free-wheeling, boozing, wenching outfielder who boasted, "I never learned anything in college."

American culture, symbolized by Coca-Cola and jazz, had come flooding into Japan, and in an unusual salute to the country's new institution of *demokurashi,* more than one team actually chose its manager by player vote. A visit by the minor league San Francisco Seals, led by the sympathetic O'Doul, further helped rekindle the country's passion for the game.

By 1950, the present two-league setup was established with pennant winners meeting in the Japan Series. Nearly all the clubs were financed by large corporations for promotional purposes. The Taiyo Whales, for example, existed solely to promote the sales of whale meat and other products of the Taiyo Fishery Company.

Amateur baseball retained its popularity. Keio-Waseda games drew their usual screaming crowds of fifty thousand–plus, and the annual summer high school baseball tournament played to packed stadiums.

But it was the pro game that really took off, helped from around 1955 by the phenomenal spread of television. The Tokyo Yomiuri Giants became the everlasting heroes of the nation with their unprecedented and still unsurpassed nine Japan Championships in a row—from 1965 to 1973. Giants first baseman Sadaharu Oh hit 868 home runs in a twenty-two-year career (1958–80), surpassing Ruth and Hank Aaron, while his colorful, ebullient teammate Shigeo Nagashima won six batting titles and became the most beloved figure in the history of the Japanese game.

Pro baseball's postwar growth paralleled that of Japan's skyrocketing GNP and by the late 1980s it was fabulously profitable, drawing nearly 20 million fans a year. Most Valuable Player awards had grown from such early post-war prizes as a barrel of *Shoyu* (soy sauce) and a live pig to expensive new cars and tens of thousand dollars in cash—all of which reflected Japan's new status as a world power. When the new Tokyo Dome, modeled after Minnesota's Metrodome, opened in 1988, it cost forty-five hundred yen (about thirty-five U.S. dollars) a ticket for choice infield seats.

Although Japanese teams still had difficulty defeating major league teams in periodic postseason encounters, their game grew stronger and more clearly defined. It became as clear an expression of the Japanese character as one could find, reflecting the real life and spirit of the people.

$$\otimes \qquad \otimes \qquad \otimes$$

Baseball's grip on Japan's collective psyche is due, ultimately, to the fact that it suits the national character. Introduced to a people whose very identities were rooted in the group, but who, oddly enough, had no group sport of their own—only one-on-one competitions like kendo and sumo—baseball provided the Japanese with an opportunity to express their renowned group proclivities on an athletic field. Indeed, over the years—and despite Oh's home runs—it has been the team aspects of the game, the sacrifice bunt, the squeeze, the hit-and-run, that have come to characterize Japanese baseball. (In fact, when the Hanshin Tigers of 1985 set an all-time league record for home runs by a team, 219, they also set a similar mark for sacrifice bunts, 141.)

Unlike other group sports, baseball also comes with a built-in individual confrontation—a test of wills—which, as we have seen, also gave it its initial appeal to fans of the martial arts and sumo. The "get-set" ritual in sumo, for example, with its squatting, stamping, and fierce glaring, has its equivalent in the war of nerves the pitcher and the batter wage, which involves delaying tactics like calling time and cleaning spikes.

Perhaps another reason for baseball's attraction for the Japanese is its relatively slow pace. As any Western businessman familiar with Japan will agree, the Japanese are extremely careful. They like to fully discuss and analyze a problem before reaching a decision. On a baseball field the natural break between pitches and innings allows ample time for verbose and dilatory strategy sessions, since the game is never over until the last man is out. Japanese pro games—like Japanese business meetings—can seem interminable.

As each new situation arises, there is so much discussion on the field and in the dugout, involving managers, coaches, players, and even umpires, that most games last well over three hours. Indeed, the average Japanese game is more like a board meeting at Mitsubishi than an athletic event.

Said Warren Cromartie, "Managers in Japan are afraid to make quick decisions, because they are afraid of making a mistake. They have to discuss everything to death with their coaches before they make a move. I played one half-inning in Osaka that took forty-five minutes. That must be a world record."

Japanese baseball has, on occasion, even invited comparison with Kabuki, a traditional, highly stylized form of theater in which performances last four to five hours. The leisurely pitch-by-pitch format of baseball, many Japanese say, is not without its similarities to a Kabuki dialogue which depends on the dramatic use of *ma* (pauses). An admirer of a top relief pitcher, Yutaka Enatsu, once explained his success by saying, "He was good because he knew how to use the *ma*. He waited for just the right moment—a momentary lapse of concentration by the batter—to deliver his pitch."

Finally, baseball seems ideally suited to the well-known statistical bent of the Japanese. The postwar baseball boom gave rise to a number of sports dailies—fourteen in all, counting regional editions—with a total readership of 30 million. They provide enough data to satisfy a bookkeeper—ten-column box scores, batter-by-batter accounts of every game, detailed listings of the top thirty hitters in each league, and complex player-ranking formulas. Graphics during televised games show the inning, score, number of outs, and the ball-strike count on each batter after every pitch. Some stations even indicate the speed of every pitched ball as well as its location on a superimposed strike zone.

A Japanese writer once summed up his country's love for baseball by saying, "Baseball is perfect for us. If the Americans hadn't invented it, we probably would have."

He understated his case.

3

A Philosophy

*I'll tell you the big difference between Japan
and the U.S. In the U.S. we believe that a player
has a certain amount of natural ability and
with practice he reaches a certain peak point,
but after that no amount of practice will make
him better—because after a certain point your
ability reaches its limits. But the Japanese believe there is no peak point. They don't recog-
nize limits.*

Chris Arnold,
Former San Francisco Giant and Kintetsu Buffalo

Choji Murata believed in spirit and hard work—that if a
man tried hard enough, he could do anything. He had
employed that philosophy to make himself the best
pitcher in Japan. Through constant effort he had developed a forkball that visiting U.S. major leaguers who faced
him said was impossible to hit.

He had been drafted in 1967, from a high school in
Hiroshima, by the Pacific League Lotte Orions, the least-
popular team in the country. The Orions played in the
heavily polluted industrial city of Kawasaki. Their home
park, Kawasaki Stadium, was a chipped and weathered
postwar structure—usually empty—with assorted bumps
and holes in an outfield Murata's teammates compared to
playing in a vacant lot.

But Murata did not mind. All he cared about was pitching. He went on to win every pitching honor there was to

win. In 1976, his best year, he won twenty-one games and led the league in strikeouts, with 202, and an ERA of 1.82. He pitched five one-hit games in his career and was twice voted league MVP. In 1981 and 1985, he won his first eleven games in a row.

Murata thought a pitcher should never stop working. He threw a hundred or more pitches every day in practice and in games he would throw every pitch as hard as he could—which in Murata's case was over ninety miles per hour. This was counter to the advice of American sports physicians who usually recommend pitchers take three to four days of moderate rest between starts. However, Murata did not concern himself with such things.

But one day early in the 1982 season he felt a strange twinge in his right elbow and found himself unable to pitch normally. His arm hurt every time he tried to throw and he was forced to go on the disabled list. The team doctor could find nothing wrong, so Murata decided that he would "pitch through the pain."

Every day he would go out and throw a ball against a concrete wall in his neighborhood. Pain shot through his arm with every pitch, but he continued to throw, hoping somehow to make the pain disappear by sheer will.

His wife said that what his arm needed was rest. So did his American teammate Leron Lee. But Murata was an advocate of the old dictum that a man should pitch until his arm falls off. He was a purebred Hiroshiman, and Hiroshimans were known for their special brand of perseverance. So he kept it up. He continued to throw until his arm ached so badly that he could not even raise it above his shoulder.

Murata tried everything to heal his injured elbow: acupuncture, electrical shock, massages. One fan, a Japanese-American living in Los Angeles, wrote him a letter about the miraculous comeback pitcher Tommy John had made. When John had ripped a tendon in his left elbow, an orthopedic surgeon named Frank Jobe performed an unusual operation that saved his career. He replaced the damaged tendon in the left elbow with one from the right, and after a year of therapy, John was able to come back and pitch many more seasons in the big leagues.

Murata's wife saw the letter and said, "Maybe this is your chance." Murata blanched. He felt a chill down his spine. He didn't even want to think about that possibility. In Japan, it was said that once you had surgery on your pitching arm, you were finished. Sports medicine had not yet developed into the specialty field that it was in other countries.

Still Murata had to do something. His children in primary school were being teased that their father was all washed up. So he went to Tokyo University Medical School, the best facility in the country. But after extensive examinations, doctors there could find no trace of damage. The bone and muscle were normal, they told him. He went to other clinics. But everywhere, the answer was the same: "There is nothing wrong with your arm."

He tried a masseur who bent and twisted his arm so violently he thought it would pop out of its socket. When the massage was finished, Murata's arm was black-and-blue, and when he tried to throw, the pain was so intense he doubled over.

But he kept on trying to throw. He thought if he just kept doing it, he could somehow conquer his affliction. A year had passed. Finally, a solicitous Lotte official asked him to stop throwing. "What if you hurt yourself so much that you can never pitch again? Please rest until your arm heals."

Murata replied, "A man should pitch until his arm falls off."

Lotte formally ordered him to cease and desist until they could find out what the problem was.

Murata fell into a deep depression. His wife would wake up in the middle of the night and find her husband out of bed, sitting by himself in the living room.

By the middle of 1983, the newspapers had declared it official: Murata was finished.

Murata practiced Zen. He read books on Zen philosophy and on occasion he meditated. Every year in the off-season, during the coldest part of the winter, he would go to a forest temple on the Izu Peninsula, south of Tokyo, where he would fast and meditate while standing seminaked under an icy waterfall.

Zen was a familiar word in the lexicon of the Japanese athlete. Legendary seventeenth-century samurai swordsman Musashi Miyamoto, wrote, "The Way of the Sword is Zen." Four centuries later, Kawakami, "The God of Batting," wrote, *Bēsubōru* is Zen." Sadaharu Oh's batting teacher was an aikido instructor who emphasized the value of Zen in improving concentration.

Murata was more serious about Zen than most. And now, he went to the Izu temple to seek a final solution to his problem. There, a Zen master named Takamatsu gave Murata painful massages and told him that only through inner strength could his arm be healed. "No one can heal it for you," he said. "You have to do it by yourself."

Murata followed his advice. Each day he would stand under the icy waterfall to meditate. And each day Takamatsu continued his massages. He produced a snakeskin which had been soaked in *shochu* (a kind of potato whisky) for eight years and wrapped it around Murata's elbow to help draw out the poison inside. For weeks Murata followed the same daily routine, and then it was time to go home.

Back in Kawasaki, he picked up a ball and tried to throw, but found that the pain was still there, as intense as ever. Worse yet, he now had an ugly excrescence on his elbow. Said teammate Lee, who saw Murata's arm one day at the Lotte park in Kawasaki, "The sight of it made you want to puke."

Murata began to think that maybe he never would pitch again. He said as much to his wife and reminded her of a promise he had made when they got married. He had vowed to be the best pitcher in Japan and that if the day ever came when he didn't think he was the best anymore, well, if she wanted to leave, it was okay. He would understand.

She became indignant. She had been a patient, loyal, and supportive wife, she said, and she wasn't sharing all this pain and agony with him just so she could be the wife of a great pitcher. Didn't he understand that? She said she would never leave him. She also told him to stop thinking about retiring.

So, finally, Murata was faced with the unthinkable. More than two years after he had first felt that funny twinge in his arm, he went to Los Angeles with his wife to see Dr. Jobe. It was his only remaining option.

Jobe examined Murata's arm and told him that the tendon had been severed. The bone and the nerves were okay, he said, but the tendon was cut and he could not believe Murata had actually been trying to throw with his arm in such a condition.

Jobe said that he would have to operate. He would take a tendon from Murata's left wrist and put it in his right elbow. The operation would be easy, he said, but the rehabilitation would not. It would take a year of very hard work to reach the stage where he could pitch again. It took a special kind of person to make that commitment. Tommy John had been that kind. Was Choji Murata?

Murata said yes. By all means.

The operation was a success. Although Murata suffered considerable pain afterwards, he initially refused to ask for a painkiller. He thought it would be unmanly (and, as he later confessed, he had an intense phobia of injections).

Murata thus began the long process of coming back. At first, he could barely make a fist, but he stuck with it. He exercised daily and soon he was able to lob the ball across his living room. In September 1984, he pitched an inning in relief, after 1,070 days on the sidelines.

The most difficult thing about Murata's comeback, perhaps, was following Jobe's orders not to pitch so much. Jobe had explained certain scientific facts of life about pitching:

> Pitching is an unnatural motion. The human arm, be it Caucasian, black, or Oriental, is not constructed to throw a baseball. Every time a starting pitcher pitches, he gets a sore arm. He experiences tiny muscle tears in his arm. A starting pitcher who throws a nine-inning game should rest until his arm can regain its normal structure.

Jobe warned Murata that in his case, six days of rest was imperative between each appearance. And that meant rest, not throwing a hundred pitches a day as Murata had done previously.

Murata complied, however reluctantly. The next year, he compiled a record of 17–5, with 93 strikeouts, winning Comeback of the Year honors. At the end of that 1987 season, he and his wife flew to L.A. to personally thank Jobe for all he had done.

Murata's success started a new trend in Japan. Several other pitchers followed his path to L.A. for arm surgery and found their careers resurrected. Suddenly, going to see Jobe had become a fad.

But Murata was not happy about that. He thought some of the younger players went under the knife all too quickly, that their comebacks were too easy. Suffering built character and character is what made the difference between winners like Murata and weak-kneed losers. Modern medicine may have rebuilt his arm, but something else had made his career.

One afternoon in 1987 at a Kawasaki coffee shop, he talked to a young writer about the proliferation of machines and electronic instruments in modern-day life.

"Do you use a word processor?" asked Murata.

"No, I don't," replied the young man, "I use a pencil."

"Good," he said nodding his approval, "You can't get any heart into your work with one of those things."

A man who lost touch with the natural way of things— things like pain and suffering, and who didn't have to try hard, would lose touch with himself.[1]

⚾ ⚾ ⚾

By the time Japanese professional baseball had celebrated its fiftieth anniversary, it had become a mirror of Japan's fabled virtues of hard work and harmony, and a game that was barely recognizable to Americans.

"This isn't baseball," grumbled former Dodger Reggie Smith after his first season as a Tokyo Giant. "It only looks like it."

Like the U.S. game, the Nipponese version is played with a bat and ball. The same rulebook is used, but that's where the resemblance ends. Training, for example, is nearly a religion. Baseball players in America start spring training in March and take no more than five or six weeks to prepare for the six-month season. They spend three to four hours on the field each day and then head for the nearest golf course, swimming pool, or couch. Some, like Pete Rose, have said that even that is too much.

Japanese teams begin with "voluntary" training in the freezing cold of mid-January. Each day they're on the field for a numbing seven hours, and then it's off to the dormitory for an evening of strategy sessions and still more workouts indoors. Players run ten miles every day, including periodic climbs up and down the stadium steps.

---

1. Murata did in fact try to advise the younger starter on the Orions not to throw so much in practice. "I tried to teach them to take care of their arms," he said, "but they ignored me. They still think pitching hard everyday is the only way to success. Some things are hard to change."

Said Warren Cromartie, who spent five consecutive Februaries in Japan, "It makes boot camp look like a church social."

During the season, such hard training continues. Whereas many American players curtail their pregame midsummer workouts to conserve energy for the game, the Japanese often step up theirs—believing among other things that extra work is a good way to beat heat fatigue. As Sadaharu Oh once put it, "The hot weather does in those players who haven't trained hard all along."

"It's baseball all your waking hours," said American Steve Ontiveros, a former Cub who played in Japan. "For a night game, I would get to the stadium at 2:00 P.M. and some of the Japanese players had already been running for thirty minutes. On travel days we headed straight from the airport for a four-hour workout—even in the middle of August. I heard Japan was a nice country, but I never got a chance to see it. I was always practicing."

The Japanese game is strictly organized around a plethora of rules to ensure that each player is not only well-trained physically but also has the right mental attitude. Among the rules the Tokyo Giants instituted one year for their practice sessions were: "Report to the field fifteen minutes early, do not engage in private conversation on the field, encourage your teammates in a loud voice, run when moving from place to place." The Seibu Lions, perhaps Japan's strictest organization in the two pro leagues after the Giants, have a season-long ban on drinking, smoking, and appearing in commercials. (When star pitcher Osamu Higashio was discovered to have gambled at mah-jongg against known *yakuza* (gangsters), the team suspended him for half a year and cut his salary by 40 percent.)

Clubhouse walls are covered with slogans to spur the players on: without Self-Sacrifice There Can Be No Real Team; You Are The Master of Your Own Fate; Cry in

Practice, Laugh in the Games; Self-Reflection Is the Bread of Progress.

To Americans used to the notion that an individual is responsible for himself and that performance on the field is the only thing that matters, the Japanese system can seem incredibly restrictive. Charlie Manuel, a former Minnesota Twin who played in Japan, said, "I've never experienced anything like it in all my years of baseball. The coaches even told me when to change my socks."

For Americans baseball is a job. For the Japanese it is a way of life. From the younger players who live in the team dormitory year-round (and take turns raising the team flag every morning) to the older veterans who may organize impromptu workouts in the brief off-season, the story is the same: total commitment.

The Japanese believe that good players are made, not born, and that only through endless training can one achieve the unity of mind and body necessary to excel. The famed Kawakami claimed inspiration from the afore-mentioned samurai Musashi Miyamoto, who taught that the key to master swordsmanship was the motto, "One thousand days to learn, ten thousand days to refine."

Through years of constant practice, Kawakami developed his concentration to a state where, he said, a pitched ball would "stop" for him before he went into his swing.

Sadaharu Oh incorporated a drill into his routine in which he would slice away with a sword at a tiny piece of paper suspended by a string from the ceiling. Said Oh of his 868 home run career, "I achieved what I did because of my coaches and my willingness to work hard." When Oh signs autographs, he signs with the word *doryoku* (ef-fort). So does former star Koji Yamamoto, who hit 536 home runs in his eighteen years with the Hiroshima Carp.

Such attitudes strike a responsive chord in the Japanese psyche. The traditional view in this rich but cramped and resource-poor land is that nothing comes easily, and that only through *doryoku* and the ability to persevere in the face of adversity can one achieve success.

Indeed, in a 1982 survey conducted by NHK, Japan's equivalent of the BBC, the word *doryoku* was chosen as the "most-liked" word by those polled. The rest of the top ten, in descending order, were *patience, thanks, sincerity, endurance, love, harmony, kindness, friendship,* and *trust.*

Six years later, Toshiyuki Ueda, a young editor at Kodansha, a leading Japanese publisher, said, "Youth in Japan is changing, but if that same survey were taken today, *Doryoku* would still be there at the top, along with *love* and *harmony.*

No one embodied *doryoku* more than Koji Yamamoto's teammate Sachio Kinugasa, who stepped into the Carp starting lineup at third base on October 18, 1970, and did not miss a game until he retired on October 22, 1987. He played 2,215 consecutive games, the longest streak in the history of professional baseball.

When, on June 13, 1987, Kinugasa bettered Lou Gehrig's record for durability of 2,130 games in a row, it was cause for jubiliation unseen in Japan since the days when Sadaharu Oh was passing Babe Ruth and Hank Aaron in career home runs.

It was a triumph of will, they said. Kinugasa had overcome slumps, injuries, and broken bones on the way to his record. And whereas there had been grousing by Americans in Oh's case—that he had achieved his record by playing in small parks, against inferior pitching, and that throughout his career he had used compressed bats which propelled the ball considerably farther than normal bats—no one could disparage Kinugasa's accomplishment.[2]

---

2. Compressed bats are banned in the U.S. and were subsequently phased out in Japan after Oh's retirement.

It took Kinugasa seventeen years to do what Gehrig had done in fifteen, because Japanese teams play 130 games a year, compared with the 154 played in the U.S. major leagues in Gehrig's time. On the other hand, Kinugasa endured tough Japanese-style pregame workouts that few major leaguers ever experienced.

Rich Lancelotti, Kinugasa's American teammate in 1987, said, "He worked as hard as anybody on the team. Given the amount of energy he expended in practice. It was as if he played a doubleheader every day of his entire career.

Kinugasa was more than just an everyday player. He hit 504 home runs and was one of the few Japanese to reach 2,000 hits, the benchmark for the Japanese game, given the shorter season. In 1984, he led the Central League in RBIs with 102, and was named the league's Most Valuable Player. His lifetime average was .270.

The exploits of Kinugasa and home run hitter Koji Yamamoto moved people in Hiroshima to tears. Together they elevated the Carp from a perennial second-division team to a constant contender, winners of five pennants and three Japan Championships. It was a club that symbolized the remarkable climb of Hiroshima from the horrible ravages, both physical and psychological, of the atomic bomb, to a bustling, thriving metropolis.

Kinugasa was not physically big; he stood five feet nine inches tall and weighed 165 pounds. But he was strong and he had a big American-style swing—much to the chagrin of Carp coaches who preferred batting technicians—which he employed to set the all-time Japanese strikeout record of 1587. Kinugasa swung so hard that for many years he suffered from whiplash.

Kinugasa is a dark-featured man of easy smiles, a flashy dresser who likes flashy cars. He spent his signing bonus on a big Ford Galaxy—back in the days when the Japanese thought American cars something worth buying. He also had a reputation as a hard-drinking hell-raiser.

Yet, before going to bed, each and every night of his eighteen-year career, he always swung a bat. He would be drinking in a bar with teammates, when suddenly he would disappear and return an hour or so later. Nobody knew until many years into Kinugasa's career that he was off, alone, taking shadow swings.

The story is told of the time in the summer of 1970, Kinugasa's third year in professional ball, when he staggered back to the Carp dormitory at dawn, dead drunk. Coach Junzo Sekine, who had been working one-on-one with Kinugasa every night, was waiting for him. "You forgot to practice your swing," he said.

Kinugasa swung his bat one hundred times before he crumpled to the floor, crying from exhaustion.

Clyde Haberman, former Tokyo bureau chief of the *New York Times*, expressed Kinugasa's appeal well when he wrote:

> (Kinugasa) is a rock of consistency, and, as such, the hero. The *sarariman*—the Japanese word is taken straight from English, *salaryman*—is Japan's average Joe. He is the guy who puts on a blue suit every morning, rides the train to work for an hour and a half, puts in ten–twelve hours, drinks late into the night with his colleagues, then heads home for a few hours' sleep so that he can start all over again the next day.
>
> Like the *sarariman*, Kinugasa is there as promised every day.

Kinugasa suffered five broken bones over the years, yet he never missed a game. His record was in the greatest danger in August 1979 when Yomiuri Giants pitcher Takashi Nishimoto hit him in the back with an errant pitch. He was taken to the hospital in an ambulance, where doctors diagnosed his injury as a fracture of the left shoulder blade and ordered him not to play. His streak then stood at 1,123 games.

Kinugasa endured a fitful night. The next day he taped up his shoulder, went to the park, and stepped into the batting cage. For the next ten minutes, he swung his bat hard, as always, showing his manager that he could still play.

His remarks about that day have been repeated many times in the Japanese media: "It would have been even more painful for me to stay home. If I played and swung the bat, the pain in my shoulder would last only an instant. If I had to stay home and watch the game on TV, I'd hurt all over for three hours."

Verbal accolades came from every quarter when Kinugasa passed Gehrig. "Extraordinary moral strength and superhuman endurance," went a *Yomiuri Shimbun* editorial. "Kinugasa's great record is due to . . . physical toughness, diligence, endurance, and strict observance of the rules and manners of team spirit."

The then prime minister, Yasuhiro Nakasone, presented Kinugasa with a silver bas relief of Mount Fuji— that "beautiful, noble mountain of perfect symmetry and without blemish."

At times, Kinugasa seemed embarrassed by being held up as a paragon of Japanese virtue. "If we have a game, I want to play," he said, "That's all. A true sportsman is somebody who plays as long as he can."

It may be that Kinugasa had a special motivation for succeeding. His father had been a black American soldier stationed in Okinawa after the war and had deserted the family. It was the only thing Kinugasa was really sensitive about. The subject was not mentioned in either of his authorized biographies and there were standing orders on the Hiroshima team never to talk about it.

As a boy growing up in Kyoto, Kinugasa endured the taunts of other schoolchildren and it apparently took him years to come to grips with his background. His former roommate, Tatsuo Okitsu, a Carp infielder, told a reporter

about the time he found Kinugasa up late at night studying English.

"I asked why," said Okitsu, "and he said he wanted to
go to America to look for his father because he'd never
met him. I told him he'd do better working more on his
swing instead of English.

"If you become the number one player in Japan, he'll
come to see you," I told him. He nodded with tears in his
eyes.

Kinugasa's father never came, but for one shining summer in 1987, Kinugasa was indeed number one.

        Ⓒ   Ⓒ   Ⓒ

The capacity for *doryoku,* many Japanese coaches have
long maintained, must be cultivated through practice.
Consequently an integral part of spring training routines
are *gattsu* (guts) drills designed to push a player to his
limits. The record for the 1980s was held by a player
named Koichi Tabuchi. In 1984, the year of his retirement at age thirty-eight, he capped off a day of workouts
in spring camp by fielding nine hundred consecutive
ground balls. It took two hours and fifty minutes before he
slumped to the ground, unable to get up.

Americans generally consider such training valueless.
They believe that forcing a player to practice when he is
tired only creates bad habits and adds to the likelihood of
injury. Yet to Japanese like Kennichi Ishida, a former
writer for the *Nikkan Sports,* those critics are overlooking
the Zen ramifications of the drills. "These drills are primarily mental. Yes, they do wear a player out, but that is
necessary in order to develop his spirit. Athletics are essentially an act of will. You can always do more than you
think you are capable of. It is our philosophy that only by
pushing a player to his limits can he discover and develop
the power to surpass them. And that is what these drills
accomplish."

The Japanese system of player development through endless practice and physical drill doesn't always work the way it's supposed to. Consider the case of one rookie pitcher who began his professional career in the mid-1970s. He was, his manager believed, a potential star, but being rather frail of build he had difficulty keeping up with his team's torturous spring training. By the time his turn for pitching practice came around, he was so tired he could barely get the ball over the plate.

To correct the problem, the coaches devised a special routine for him to follow every day after regular practice. First he was forced to run from one stadium foul pole to the other (a distance of about 150 yards) fifty times. As an additional test of his resolve, coaches would station themselves at either end of his run to yell *bakayaro* (stupid S.O.B.) every time he finished a lap. This was followed by a special pitching practice in which any bad pitch would prompt another flurry of insults. To wrap up the day, he was required, like all rookies, to pick up loose balls and other pieces of equipment and carry them back to the clubhouse.

In the manner of most Japanese players, he kept a stiff upper lip and gave it all he had. His special training went on at periodic intervals with no visible improvement. And during his third season, he found himself in a mental institution in Osaka, the victim of a nervous breakdown.

⚾   ⚾   ⚾

The U.S. is a land where the hard individualist is honored. The typical American player is one like Darryl Strawberry or Don Mattingly, who lives by the rule "I know what's best for me."

In Japan, however, the word for individualism, *kojin-shugi*, is almost a dirty word. The only ones who know what's best are the managers and the coaches. They have the virtues Orientals most respect—age and experience, hence knowledge. Their word is law. And they demand that everyone do everything their way. The traditional Japanese ideal is a humble, uncomplaining, obedient soul like Giants star Tatsunori Hara, who was once chosen in a poll as the "male symbol of Japan."

Hara was frequently compared in the Japanese press to Cal Ripken, Jr., who visited Japan in 1984 with the Baltimore Orioles and again in 1986, with a group of major league All-Stars. Ripken was Hara's counterpart, the writers said. Both had been raised by baseball fathers (Cal Ripken, Sr., managed the Orioles in 1987–88, while Hara's father Mitsugu became famous when he guided tiny Miike High of Kyushu to a national championship). Both were infielders, big stars in their early twenties, league MVPs in 1983, and quiet, likable young men.

Yet, that was where the similarities ended. In other aspects, the two were poles apart.

Ripken was typical of the successful athlete in America. Once he had mastered the fundamentals of baseball as a youth, he improved by emulating the players above him, innovating and improvising along the way. By the time he reached the big leagues, he had developed a batting form that was unique—fists horizontal, bat pointed back—and a fielding style that was unorthodox: He would sometimes backhand ground balls that came directly at him. His style was different, but it worked for him.

"I've never really taken much advice from anyone," he said, "be it my father or any other coaches. I've always been able to figure things out for myself." Japanese reporters and coaches were aghast when they heard him say that.

By contrast, people had been telling Hara what to do all his life; first his father, then a long succession of Giants instructors, all of whom believed that form, orthodox form, was all important. Hara had learned how to bat and field by the numbers. He looked like a carbon copy of every other player in Japan.

It was significant that if Hara wasn't hitting, TV cameras

frequently zoomed in on the Giants batting coach, sitting on the bench, shaking his head, as if to say, "I taught him proper form, why can't he hit?"

It is doubtful that any American player had ever been as closely supervised as Hara. He had been groomed for stardom almost from the time he was born. He was only three months old, as the story goes, when his father picked him up and dropped him on the family *futon* (sleeping quilt), to test his son's reflexes. The baby immediately flexed his legs and absorbed the impact. Hara Senior gauged the results and said, "Hmmm. I've got myself a star here."

When Hara reached the age of three, his father began to train him for baseball, starting with a daily routine of twenty pushups and a four-kilometer run up and down the hills of his neighborhood. As Hara got older, the routine became progressively harder.

Hara starred in high school and college under his father and was drafted by the Yomiuri Giants, who needed a cleanup hitter to replace the retiring Oh. As a rookie in 1981, he hit .262 with 22 home runs and was more popular than the Emperor. He was a strapping six footer, with Prince Charming good looks, and marriage proposals from adoring female fans flowed into the Giants front office every day. Film studios tried to sign him up, but Hara had to refuse them. He was expected to concentrate only on baseball.

Hara went on to have many fine seasons, averaging .285 and 31 home runs a year for his first eight years. He won his 1983 MVP for hitting 32 homers, driving in 103 runs, and hitting .302, while helping the Giants win the pennant.

But fans, commentators, and coaches were never satisfied. They complained that he struck out too often in key situations, that he couldn't hit a decent forkball, that he couldn't hit the 40-homer mark. He did not have the mark of greatness of an Oh or Nagashima.

His critics said that Hara was not tough enough. That was the problem. Once Hara had a wisdom tooth extracted before a game and his jaw became so swollen and painful he had to lie down in the stadium first aid room. When he did not play that evening, retired Carp star Koji Yamamoto, the *doryoku* man, publicly took him to task in a newspaper column, implying that a real cleanup hitter would have been in the lineup.

The next day, a photographer asked to photograph the inside of Hara's mouth, as evidence he really was in bad shape. Hara angrily refused. That night, his face still badly swollen, he returned to the lineup and hit a home run.

Programs were continually being devised to make Hara more productive. He was sent on a *yamagomori* (spiritual retreat to the mountains.) He was put through extra batting practice and conditioning drills—one spring camp he took fifteen thousand swings in two-and-a-half weeks, and former Giant coaches and managers paraded out to the park to make minute analyses of Hara's batting form to see if they could improve upon it. The reasoning seemed to be that if everyone kept trying, together they could find a way to make Hara a better player.

Hara obediently listened to his coaches and followed their advice. Yet nothing much changed. He kept churning out roughly the same statistics every year.

Said Reggie Smith, who played with Hara for two years, "He had so many different people telling him what to do, it's a wonder he could still swing the bat. They turned him into a robot, instead of just letting him play naturally and expressing his natural talent."

Added Cromartie, who played with Hara for five years, "I'd try to tell him to ignore the coaches, to play his own game. But he couldn't do that."

Smith's and Cromartie's attitudes were typically American. They maintained that individual initiative was a key ingredient in any endeavor. They thought Hara would do just fine if everyone would leave him alone. But few Japanese were willing to buy that argument. They believed that the individual was nothing without others and that even the most talented people need constant direction.

Indeed, the relationship between teacher and student, and by extension, coach and player, is one of the fundamental characteristics of Japanese society—in fact, of Asian life as a whole. It is rooted in the master-disciple relationship found in Zen and the martial arts. Oh has continually credited his success as a home run hitter to his chunky batting coach Hiroshi Arakawa, the man who introduced Oh to his famous foot-in-the-air stance. As Oh said many, many times, "I would have been nothing without Arakawa."

The gap between Japanese and American thinking on this point is not easily bridged. To the American criticism that Hara was overcoached, the Japanese would invariably retort, "Just think what a truly great player Ripken could be if a coach could iron out those flaws in his form."

⊗　　　⊗　　　⊗

The concept and practice of group harmony or *wa* is what most dramatically differentiates Japanese baseball from the American game. It is the connecting thread running through all Japanese life and sports. While "Let It All Hang Out" and "Do Your Own Thing" are mottoes of contemporary American society, the Japanese have their own credo in the well-worn proverb, "The Nail That Sticks Up Shall Be Hammered Down." It is practically a national slogan.

Holdouts, for example, are rare in Japan. A player usually takes what the club deigns to give him and that's that. Demanding more money is evidence that a player is putting his own interests before those of the team.

In 1984, when the Chunichi Dragons' top batter Yasushi Tao hit .353 to win the CL batting crown and asked for a big raise, he was traded. Praiseworthy, by contrast, was a Seibu Lions outfielder who, in the same year, refused a raise offered by his club because he had missed too many games as the result of an injury.

The players may not like this state of affairs, especially since the minimum salary is only about one-third of what it is in the U.S. major leagues, but in Japan, social pressure is strong and the media are vigilant. When a pitching star named Suguru Egawa asked for a 10-percent raise one year after slipping from 16 wins to 15, a leading sports daily ran the headline, "Egawa! You Greedy SOB!"

A players' union was formally established in 1985, but union leader Kiyoshi Nakahata of the Giants quickly declared on nationwide television, "We'd never act like the U.S. major leaguers. A strike would be going too far." Indeed, in a subsequent survey taken by the *Asahi Shimbun,* only 28 percent of the players polled said they would ever agree to a walkout.

In the pressure-cooker world of U.S. pro sports, temper outbursts are considered acceptable, and at times even regarded as a salutary show of spirit. In Japan, however, a player's behavior is often considered as important as his batting average. Batting slumps are usually accompanied by embarrassed smiles. Temper tantrums—along with practical joking, bickering, complaining, and other norms of American clubhouse life—are viewed in Japan as unwelcome incursions into the team's collective peace of mind. They offend the finer sensitivities of the Japanese, and as many American players have learned the hard way, Japanese sensitivities *are* finer.

When Hiroshima Carp All-Star shortstop Yoshihiko Takahashi threw down his glove in anger and disgust after committing an error during a game in 1984, his manager Takeshi Koba slapped his face, right there in front of several thousand fans. "A player's glove is his most important possession," a journalist explained the next day. "He should treat it with respect as a samurai would his sword."

When Giants top pitcher Takashi Nishimoto ignored the instructions of a coach in practice one summer day in

1985, the coach punched him between the eyes. Nishimoto was also forced to apologize and pay a one-hundred-thousand-yen fine for insubordination.

Moreover, untoward behavior is also seen as a sign of character weakness and a "small heart," as well as being detrimental to the team's image overall. In Japan, a "real man" is one who keeps his emotions to himself and thinks of others' feelings.

Shortly before opening day in 1987, Takahashi found himself in hot water again. He had balked at attending a team rally in downtown Hiroshima, complaining, "We should be concentrating on baseball. How the hell can we do that with all these other functions?" For this the Carp owner banished Takahashi to the farm team for three weeks. Irrational? Perhaps. Without the mainstay of their infield and one of their best hitters, the Carp, defending league champions, fell behind in the early going and never did catch up, finishing second. But any games lost because Takahashi was unavailable were not as important as the example that had to be set.

The lengths to which Japanese team officials will go to preserve the team's *wa* can be alarmingly final—as a veteran pitcher named Takenori Emoto can attest. Emoto had a wicked slider which he used to win 113 games in ten years. But he was the nail that stuck up in more ways than one—from his six-foot-four-inch bamboo-shoot frame to his defiant attitude, which frequently got him into hot water. Once, for example, he let his hair grow over his ears in defiance of the team's short-hair policy. The general manager had to threaten him to release him before he would get a haircut.

Playing for the Hanshin Tigers in 1981, Emoto bridled at the way the Tigers manager kept using him—shifting him back and forth between starting and relief. One August night, after being yanked from a game in which he had been pitching well, Emoto stalked back to the dugout

and into the runway, where reporters heard him complain angrily, "I can't pitch with this kind of stupid
managing."

The next morning, the Emoto Rebellion was front-page
news in all the sports dailies and Emoto found himself the
target of much editorial wrath for his willful conduct.
Wrote one newspaper editor, "Players should just shut up
and do as they're told."

Emoto announced his "voluntary retirement" from the
team to "accept responsibility" for the incident. However, his retirement later revealed itself to be not so voluntary when the Tigers, who still owned the rights to
Emoto, rejected all trade overtures from other teams.

If Emoto expected his fellow players to come dashing
to his defense, he was sadly disappointed. Said Koji
Yamamoto, then head of the players' association, "It's too
bad Emoto had to commit hara-kiri like that." And then
dropped the matter.

"I didn't want to quit then," said Emoto, an unchas-
tened pariah. "I felt I had a couple of more years and even
thought about going to America to try my luck. But the
Tigers wouldn't even allow that. I was completely black-
balled."

Adversity sometimes has its blessings, however. Emoto
went on to write a series of books about behind-the-scenes
life in pro baseball which became enormous bestsellers.
His candid revelations, including a description of
Sadaharu Oh's penis, which he had supposedly espied in
the dressing room before an All-Star game, made Emoto
a TV celebrity and a very wealthy man. Pacific League
public relations director Pancho Ito referred to him as the
"Jim Bouton of Japan."

⚾   ⚾   ⚾

Wa and *doryoku* have long been regarded as indispensable elements in any successful organization in Japan.

They were emphasized by the most successful Japanese manager of all time, Tetsuharu Kawakami, who piloted the Giants to eleven league championships in his fourteen years, including nine consecutive Japan titles, from 1965 to 1973. They were also stressed by those business leaders who helped fashion Japan's economic miracle during that same era, many of whom were, not coincidentally, ardent Kawakami fans.

Wa is the motto of large multinational corporations, like Hitachi, while Sumitomo, Toshiba, and other leading Japanese firms send junior executives on outdoor retreats, where they meditate and perform spirit-strengthening exercises, wearing only loincloths and headbands with *doryoku* emblazoned on them.

After Kawakami retired in 1974, he occasionally lectured business groups around the country on his managerial principles. Some of them, as delineated in a bestselling book, are: "Most players are lazy. It's a manager's responsibility to make them train hard." "Courteous players make for a strong team. It's a manager's responsibility to teach them proper manners." "Leaders who are thought of as 'nice people' will fail." "Lone wolves are the cancer of the team."

"If your leading salesman opposes you," he would tell executives, "fire him. For if you allow individualism, it will surely spoil your organization."

Kawakami's system came to be known as *kanri yakyu* (controlled baseball), because he controlled all aspects of his players' lives. He even forbade them to read comic books in public for fear it would spoil the team image.

After Kawakami, the foremost practitioner of *kanri yakyu* was Tatsuro Hiroka, a lean and hard disciplinarian who won four pennants and three Japan Series titles in his seven seasons as a manager (1977–79, Yakult, and 1982–85, Seibu), before retiring.

He gave the term *kanri* new meaning. He put his teams on a strict natural-foods diet—fish, soybeans, brown rice, tofu salad, and bean curd soup. The pregame meals he instituted on the road were so skimpy that his players surreptitiously supplemented their diets with *onigiri* (rice balls).

He would call his players at night to make sure they were in bed by his midnight curfew and would counsel his players on family and other private matters, even their sex lives, if he felt it would improve their ability to play baseball.

More than once, Hiroka confined his squad to quarters while on the road as punishment for bad play. One season, he went four solid months without giving his charges a single day off. He often slept at the stadium.

Like Suishu Tobita, Hiroka had attended Waseda University and he adhered to the theory that sports must be played according to *budo* (the "way" of the military arts) which implies a yearning for spiritual as well as physical perfection. One winter, he sent the Lions' shortstop and team captain to an icy mountain river, hoping acts of self-immersion would strengthen the player's spirit and help make him a better leader. "I've done it myself several times," said Hiroka. "It gives you something others don't have."

In 1984, Hiroka ran an "autumn camp" for the younger players on his squad, and some veterans as well, that surely qualified for the *Guinness Book of World Records.* Lasting fifty-nine days, from season's end to late December (a time when most American ballplayers are relaxing in front of a television), it consisted of an average of nine hours of daily drills, including 600 swings a day for each batter, 430 pitches a day for each pitcher, as well as swimming and aikido—a kind of self-defense—sessions.

One of his former players, American Steve Ontiveros, recalled the one year that Seibu Hiroka didn't win a pennant.

Hiroka called a meeting in the middle of the season to ask us what we thought was wrong with the team.

Some of the group told him he was too strict. They said that baseball wasn't fun with him as a manager, which it wasn't.

But he just shot back and said that "Baseball isn't supposed to be fun." He said, "It's your job and it's your duty to do it well."

That's the way he was.

The implacable Hiroka once suspended three of his players for two weeks, after they had publicly objected to their names being put on a trading list. When Hiroka won his first Japan Series title with Seibu, he was quoted as saying, "This year was a battle between me and the players. And I won."

⚾   ⚾   ⚾

Not all modern-day managers in Japanese pro ball have been *kanri yakyu* advocates. Kazuhisa Inao, who managed Lotte (1984–86), had no curfew. He liked to drink and play pachinko with his players, claiming it was a good way to get to know them. Inao had pitched for the old Nishitetsu Lions, who were famous for their late-night carousing and for winning games with tremendous hangovers. When Inao's former teammate Hiroshi Oshita managed the Toei Flyers, he had only three rules: no fines, no curfew, and no signs. His practices were almost nonexistent. (Oshita had to resign after a year because a game-fixing scandal hit the team.)

Yet, the successes of Kawakami and Hiroka had convinced many managers that the sword was indeed mightier than the sake cup. Michiyo Aritoh, who replaced Inao, called a meeting in mid-May of his first season and announced there would be no more days off until the week-long All-Star break in late July. Then, when the break came, he held daily two-hour mini-camps in ninety-five-degree heat. Said Leron Lee, who participated, "One day, two of our pitchers were ordered to throw five hundred pitches without rest. It took one hour and forty-five minutes. They could hardly stand up when it was over."

Aritoh's regime was so tough that one of his players admitted, privately, that he sometimes faked an injury to get some rest, saying, "If I followed his way all year, I'd collapse in no time."

Minoru Murayama, who took over as manager of the Hanshin Tigers in 1988, ordered his players to remove their caps and bow when he and the coaching staff walked on the practice field.

There are, to be sure, more and more young players who scoff at terms like "fighting spirit," in the fashion of many young Japanese company employees who have no compunction about leaving the office at five o'clock or even changing jobs. Chunichi Dragons star Hiromitsu Ochiai, who won three triple crowns, was their hero through most of the 1980s. In interviews, he would say things like, "It's better not to practice at all than to practice too much," followed by the equally blasphemous, "I'd play for any club as long as they paid me enough." His five-minute pregame workouts became famous, or rather infamous, in Japanese baseball.

But tradition dies hard, very hard in Japan. And although Ochiai may have had his admirers, he did not have imitators.

Hanshin Tiger relief ace Kazuyuki Yamamoto declared in 1985, at age thirty-five, that he would go to play in the U.S. major leagues. It was a long-held dream. As soon as he announced this intention, however, pressure to make him stay was applied from several quarters, including petitions from fans, newspaper editorials, and a public plea from his mother. "Don't go, my son!" ran an emotional headline in one major sports daily. "Think of what you owe the team."

It took one week for Yamamoto to change his mind.

4

You Gotta Have Wa

These guys never speak up.

Once the manager pulled me out of the game in the third inning. I'm hitting cleanup, mind you. So I went up to him on the bench and asked why. He said, "You didn't get a hit."

I said, "Neither did so-and-so and so-and-so," and went on down the lineup.

He got mad and kind of waved me away. And he sat me down for three days.

So I had to go to him and apologize. He said, "I had to bench you to show you that you can't get away with that."

"Get away with what?" I said. "I didn't do anything. Jeez. You got to be kidding me."

He said, "I got to show the other players that you can't do that."

I said, "Are you kidding me? These other players would never . . . They run in the hallway to cough. They're afraid to say anything."

Sometimes you just got to stand back and say, "Hey, wait a minute."

Rich Lancelotti
1987 Central League Home Run Champion

If you asked a Japanese manager what he considers the most important ingredient of a winning team, he would likely answer *wa*. If you asked him how to knock a team's *wa* awry, he would probably say, "Hire an American."

Foreign ballplayers, most of them refugees from the American major leagues, have been an active part of Japanese baseball since the postwar era. And for most of that time, there has been a limit of two per team. The somewhat lower level of play in Japan has given these *gaijin* a temporary reprieve from the athletic scrap heap. And although the Japanese have paid the *gaijin* high salaries, it hasn't always been a mutually rewarding experience.

Money is a particular sore point. Foreigners always make two to three times as much as Japanese players of comparable ability. This fact, combined with the free Western-style house and other perks that the *gaijin* seem to view as inalienable rights, sets them too far above their teammates.

Despite the special treatment, the foreigner is often unable to adjust to the different style of play in Japan. Roughly half of all new *gaijin* recruits each year are not invited back for a second. Said one American of his initial season, "I was in a daze for six months."

In 1981, the Yomiuri Giants signed former major leaguer Gary Thomasson to what was then the highest-paying contract in the history of Japanese baseball: three years at a total of $1.2 million. This compared to the $270,-000 a year earned by the highest paid Japanese player, Koji Yamamoto of the Hiroshima Carp. While Yamamoto was winning his third straight home run crown with 44 homers, Thomasson compiled a batting average of .261, hit 20 homers, and struck out 132 times. The Giants benched him during the last week of the season, perhaps to spare Thomasson the embarrassment of breaking the Central League strikeout record of 136, held by another American named Lee Stanton. Thomasson was dubbed "The Giant Human Fan" by Japan's merciless sports press, which also frequently spelled his name using the Chinese character *son*, meaning "loss" or "damage." He was released the following year.

But finance is only part of it. Deportment is the rest. Although few Americans hold Japanese batting or pitching records, many have established new lows in the area of bad conduct. Records for most smashed batting helmets, ejections from games, and broken clubhouse windows, for example, are all held by individual *gaijin*. Indeed, the clash of free-spirited individualism with Japanese groupthink has perhaps caused more grief than all the American strikeouts and errors put together.

There was ex–San Francisco Giant Daryl Spencer, for example. Like most former major leaguers, Spencer insisted on following his own training routine, and it was considerably easier than his teammates'. One night, as he was lackadaisically going through his pregame workout, his manager on the Hankyu Braves, Yukio Nishimoto, decided something had to be done.

"You don't look sharp, Spencer-*san*," he said, "You need a rest."

"What do you mean, I need a rest?" Spencer growled. "Who's leading this team in home runs, anyway?"

"I don't think you can hit this pitcher," Nishimoto said.

"I can't hit him? I'm batting .340 against that guy."

"Not tonight. That's my feeling. You're out."

That was too much for Spencer to take. He was in the dressing room changing into street clothes when he heard his name announced in the starting lineup. Nishimoto had put Spencer down as the third batter, but only because he was planning to "fool" the opposition by inserting a pinch hitter in the first inning.

Now Spencer was smoldering. When the game began and he heard the name of the second batter over the loudspeaker, he decided to get even. Clad in his shorts and shower clogs, he headed for the dugout. Grabbing a bat and smirking in the direction of Nishimoto, he strode out to the on-deck circle to take a few practice swings.

Spencer's entrance delighted the fans, and his picture

was in all the papers the next day. Nishimoto, however, was not amused. He ordered Spencer off the field and slapped him with a suspension and a two-hundred-dollar fine. Spencer paid up, later reporting with a wide grin, "It was worth every penny."

Other Americans have followed in Spencer's shower-clogged footsteps.

Willie Kirkland, who had played for the Giants, Indians, Orioles, and Senators was a happy-go-lucky sort who liked to tease his teammates. One day Kirkland was bemusedly watching an aging infielder who had recently been elevated to player-coach straining through a batting drill. "Hey, man, you're a coach now," Kirkland yelled playfully. "You don't have to practice anymore."

The player-coach took Kirkland's jest as a comment on his declining usefulness and he launched a roundhouse right that barely missed the American. It took half a dozen men to restrain the coach. "I was just joking," Kirkland protested, "He was making fun of me," the unappeased coach retorted.

The Japanese didn't find Richie Scheinblum a barrel of laughs, either. A noted clubhouse wit in the U.S., Scheinblum spent his two years (1975–76) as a Hiroshima Carp baiting the umpires. Shane, as he was known on the club's official roster, was frequently agitated by the plate umpire's idea of Scheinblum's strike zone; that is, it was considerably larger than the one Shane had in mind.

Scheinblum searched for a Japanese phrase to convey his sentiments to the men in blue, something that would really get under their collective skins. A Japanese friend came to the rescue, and soon Scheinblum was muttering, "You lousy Korean" to arbiters who crossed him.

There is, historically, not much love lost between Koreans and Japanese, and to the umpires, Scheinblum's taunts were intolerable. To stop him, they imposed a stiff fine each time he uttered the dreaded epithet. When

Scheinblum finally departed Japan, no cries of "Come back, Shane!" were heard—at least, not from the umpires.

It was not until Clyde Wright came along that the rules of behavior for foreigners were to be finally codified. Wright, a pitcher of some note with the California Angels, Milwaukee Brewers, and Texas Rangers, made his first Japanese appearance in Japan with the Yomiuri Giants in 1976. A self-described "farm boy" from eastern Tennessee, Wright was regarded by those who knew him in America as a "tough-as-nails" competitor who didn't believe in hiding his feelings.

The Giants, of course, were by a million miles the most popular team in Japan, and their manager, Shigeo Nagashima, was indisputably the most beloved sports figure in the land. As a player he had been personally responsible for the most exciting moment in Japanese baseball history: a game-winning (or *sayonara*) home run in the first professional game Emperor Hirohito ever attended. He had charisma that no one, not even famed teammate Sadaharu Oh, could match.

The Giants were also the self-appointed custodians of national virtue. Popular belief had it that their players were neater, better mannered, more disciplined, and more respectful than those of other clubs. Their *wa* was in better tune.

In early 1977, when one writer, a former Giants player turned magazine reporter, suggested otherwise in print, he was banned from the Giants' home stadium, Tokyo's Korakuen, for a whole year. Among his horrifying revelations were: (1) Some Giants players did not like other players on the team; (2) A few players thought Nagashima could be a better manager; (3) Some younger Giants living in the team dormitory did not especially care for the Saturday night 10:00 P.M. curfew; (4) Some Giants wives objected to the season-long "energy-conserving" rule forbidding them to request sexual relations with their husbands. It was tame material as far as exposés go, but to the shoguns of Yomiuri, the Giants' name had been desecrated, and someone had to pay.

Wright also faced the difficulty of being a foreigner on a team that traditionally liked to consider itself pureblooded—Oh's Chinese ancestry and the few closet Koreans on the Giants notwithstanding. Wright was only the second non-Oriental *gaijin* to play for the team, and the sight of a fair-skinned American in a Giants uniform was a bit unsettling to the Japanese multitudes.

Wright, like many other *gaijin,* seemed to the Japanese to be of a breed apart. He was a muscular and hairy six-footer who seemed selfish and crude to Giants fans, many of whom considered themselves the height of refinement.

Wright soon gave them reason to be more unnerved. In the sixth inning of an early-season game, with the score tied 1–1, Wright allowed the first two batters to get on base. Nagashima walked out on the field to take him out of the game. Few American managers would have removed him so abruptly. It was Nagashima's feeling, however, that Wright was getting weak and that was that.

When Wright realized what was happening, he blew a gasket. To the horror of fifty thousand fans and a Saturday night TV audience of millions, he brushed aside Nagashima's request for the ball and stormed off the mound, an angry scowl on his face. Halfway to the bench, he threw the ball against the dugout wall, cursed, and disappeared inside.

Once inside, he kicked over a trash can, ripped off his uniform, shredded it and flung it into the team bath. Amidst a rapid-fire discharge of obscenities, he finally said something that the official team interpreter was able to understand, "Stupidest damn baseball I've ever seen. If this is the way the Giants treat their foreign ballplayers, I'm going, I've had it."

Nothing like this had ever happened on the Giants. Other teams had problems, but not the proud Kyojin, as the Giants were called in Japanese. No one had ever shown this much disrespect for Nagashima. "Crazy" Wright, as he was instantly renamed by the press, became headline news in the sports dailies the next day. Letters, telegrams, and phone calls poured into the Yomiuri offices. Outrageous! Inexcusable! Wright should be released. Deported. Shot. Drawn and quartered. And not necessarily in that order.

Only Nagashima kept his cool. First he patiently explained to his American pitcher that what he had done was not "stupid" baseball but simply the Japanese way of playing the game. It's a group effort. Then the manager faced the angry masses. There would be no disciplinary action. He was glad that Wright cared so much about winning. And he wished that some of his Japanese players would show as much fight.

Such benevolent words from the prince of Japanese baseball dissipated much of the public's antagonism toward Crazy Wright. It did not, however, pacify the front office. Management was not as eager as Nagashima-*san* to let Western ways penetrate the organization. They issued a set of ten rules of etiquette that Wright and every other American player the Giants might henceforth deem worthy of their uniform would be obliged to obey.

The Japanese press quickly gave it a name: The Gaijin Ten Commandments. This is how they went:

1. Obey all orders issued by the manager.
2. Do not criticize the strategy of the manager.
3. Take good care of your uniform.
4. Do not scream and yell in the dugout or destroy objects in the clubhouse.
5. Do not reveal team secrets to other foreign players.
6. Do not severely tease your teammates.
7. In the event of injury, follow the treatment prescribed by the team.

8. Be on time.
9. Do not return home during the season.
10. Do not disturb the harmony of the team.

Willie Davis, then a practicing Buddhist, thought it would be different for him. Davis was one of the best all-around American players ever to come to Japan. He was a seventeen-year veteran of the major leagues and a former captain of the Los Angeles Dodgers. He had been an All-Star, he could run like a deer and hit and field with a grace and skill that few American big-leaguers, let alone Japanese, possessed. Even at thirty-seven, Davis could have continued to play in the U.S.—in fact, when he departed Japan two years hence, he spent a season as a pinch-hitter for the California Angels—but when the chance to go to Japan came in 1977, he took it. Not for the money (one hundred thousand dollars—an eye-popping sum in those days in Japan), he insisted, but "for the good of baseball." Whatever that meant.

Davis was a product of his times, of America's "quest for meaning." While others were exploring the wonders of Transactional Analysis, est, and the like, Davis was a devout member of the Soka Gakkai, the Nichiren Buddhist sect that had America chanting. Because Japan was the birthplace of the Soka Gakkai, Davis assumed he would be right at home. It was a misguided assumption.

The religion's sacred chant, *namu Myoho renge-kyo*, was an important part of Davis's daily life. He did it faithfully, because it brought him inner peace. When he joined the Dragons, he naturally continued this practice—in the morning, at night, in his room, in the team bath, and on the team bus. When not intoning the chant himself, he would play tapes of it on a portable cassette recorder.

Davis reasoned that the chanting would be music to his teammates' ears. Instead, it drove them nuts. They complained there was no peace and quiet on the team; they couldn't sleep. The incantatory chant that supposedly would bring inner harmony to anyone who regularly intoned it was rapidly eroding the Dragons' collective *wa*.

What particularly annoyed the Japanese players was Davis's locker-room chanting. Before each game, he would pull out his beads, and off he'd go, "Namu Myoho renge-kyo, namu Myoho renge-kyo, namu myoho renge-kyo, . . ."

"He'd pray that he'd do well, that the team would win, and that nobody would get hurt," his manager, a Japanese-Hawaiian named Wally Yonamine, says, "but it gave the others the feeling they were at a Buddhist funeral." Buddhist funerals, it seemed, were the only time most Japanese were heard such chanting.

When the game began, Davis was a ball of fire—at least during the first half of the season. He was by far the most feared Dragon hitter, and on the base paths he displayed a flair that the Japanese had never seen before. Nonetheless the team was in last place. Key players were injured, and the pitching was subpar. Team *wa* was out of whack, and many Dragons blamed their American Buddhist for it.

It was more than the chanting, which Davis soon toned down to please his teammates. There was, for example, the matter of his personal attire. Davis liked his Dragon training suit so much he had half a dozen made in different colors. He wore them in public, agitating club executives, who felt Davis was tarnishing the team's dignified image.

Davis would sometimes practice in stocking feet and he once appeared for a workout with his comely wife, who was wearing hot pants and who jogged with him on the field. "It's so . . . so unprofessional," one sportswriter observed. "Davis is destroying our team's spirit in training," grumbled a player. "We can't concentrate on what we're doing."

Several players complained that Davis had special privileges. They referred to him as "Davis the king," and as "Davis, our precious black *gaijin.*"

Yonamine was caught in the middle. "I'd try to tell them not to worry about it," he said. "Forget about how much money a man makes or how little he practices. What he does in the game is all that counts." Few Dragons were willing to accept that piece of American advice.

Davis's biggest liability was his garrulousness. "People didn't understand him," said a team official. "He was loud. He'd get excited. He'd yell a lot and wave his arms. It was all in English and people didn't have the faintest idea what he was saying, but it looked as though he was arguing."

Once he reproached a teammate for not attempting to score on a play that Davis had initiated. "Why didn't you try for home?" Davis shouted. That was the wrong thing to do, because the player was not only the team captain, but also a player-coach. In Japan, a player does not yell at a coach, much less question his judgment.

In August of 1977, when Davis had 25 home runs and a .306 batting average, he broke a wrist in a collision with the outfield fence. It put him out for the year. The Dragons immediately went on a winning streak. During the last two months of the season they had the best record in the league and missed finishing second by a hair.

"It's our pitching," Yonamine insisted. But if you listened to Dragon supporters and students of Japanese baseball, it was all because team *wa* had been restored.

"I knew Willie as well as anyone," said Jim Lefebvre, a teammate of Davis's on the Dodgers. "He had his quirks, but then we all do. He was named captain, and you're not chosen captain of a team like the Dodgers if you're a real troublemaker. If you can't get along with somebody like Willie, you don't belong on a baseball team."

The Dragon front office apparently felt that it was Davis

who didn't belong on a baseball team—at least not theirs. They traded him, and at the start of the following season the most exciting player ever to wear a Chunichi Dragons uniform was laboring in the backwaters of Fukuoka, contemplating the infinite and subtle mysteries of *wa* while playing for the lowly Crown Lighter Lions.

Of course, not every American who came to Japan wrought havoc on his new team. There have been some, like Clete Boyer and George Altman, who did their best to please their Japanese hosts. In turn, the Japanese liked them, describing their demeanor as *majime*—which means serious, sober, earnest, steady, honest, faithful. They did everything that was asked of them. They kept their mouths shut, their feelings to themselves.

Some, like Boyer, paid a substantial price for the goodwill they engendered. The former Yankee fielding whiz had three reasonably good seasons for the Taiyo Whales, but in his fourth year, 1975, when he began to reach the end as a player, he ran smack up against the cultural wall.

Boyer decided that he needed to be used more sparingly, and he asked the club to rest him every third game. "I hit well in the first two, but then I get tired," he explained. "I'd do a better job with an extra day off."

The team argued that what Boyer needed was not more rest but more training. Because he was older, the trainer reasoned, Boyer would have to work harder to keep up with the others. The team owner, after considering the probable reaction of the fans to an eighty-thousand-dollar-a-year *gaijin* sitting on the bench a third of the time, agreed with the trainer. Boyer reluctantly acquiesced. In an effort to keep his energy level up, he took massive vitamin injections that left his arms black-and-blue and he worked very hard. Still, he finished the season hitting .230 and then retired to coaching. His goodwill, of course, remained intact.

Jim Lefebvre, too, obeyed all the rules. Yet he ended up

incurring the largest fine in Japanese baseball history. His manager on the Lotte Orions, Masaichi Kaneda, Japan's only four hundred-game winner and the "God of Pitching," had personally recruited and signed Lefebvre—to a multiyear contract worth one hundred thousand dollars a year—and had predicted that Lefebvre would win the Triple Crown. Lefebvre hit only .265 with 29 home runs his first season. Hampered by a leg injury, he fared even worse in succeeding years.

Kaneda was so embarrassed that he resorted to open ridicule of his "star" in an effort to regain lost face. Once, after Lefebvre had committed a particularly damaging error, Kaneda apologized to the other players for the American's "poor play." Another time, after a similar misplay, Kaneda temporarily relegated his *gaijin* to the farm team. In Lefebvre's third year, Kaneda took him off the roster completely for half the season, retiring him as a player and "promoting" him to being a coach of a minor league team.

Lefebvre tried logic in appealing to Kaneda. "Look, you won four hundred games, right?" he said, "That makes you the winningest pitcher in Japanese history, right?"

"Right," Kaneda proudly replied.

"You also lost two hundred fifty games, didn't you?"

"Yes."

"Then that also makes you the losingest pitcher in Japanese history."

"Yes, but . . ."

"But, what? Don't you see? Even the greatest in the game have bad times. Give me a break, will you?"

But Kaneda kept up the pressure. And the unhappy Lefebvre endured it until his fifth season. After being summarily removed from the lineup in the middle of an important game, Lefebvre finally lost his control. Walking back to the bench, he threw his glove at the dugout wall, producing a rather loud *whack*.

Kaneda, sitting nearby, assumed that Lefebvre had thrown the glove at him. He sprang to his feet and raised his fists. "You want to fight me?" he yelled. Lefebvre, who saw his playing career rapidly coming to an end anyway, stepped forward to meet the challenge. Coaches intervened, but after the game Kaneda levied a ten-thousand-dollar fine against his "troublemaker" and suspended him indefinitely.

"It was a big game, and I wanted to stay in it," said Lefebvre, "but what made me even madder was the way Kaneda took me out. He waited until I'd finished my infield warm-ups, then he came and waved me out. That's embarrassing. But I certainly wasn't trying to throw the glove at him. It missed him by five feet."

Kaneda wasn't interested in Lefebvre's version of the incident. If he had misunderstood his *gaijin*'s intentions, perhaps others on the team had as well. What would they think if it appeared that the "Emperor of Pitching" tolerated that sort of behavior?

Refused a private audience with Kaneda, Lefebvre took his case to the public. He called a press conference. Yes, he had lost his temper. That he regretted. But no, he was not guilty as charged. A standard fine of fifty thousand yen (then about two hundred fifty dollars) would be okay. But there was no way he would pay the outrageous sum of ten thousand dollars. There was no way he *could* pay it. Kaneda was just getting back at him for his failure to win the Triple Crown. Or Kaneda was making him the scapegoat for everything else that was wrong on the team. Or, perhaps, Kaneda was simply taking this opportunity to demonstrate his skills as a *"gaijin* tamer." Whatever the reason, Lefebvre wasn't going to take it all lying down.

When Kaneda heard that he was being openly opposed, he called his own press conference and vowed that Lefebvre would "never, ever again wear the uniform of the Lotte Orions."

Lefebvre was in limbo for weeks, while the coaching staff and management covertly worked to find a solution. At one stage they suggested secretly dropping the fine but making an announcement that Lefebvre had paid it. As long as Kaneda, and his public, didn't know the truth, they concluded, Kaneda's ego and image would suffer no damage. Lefebvre refused. He had his own ego and his own image to worry about. He appealed to a highly placed baseball official in the U.S., whom he refused to identify publicly. The official made a call to Kaneda and the next day the fine was quietly dropped. Lefebvre was allowed to put his uniform back on and finish the season— which, not surprisingly, was his last.

Obviously, it took a certain strength of character to survive in a country as radically different as Japan. In the years since 1962 when Don Newcombe and Larry Doby became the first ex-major leaguers to play in Japan, hardly a season has passed without a controversial incident involving a *gaijin* player.

The ways in which Japanese and Americans could get on each other's nerves seemed infinite in their variety.

Chris Arnold from the San Francisco Giants joined the Kintetsu Buffaloes in 1978 and, almost immediately, had a run-in of his own with Buffaloes manager Yukio Nishimoto. Nishimoto had just moved over from the Braves, and was becoming wise in the ways of dealing with intemperate Americans.

In the eighth inning of one early April game, Arnold made an error playing second base, and Nishimoto, as Japanese managers are wont to do, immediately removed him from the game to placate the fans. It was a way of maintaining *wa* in the stands. Arnold, an intense man, returned to the bench. Outraged, he hurled his glove in anger at Nishimoto's feet.

"I'm a major leaguer," he screamed for all the fans to hear. "You can't treat me this way." Arnold's interpreter ushered him away before any further damage could be done, but the next day at practice, phase two of the confrontation took place.

Arnold was in the batting cage, taking practice swings, when Nishimoto approached. Suddenly, there was complete quiet on the field, as everyone stopped to watch.

"You no like the way I manage?" said Nishimoto in halting English.

"No, it's not that," replied Arnold, looking around nervously and turning red. "I just felt embarrassed by being removed like that in front of the fans. It's your right to take me out, but couldn't you have waited until the end of the inning?"

Nishimoto gave Arnold a cold stare and repeated, "You no like the way I manage?"

Arnold, fidgeting, answered, "No, it's just that I'm not used to the Japanese way. I was upset with myself for making the error. But I had three hits in the game, and still you took me out. It's natural to be upset."

Nishimoto's gaze was pure steel. "You no like the way I manage?" he said for the third time.

Suddenly, Arnold realized that Nishimoto hadn't understood a word he had said. He hurriedly called over his interpreter, explained himself once again, and this time added an apology in one of the few Japanese phrases he had managed to learn, *"Domo sumimasen."*

At this, Nishimoto turned and stormed off the field. All the coaches and all the other players followed him, even the batting practice pitcher. Arnold was left standing alone on the field, He was embarrassed, angry, confused, and more than a little scared. "What the hell is going on?" he asked himself.

The next day, when Arnold arrived at the Buffalo clubhouse, no one spoke to him. No one would look at him. He was called into Nishimoto's office, half-expecting to be given his release. Instead, behind closed doors, Nishimoto explained through his interpreter the facts of life for a *gaijin* in Japan—or, at least, the facts of life for a *gaijin* on Nishimoto's team.

"You see, Arnold," he explained, "If I show that I have the power to take Americans out of the game and to control them if they get angry, then the other players will fall in line. That's why what I did yesterday, and the day before yesterday, was necessary."

"Don't you think that's going too far?" blurted Arnold. "What about my feelings? I have my pride you know."

"I understand your feelings, however there are more important things," the manager answered.

Arnold was dumbfounded. He swallowed his pride and bowed to Nishimoto's power. He promised to try to exercise more self-control in the future.

Following the meeting the clubhouse freeze quickly thawed. For the next three years, Arnold refrained from shouting at his manager. And Nishimoto, for his part, also behaved. Whenever he removed Arnold from a game, he did it in a way that showed consideration for his *gaijin*'s feelings. Cross-cultural understanding had been achieved . . . the hard way.

Japanese team officials understandably grew weary of the perennial conflicts wrought by their foreign imports and tried to be more selective in signing Americans. By the late 1970s character checks became a standard part of their recruiting process, and frequently they were rewarded with even-tempered types who kept their feelings to themselves and fitted into the Japanese system.

One of them was Felix Millan, a former Atlanta Braves and New York Mets second baseman, who was the quintessence of propriety. When he arrived in 1979 for his second season as a Taiyo Whale, coming off a .287 year, he politely refused an offer to let him train as he wished and instead endured all the rigors of a Japanese preseason camp with his teammates. When he was benched on opening day, he sat quietly in the dugout, a shy smile on his face, intently watching the action. When he got his chance to start a week later, he went 4-for-4, won his spot back, and eventually won the batting title as well, with an average of .324.

Then there was ex-Yankee Roy White who played with Yomiuri for three years in 1980–82 and was only the second *gaijin,* after Yonamine, ever invited to join the Giants OB (Old Boys) Club. It was as much a tribute to his quiet, unobtrusive personality as it was to his dependable play on the field—his best year was 1980 when he hit .298, with 29 home runs.

Here was a man who did not have fits of apoplexy if asked to bunt. He did not threaten to firebomb the clubhouse if prematurely removed from a game. In the middle innings of one contest against the Whales in Yokohama during his first season, White was ordered to squeeze bunt, which he did successfully, and as a result, the Giants were able to win the game.

"I like the squeeze," he said pleasantly. "I don't think that Nagashima should have to cater to me, just because I have been in the major leagues with the Yankees."

White's ingratiating remarks were music to the ears of Giants fans. "I played with Mickey Mantle and Roger Maris and won a World Series," he would say. "Now I'm playing with Sadaharu Oh under Shigeo Nagashima. To win a championship with them would be the pièce de résistance."

The following year, that's exactly what happened, with White hitting a dramatic ninth-inning home run in Game 2 of the Japan Series.

Not once in his entire Japanese career did White ever raise his voice to an umpire, a teammate, or an opposing player—not even when downed by an obvious beanball attempt. The Japanese could not quite believe he was really an American. One Tokyo sports columnist was so enamored of him that he wrote, "It's too bad White isn't a Japanese. Then he could stay here forever."

The list of gracious *gaijin* also included courteous Leron Lee and his equally well-comported brother Leon. Said a veteran baseball writer of the Lees, perhaps hiding his disappointment, "There's nothing bad you can say about them. They do good in the games. They never argue with the umpires. They never throw their bats. And they're always polite to the fans. They even like each other. There must be something wrong with them."

Leon deserved some sort of prize for diplomacy. He would give the following advice to newly arrived Americans:

> Try to be as humble as you can, especially if you have a good season. Because acting like a big star just causes more trouble for you.
>
> Americans have to understand that managers will test you to see if you're a team player. They single you out. Take you out of a game, or make you bunt just to put you in your place and make sure you don't get a big head. When that happens try not to get angry. I've been blamed for errors that were some other guy's fault. I just nod and say I'm sorry in front of everybody and it's okay. And it makes my teammates happy because it takes the load off of them.
>
> In my first year in Japan, our batting coach kept trying to show me how to hold the bat whenever reporters or managers were around. I told him, "I'm just fine with my own style." He said, "You don't have to listen to anything I'm saying, but just act as if you are. I have to look like I'm doing my job."
>
> The Japanese are very face-conscious, so you should at least let the coaches pretend they are teaching you something.

If the Japanese are industrious and harmonious, they are also gloomy and cynical—their attitudes tempered by centuries of earthquakes, typhoons, and a recent war that devastated their country. They are, in some ways, the most skeptical people on the face of the earth.

It is the Japanese habit to divide social interaction into two categories: what people say and what people really think. They have words for both: *tatemae* (principle, what is expected) refers to what one says to please others, while *honne* means one's real feelings. All peoples make such distinctions to some extent, but since the Japanese place such a premium on social harmony and so abhor confrontation, they have refined the suppression of their *honne*, in favor of *tatemae*, to a high art.

Not surprisingly, they are suspicious of *tatemae* in others and are particularly dubious of excess civility on the part of foreign players. When people like White told them how much they liked Japan, their initial reaction was a simultaneous mix of gratification and disbelief.

Many Japanese would internally translate the phrase, "I love Japan," from the mouth of a *gaijin*, to "I can't stand this place, but the pay is good." They suspected that good behavior on the part of an American was just a cover for the real nature lurking inside.

"It's all an act," said one reporter of White and the Lees. "*Gaijin* are only here because they are no longer wanted in the States. They are only here for the money. And we shouldn't forget that." He went on to speculate, "It must be the sagging dollar, the recession in the U.S. Americans have it good in Japan and they're afraid of losing what they have." Of course, if a *gaijin* ever did come out and openly say that he had only come for the money, well, the press would be quick to pounce on him with righteous indignation.

The fact of the matter was that Americans, at least, did have mixed feelings about Japan. Many of them did not like the massive urban crowds, the eye-watering pollution, the ubiquitous power lines, and the smallness of it all: Some of the larger players could not sit comfortably in coffee shop seats.

Others, however, were attracted to the pleasures that great cities like Tokyo and Osaka could offer. There were lots of discotheques and bars and good-looking, well-dressed women, who had a softer brand of femininity than the ones back home. (When Johnny Bench was asked what impressed him most after a month-long visit to Japan, he replied, "The girls. I couldn't believe how clean they were.") What's more, Japanese were well-mannered people as a whole and the country was safe. As Millan once put it, "There are no killings in my neighborhood, man."

Of Japanese baseball, however, the Americans were unanimous in their dislike. It was like nothing they had ever encountered before and when they got together for drinks, what would start out as a social evening would become a nonstop bitch-and-moan session. Their coaches and the press were always harping about proper form and fighting spirit and *wa* and just wouldn't leave them alone.

Despite the good-conduct medals earned by some people, Americans, just by virtue of their being Americans, created trouble. Americans might be okay in the abstract, Japanese thought, but face-to-face was something else. Some Americans could ruin a Japanese day merely by walking into the same room. They were everything that their hosts were not. They were bright and positive, but they were also loud, frank, assertive, too familiar, and uncomfortably democratic.

Conflict just seemed to be in the nature of things, the respective cultures too different—like sushi and sirloin—to ever go well together.

By the early 1980s, the Japanese print media had come up with a special way of referring to the foreign baseball player in Japan. They removed the character *gai* 外 , which means "foreign" or "outside," from *gaijin* (外人), or "foreign person," and replaced it with the homonym *gai* 害 , meaning "harm," to make 害人 "harmful person."

Having 害人 in the sports daily headlines, some editors claimed, stimulated sales. One reporter for a Japanese evening paper, in fact, confessed, "Frankly, when it comes to *gaijin,* negative or controversial stories sell better than positive ones."

And oh, how the stories kept coming. In 1980, it was thirty-six-year-old Chuck Manuel, on his way to winning a home run title, who took a week off in June to attend his son's high school graduation ceremony back home in Virginia.

Japanese were dumbstruck when they heard the news. They could not conceive of anyone acting that way. If there was a job to do and they were needed, they would never think of leaving. Work always came first, be it at the factory or at the ballpark.

The Japanese looked at the American ballplayer and saw in him an overpaid version of the American worker: indolent, indifferent, and always demanding something. As a Japanese reporter who had spent a year in the U.S. expostulated for the *Sports Nippon:*

> Americans seldom work hard and are constantly complaining. No matter how busy the work situation might be, they have no compunction about just picking up and going home, if they can.

It was no wonder the American economy was falling to pieces.

Manuel, for his part, was unconcerned. "I can play baseball anytime," he said. "My son's graduation only comes once."

The following year, the Bad Guy Award went to Pete LaCock, the former Cubs and Kansas City Royals reserve. LaCock got off on the wrong foot by publicly admitting he was not worth the eight hundred thousand that the Taiyo Whales were paying him for two years.

Then his manager became upset because LaCock would not apologize when he made an error. "LaCock always has some excuse," he complained. "He never accepts responsibility."

After being ordered to sacrifice bunt in one game, he returned to the bench, threw his batting helmet down, kicked over an upright ashtray, and, as the *Tokyo Chunichi Sports* reported it, "let forth a stream of dirty slang words. Although it was not all understandable, one could catch the English word *fucking* and that was clearly intended as a criticism of the manager."

Moreover, LaCock, like practically every other American player in the country, complained emphatically that he was a victim of discrimination on the part of the umpires. Once, after being called out on a third strike, he handed his bat to the arbiter and said, "Here. You're taking the bat out of my hands, anyway, so you might as well have it." Such behavior was embarrassing to the Whales.

These and other acts, such as the time LaCock strolled into the Yomiuri clubhouse area to continue a pregame conversation with Giants *gaijin* Gary Thomasson, combined with his record of .273 and 10 homers, led to his release at the end of the year—even though the Whales were obligated to pay him off in full.

Nineteen eighty-four turned out to be the blackest, most traumatic season Americans and Japanese ever inflicted on each other.

That year, three *gaijin* unceremoniously walked out on their teams and their fat contracts in midseason. One was Jim Tracy, who quit the Taiyo Whales in protest over being precipitously removed from a game. Another was Don Money, the one-time Milwaukee star, who, after hitting eight home runs in April, deserted the Kintetsu Buffaloes because he did not like his apartment or the antiquated facilities used by his team. Said Money of the Buffaloes' clubhouse, "It looks like a bomb hit it."

Money's young teammate, Rich Duran, joined the exodus shortly thereafter, despite having hit 12 home runs in the first two months of play. He said he couldn't hack the harsh workout the coaches put him through. The Japanese thought he was just trying to emulate his fellow Americans.

The sports press roundly decried the foreign devils. A reporter for *Nikkan Sports* found a genetic explanation for their behavior. "All of these men are Anglo-Saxons," he wrote, "a class of people that has too much pride. . . . Hitler aside, the history of mankind shows us that human beings with the sense of being chosen people will eventually act in a willful and egotistical manner."

The failure of the highly touted Bump Wills to do well in Japan further intensified the growing wave of anti-American sentiment. Wills, a thirty-year-old former major league All-Star second baseman signed a four-year contract in 1983 with the Hankyu Braves worth $1.6 million. In his first season, he had several heated arguments with his manager, Toshiharu Ueda. By the middle of his second season, he was sitting on the farm-team bench with a batting average in the low .200s, awaiting his release.

At the end of the year, despite the fact that Wills's American teammate Gregory ("Boomer") Wells had won the Triple Crown (the first American and only the fifth player in the history of the Japanese game to accomplish the feat), feelings ran so high that the pro baseball team owners voted to expurgate the foreigners completely from Japanese baseball within five years.

Although the committee never followed through on its decision, the vote symbolized how fed up the Japanese had become with the *gaijin*. It was the lowest ebb in the history of U.S.-Japan baseball relations.

Critics charged that the Americans were greedy and disloyal and lacked fighting spirit, as the Japanese would define it. Ryoichi Shibusawa, a Central League official, was quoted as saying, *"Gaijin* on certain teams have behaved in a way that could easily be called sabotage," adding that the "high salaries lavished on the foreign stars have demoralized Japanese players."

The Americans involved pleaded extenuating circumstances. Tracy claimed his manager was singling him out to teach him humility. Tracy had hit .303 with 19 home runs, but the following year he was moved down from third to sixth in the batting order because, it was said, he didn't have enough power. "You hit .260 with 40 home runs and they'd say your average wasn't high enough," Tracy complained. "Either way you lose."

Money's case was different. He had not wanted to come to Japan in the first place. At thirty-seven, after a distinguished big-league career, he had been headed for retirement on his farm in New Jersey. Moreover, he had a bad back and was not really in the best condition to play baseball anymore. But when the Buffaloes enticed him with a two-year contract worth nine hundred thousand dollars and visions of a major-league style of life in Japan, Money found himself unable to turn it down.

He had seen Japanese baseball on TV in the U.S.— games played in modern stadiums in Tokyo and Yokohama that were bulging with enthusiastic fans. He had not seen the Kintetsu home park, a decaying monument to utilitarianism with its grassless infield and prewar scoreboard, nor did he know that sparse crowds were the norm for Buffaloes contests. No one in the organization had bothered to enlighten him in that regard.

There was more, as Money later recalled:

> Someone at Kintetsu sent me a pamphlet of the apartment building we were to live in. In the drawing it was a beautiful building, surrounded by trees. We thought, Hmmm. Not bad. Then we go to Japan and the area was completely filled with buildings. No green at all.
>
> When we first got to the place and looked around, we

felt like walking back downstairs, getting into a cab, and coming back home. It was simply nothing like they told us it would be. Not even close.

The walls were filthy, the carpet completely stained. The ceiling hadn't been painted for ten years. There was no heat. The kitchen had an old, dirty, stained yellow-brown floor. The wallpaper was coming off and there were cockroaches all over the place.

What's more, it was built to Japanese standards. The cabinets were so small you couldn't put any dishes in them. The oven was too tiny for my wife to cook in.

The places of other Americans were like mansions compared to ours: You say, "This just isn't right." It turned out the building was owned by Kintetsu Railways. Then they had the nerve to say I should pay half the cost of fixing it up.

I had to travel to the park an hour and a half each way. The trains were always crowded. I'd have to carry my bats and bags. I'm standing there on the train. I'm not used to five thousand people staring at me.

It was wearying. I was getting tired—even in spring. I'd leave for the park about 1:00 P.M. for a six o'clock game. Pregame practice was about an hour and a half longer than in the States, and I wouldn't get home until around eleven at night, because the games are so long over there.

It's not like in the States where you can sit and relax and have a couple of beers in the clubhouse. In Japan, the guys are gone in fifteen minutes, win or lose.

The clubhouse wasn't the best. We had only two shower stalls and a Japanese bath. Half the time, the showers wouldn't work. The clubhouse was a complete mess. Things all over the floor. There wasn't even a decent toilet. I'd be standing there taking a whiz and some girl would walk by. I just wasn't used to it after fifteen years in the big leagues.

It all just built up and my family was very unhappy. Finally, I started talking about retiring. Kintetsu's attitude changed immediately. They started saying things like, We'll give you a brand new apartment; we'll get you a chauffeur-driven car to the park; we'll give you a salary increase.

But it was too late.

If I was a younger guy in the minors, I'd suck it up. But I never should have gone in the first place. And I would never go again.

Few Japanese were willing to sympathize with him. Most fans thought that for all the dough Money was making, he could have paid for another apartment himself (even if he did have to pay three thousand dollars a month and ten thousand dollars in key money, a form of legal extortion in Japan), and he could have rented a damn helicopter to take him to work. As for his wife and kids, well, if they didn't like it, Money should have just sent them home and stayed to do the job he had contractually obligated himself to do. That is what a Japanese would have done.

A Japanese would also have given his teammates a lot more consideration. Perhaps if Money had not left, Duran would have stayed. Who knows?

Bump Wills had the misfortune of being handpicked by Hankyu Braves manager Toshiharu Ueda, who had won five pennants and three Japan Series titles and was one of the toughest managers in Japan. He tended to treat his charges like inmates on a Georgia chain gang.

In spring camp, he would stand on the field with a megaphone, berating his players. Once, when a Braves pitcher made the mistake of showing up ten minutes late for a morning workout, Ueda made him run from foul pole to foul pole for the rest of the day. When the Braves catcher dropped a throw in an intrasquad game, Ueda kicked him in the rear end, in front of several photographers. The well-placed kick was prominently featured in the papers the next day.

In 1988 camp, a young Hankyu player was caught driving drunk. Ueda fined him one million yen (seven thousand dollars), demoted him to the farm team, and confined him to training ground quarters for three weeks.

Said Ueda in a subsequent press conference, "I've been too lenient in educating my players. Up until now, I've stayed out of their private lives. But that's all going to change."

Ueda had a personal interest in Bump. He knew Bump's famous father Maury, whom he had used as a spring-training coach many times. Because of that, perhaps, he expected something special.

Bump, however, was not at all ready for a man like Ueda. As Leron Lee, who knew both men, put it:

> It was guaranteed that Bump would not get along with Ueda. If only Hankyu had bothered to check him out before signing him. Bump was the type of guy who shot from the hip. If he didn't like something he would damn well say so. It was a trait he had inherited from his father. It was one reason why it took his father Maury until twenty-six to make it to the major leagues. Bump would have been good for some easy-going Japanese managers, like Inao, but not Ueda.

More than once, Ueda turned his acid tongue on Bump and the younger Wills felt that he was being singled out for special ridicule. "He just kept harping at me," said Bump. "It was like he was trying to make an example out of me or something."

Ueda and Braves president Sakae Okada had expected Bump to hit home runs, simply because he had once been a major league All-Star—this despite the fact that Bump was not really a power hitter. He had had his best season as a leadoff man for the Texas Rangers in 1977, his rookie year, when he hit .287 with 9 home runs and 57 RBIs.

Bump also liked to steal, having stolen as many as 52 bases one year in the big leagues. However, Hankyu already had a base stealer and leadoff batter, a man named Yutaka Fukumoto, who had 1,062 career stolen bases, held the single-season Japan record for stolen bases with 113 (in 130 games), and who had a lifetime .292 average. Said Bump, after his first few months in Japan, "There was no way they wanted me upstaging Fukumoto. Nobody stole bases on that team but him."

So Bump batted elsewhere in the lineup: fifth, sixth, and seventh. He hit .260 with 15 home runs his first season, and Ueda seemed embarrassed. In Bump's second year, things went from bad to worse. In one game in May, Bump missed a sign, swinging away and missing on a count of two balls and no strikes. Ueda exploded, and angrily yanked him out of the lineup.

Bump pleaded that it was an honest mistake. After all, he said, what major league manager would ever put on the take sign in a situation like that? But Ueda was sure it had been intentional.

"Either he leaves this team, or I do," he thundered.

Eventually, Wills was benched, then sent down to the farm team. At season's end, the Braves bought out the remaining two years of his contract.

Said disillusioned Braves president Okada to *Time*'s Neil Gross, "Maybe these guys are playing by American customs and rules. But if this kind of thing continues, I think most people would agree simply to be done with them."

⑪   ⑪   ⑪

It took a soft-spoken, blond Oklahoman named Randy Bass to redeem the American image in Japan, albeit somewhat temporarily. Bass, a peripatetic reserve first baseman who had played for five major league teams, won the Central League Triple Crown in 1985. He led his team, the Hanshin Tigers of Osaka, to their first pennant in twenty-one years, their first Japan Series title ever, and an all-time team attendance record of more than 2.6 million.

For a time, Bass came as close to being a bona fide national hero as any *gaijin* ballplayer ever has. A Hanshin Tiger cheer group chant went *Kamisama—Hotokesama—Basusama* (literally "God—Buddha—Bass"). When a marketing survey revealed that his blondish-brown beard was the most recognizable in all of Japan, Gillette Japan paid him two hundred thousand dollars to shave it off for a TV commercial.

Soon, however, it was back to business as usual. In 1986, Boomer Wells got himself into trouble by not arriving until the end of March, a time when his teammates had already been practicing hard for two months. Wells's excuse was that his wife had just had a baby. He seemed unaware that in Japan births and deaths and other such momentous occasions were not sufficient cause to miss work. (Bass had been heavily criticized when he left Japan in midseason of 1984, albeit with permission, to be at his father's deathbed. His conduct was compared unfavorably with Oh's who, in true Japanese fashion, missed not a single inning when his father died the following September.) Braves president Okada, still fuming over his Wills experience, which had been followed by an unpleasant salary battle with Wells, thought this heinous act of tardiness so disruptive of team *wa* that he publicly apologized to the Japanese players on his team for having allowed it to happen.

Then there was the "Mad Venezulean," Luis Sanchez, a relief pitcher for Yomiuri who had frequent arguments with pitching coach Mutsuo Minagawa, over Minagawa's attempts to change Luis's form. During one practice session, Sanchez threw a beanball at Minagawa, who was standing in the batter's box as a "model batter." Sanchez was later fined several thousand dollars by the Giants front office for telling reporters he thought Minagawa was "dumb."

Sanchez participated in one of the more absurd confrontations in modern sports history, when he plunked Taiyo Whales outfielder Hirokazu Kato in the leg. Kato, who spoke little English, yelled out one of the few English expressions he had managed to pick up from associating with foreign ballplayers, "Mother Fucker!"

Sanchez, not very fluent in the English language himself, understood quite clearly he was being insulted and, in an odd reversal of the usual procedure of batter charging the around, Sanchez stormed home plate—thereby insuring that Kato's attempts at cross-cultural communication were not in vain. Only speedy intervention by the catcher and the umpire prevented a fistfight.

Perhaps nothing upsets the inner *wa* of the Japanese more than the sight of a *gaijin* slugging a Japanese. It might be a normal thing for Americans to beat each other's brains out over a close pitch, but in Japan, people are expected to behave in a more civilized manner. The Japanese way of dealing with beanball pitches is to jump out of the way. Indeed, the ability to avoid being hit by an inside pitch is regarded as a fundamental technique of baseball in Japan. A batter who gets hit has no business getting angry, the reasoning goes, because it is just as much his fault for not moving quickly enough. Moreover, those who fight and get themselves ejected from games are only hurting the team by their absence.

Japanese players are all expected to emulate Sachio Kinugasa, who would leap up from the ground whenever he got knocked down by a pitch and motion to the pitcher with a smile that everything was okay. That was the Japanese way. That was Japanese cool.

To Americans a philosophy like that is only asking for more trouble and, as a result, there are beanball fights involving *gaijin* every year. One of the more memorable incidents involved the excitable Dick Davis, a former Milwaukee Brewer who had replaced Money on the Buffaloes. Davis did not mind the Kintetsu facilities, which were eventually renovated, or his housing arrangements. But he did mind a cocky Seibu Lions pitcher named Osamu Higashio, who held the all-time Japan record for hit batsmen, 150 in seventeen years.

One balmy June evening at Seibu Stadium, Davis took umbrage at an inside Higashio fastball that hit his elbow. He rushed to the mound to deliver several damaging punches to Higashio's head and face—leaving the pitcher with a swollen jaw and a left eye that was nearly closed.

The Japanese sports press swooped down on Davis like avenging warrior monks. "Unforgivable!" ran one screaming headline. Tetsuharu Kawakami, who had now been elevated to the status of Godfather of Japanese baseball, equated Davis's behavior to a national insult. "This is Japan, not America," he fumed in his *Nikkan Sports* column. "Foreigners should obey our customs. The ball field should be regarded as sacred and violence on its premises never allowed. Davis is making light of Japan and the Japanese and that is unbearable."

Kawakami neglected to note that of the eighty-four people who had been thrown out of games in the postwar history of Japanese ball, 63 were Japanese. Most of them had been ejected for manhandling the umpires. And Kawakami had been one of them.

Indeed, perhaps the worst incidence of violence ever seen on a baseball field anywhere was in September 1983, during a Taiyo Whales–Hanshin Tigers game in Yokohama. Two Tiger coaches brutally beat up an umpire in full view of a nationwide television audience. One of them even delivered a wicked kick to the genital area that doubled over the hapless man in blue. Afterward, the two coaches apologized profusely, pleaded temporary insanity, and got off with a suspension that lasted only the rest of the season.

But nobody in Japan liked to talk about that particular evening. The dark side of the Japanese character was not a popular topic for discussion in the media. Unruly *gaijin* made for much more interesting copy.

Takenori Emoto, the pitcher turned popular author, once put it this way: "All in all, it's just easier to pick on the *gaijin*. Because of the language barrier, they don't know what you're saying. Besides, they go home at the end of the season, but we Japanese have to live with each other."

For slugging pitcher Higashio, Davis was hit with a ten-day suspension and a substantial fine of one hundred thousand yen, but remained steadfastly unrepentant. "If I have any regrets," he said "it is that Higashio went on to finish the game. That means I didn't hit him hard enough."

In 1987, it was Warren Cromartie, who punched a Chunichi Dragons pitcher named Miyashita. Cromartie was also suspended for ten days and fined one hundred thousand yen. Wrote critic Kunikazu Ogawa, "Pitchers have no right to throw at a player's head, but even more than that, players have no business committing violence on the field. The intelligence level of Japanese baseball will be questioned. I'd like Cromartie to think about that."

Coincidentally, or otherwise, Ogawa used the same Japanese word, *chiteki,* that former prime minister Nakasone had used some months earlier when he made his famous remark about the low intelligence level of Americans. Said Nakasone:

> Japan is now a highly educated and fairly intelligent society, much more so than America on the average. In America, there are quite a few black people, Puerto Ricans, and Mexicans. . . . On the average, the *chiteki* level is still very low. In America, even now, there are many black people who do not know their letters.

The role of Americans in undermining team *wa* entered a completely new phase in June of 1988, when Kintetsu's Davis was arrested on possession of hashish, which is a serious crime under Japan's strict drug laws. (The news of his arrest was flashed on TV along with clips of his attack on Higashio so that there would be no mistaking the connection. The Japanese public was largely unfamiliar with marijuana and many naturally assumed his "addiction to drugs" had prompted his outburst.)

According to newspaper accounts, police had been tipped off by a neighbor of Davis's who had been irked by noisy parties held in Davis's home. Arriving at Davis's house in Osaka with a search warrant, they found fourteen grams of cannabis resin, along with three suspicious-looking pipes.

Davis protested disingenuously that he had no idea that what the police found was an illegal drug. He insisted that a friend had given it to him as a "balm" for his injured heel. But after twenty days in jail, he was released and deported. Japanese reports said he finally admitted to at least having smoked marijuana. Reports in English said he didn't. Either way, he duly impressed police officers in Kobe who interrogated him for more than 120 hours before deciding it would not be worth their trouble to prosecute.

Upon Davis's departure, one Kobe policeman allowed that Davis was one of the most obstinate suspects he had ever encountered.

Japanese could question Davis's common sense, but nobody could say he lacked fighting spirit.

5

Oendan

The wind blows from Mount Rokko
The sun beats high in the sky;
The passion of youth is beautiful,
Oh, glorious Hanshin Tigers.
Ohh . . . ohh . . . ohh . . .
Hanshin Tigers,
Fure . . . fure . . . fure . . .
Hooray . . . hooray . . . hooray.

from "The Hanshin Tigers Song,"
lyrics by Sonosuke Sato

On the outskirts of the sprawling industrial zone that is Osaka, at the base of Mount Rokko, stands a musty, ivy-covered edifice known as Koshien Stadium. It has housed the Hanshin Tigers for half a century.

At three o'clock on the day of a Tiger home night game, the gates to the outfield seats open up and a familiar ritual unfolds. Within minutes, the bleachers in the right and center field area are a sea of people, over ten thousand in all, which comprises the Tiger cheering section. Each person is equipped with the contents of a Tiger Kit, sold outside the stadium for the nominal fee of one thousand yen; a *happi* coat, a cap, and a megaphone in the Tiger colors of yellow and black.

Many young women in the crowd sport artificial Tiger tails and Tiger whiskers. Others have their hair dyed yellow and black. Several fans have their heads shaved in the shape of the Chinese character *tora,* meaning tiger. One or two carry an American flag.

In the crowd are several splinter booster groups and ad hoc organizations identified by distinctive headbands and badges. They bear names like the "I love Koshien club," the "Tiger Fanatics Club," the "Kyoto Tiger Association," the "Right Field Stands Club," and the "Tora, Tora, Tora Group."

Two hours before game time, with the bleacher crowd already overflowing into the aisles, the cheerleaders arrive, their places in the front row respectfully reserved by other fans. They have just come from the Tiger shrine, located in a nearby supermarket owned by rabid Tiger fans, where they prayed for the success of the team.

One of them, a leathery-faced man with twinkling eyes and thick callouses on his hands from waving a ponderous Tiger banner, cracks open a can of Tiger Beer, an Asahi product bearing the Hanshin Tiger logo. "It's good to be a little drunk out here," he says to no one in particular.

At 5:00 P.M., exactly one hour before the first pitch, the cheering section rises en masse to sing the Tiger song, "The Wind Blows Down from Mount Rokko." Then the chanting begins: *"Katobase Tai-ga-zu"* (Knock 'em out Tigers), *"Katobase Tai-ga-zu."* It is a resounding, deafening cry that will go on in varying forms until the end of the game approximately four-and-a-half hours away.

The fans interrupt their cheering only to celebrate the seventh-inning stretch, when they unleash a huge cloud of colored balloons.

All in all, it is an awesome display of energy. And even when the game is over, the crowd seems reluctant to leave. Many remain standing in place, still chanting as if under some magic spell.

"Baseball is a lot clearer than our daily lives," says one *sarariman,* dressed in a dark-blue suit with his tie still in place. "The strong and the best win. That's all there is to it."

For others, the attraction is even more basic. Says one

young man in a voice hoarse from screaming, "I really didn't come here to see pro ball. I just like the atmosphere." "It's like a rock concert," declares his girlfriend. "We just have a lot of fun yelling."

"To tell the truth," one of the cheerleaders, a man in his fifties, confesses, "I come here because it gives me a chance to get away from my wife." He adds with a wink, "That's also why I go on the road with the team."

There are a lot of extraordinary things about Japan's national sport of baseball: Bands that play Mahler and Beethoven in opening day ceremonies. Umpires that practice their strike and ball calling form in pregame warmups. And commentators who use sophisticated computer studies to evaluate a player's ability, then blithely cite his blood type in the popular belief that it somehow affects performance. (Types A and O purportedly make good batters, Type B makes good pitchers, and so forth.) But perhaps most unusual of all is the Japanese fan himself, who is a fascinating study in contrasts.

Generally speaking, Japanese people are reserved and tend to concentrate all their energy inside. They are shy, low-key, and only occasionally are they given to eruption, like the volcanic mountains that dot their island country. It takes several drinks after work, for example, before the Japanese *sarariman* loses his inhibitions and reveals his other, boistrous self.

Nowhere is this dichotomy more apparent than at the ballpark. Observing fan conduct there is akin to taking a crash course in Japanese psychology. The typical fan, left alone and to his own devices, will sit quietly through a nine-inning game, behaving with proverbial Japanese decorum, eschewing the sort of loud and vulgar conduct common in many U.S. major league ballparks. He will even politely return foul balls to the stadium ushers, as prescribed by long-held custom in Japanese baseball.

Yet, put him in one of the highly organized cheering groups, or *oendan,* that can be found at all baseball stadiums in Japan, and he quickly sheds his traditional restraint. Spurred on by energetic cheerleaders, and the pounding rhythm of *taiko* drums, horns, whistles, and other noisemakers, he becomes a veritable wildman, yelling and screaming nonstop for nine solid innings.

Said one New York television producer after spending an entire game in the midst of the several-thousand-member Yomiuri Giants *oendan,* "These people are lunatics! There is more noise here than the World Series and the Army-Navy game combined. How do they keep it up?"

Oendan exist at every level of Japanese sport, from amateur to professional, and date back to the nineteenth century, when they were a major presence at college baseball games—highly organized, extremely loud, and more than a little militant. Participating in the *oendan* was considered a way of demonstrating school loyalty, and postgame confrontations between rival cheering groups were a vivid adjunct to the athletic activity on the field.

In 1904, after a game in which Keio had defeated its crosstown Tokyo rival Waseda, the Keio *oendan* performed a rousing *banzai* cheer in front of the on-campus residence of the Waseda University president. Stung by this grievous insult, the Waseda *oendan* repaid in kind after the next contest, which Waseda won, with a noisy demonstration of its own in front of the Keio president's house.

By the time the third game was scheduled to be played, there was homicide in the air. Both cheering groups had swollen in size to several hundred students, fortified with members of their respective school judo clubs, who were ready to do battle. University authorities were so alarmed that they canceled the contest and any further play between the two schools was subsequently banned for the next two years.

Today, college *oendan* bear little resemblance to their fun-loving counterparts in the West. They are strictly ordered by rank and seniority, and otherwise marked by militaristic tendencies. All members wear the same black cadet uniforms and often white headbands emblazoned with a red rising sun and stirring inscriptions like *hissho* (desperate victory).

The *oendan* are also known for their association with right-wing organizations and their devotion to traditional Japanese values of loyalty and discipline. Said the leader of one *oendan*, "Japan is losing its sense of order. It's our job to help restore it."

One of the more successful college baseball managers was Kichiro Shimaoka, a rotund Wallace Beery look-alike who guided the fortunes of the Meiji University team for some thirty years. He led them to several Big Six League titles and also managed a Japanese college all-star team to a victory over the Americans in College World Series competition.

Yet, Shimaoka never played organized baseball and had only a cursory knowledge of the game. As a student at Meiji in the 1930s, he had been head of the cheering section and he was regarded as a good leader and motivator of youth. In 1939, after several years as manager of the Meiji Middle School baseball team, he was asked to step up to the college level.

Shimaoka had spirit and that was enough. He would sit on the bench and exhort his team to greater efforts. *"Yare! Yare!"* (Do it! Do it!) he would yell, and his players would play their hearts out for him.

        ⊗   ⊗   ⊗

The sun rises, the wind blows hot, the sky burns.
The Lion runs on the horizon.
Fierce, brave, beautiful;
His flying mane leaves the trail of a rainbow.
Aah . . . Lions, Lions, Lions.

> from the Seibu Lions song,
> "Lion on the Horizon,"
> lyrics by Yu Aku

With the birth of Japanese professional baseball in 1935, *oendan* naturally followed. These cheering groups consisted of a few unpaid volunteers who shared in common a passion for the home team and a strong set of lungs.

As the popularity of pro baseball soared after the war, though, the *oendan* grew right along with it. The several hundred members of the Hiroshima Carp cheering section, which grew big and brassy in the mid-1970s when the Carp emerged as a baseball power, wave so many huge carp streamers that it is sometimes impossible for the fans to see the field. The Nippon Ham Fighters *oendan* has a detachment of long-legged women cheerleaders whose high-kicking antics usually bear little relation to the flow of the game itself.

Former baseball commissioner Takeso Shimoda tried, with little success, to tone the *oendan* down for the benefit of fans who might wish to watch a game in peace and quiet.

He made three requests: (1) Do not force others to root for teams, (2) Do not use drums and other noise-making instruments, and (3) Do not wave large flags or banners. No one paid any attention. The fans, it seemed, were often as interested in watching the activity in the stands as they were the action on the diamond.

Yakult fans grew to like their lead cheerleader Masayasu Okada so much that many of those sitting in the expensive infield seats would leave in midgame to join him in the bleachers. Okada, like other cheerleaders, would follow his team wherever it played on the road, accompanied by a squadron of thirty or so assistants, everybody paying his own expenses. He once explained his hobby of twenty years by saying, "I'm just crazy about the Yakult Swallows. That's all." Then he added, "I'm just crazy period. You have to be crazy to act like this every night."

To the sky with fighting soul,
The ball soars and soars with burning flames.
Aah . . . Giants.
Ever proud of the name
Their courage lights up the field.
Giants . . . Giants . . .
Go . . . Go . . . Giants Troop.

> from the Yomiuri Giants song,
> "With Fighting Soul,"
> lyrics by Sanpei Tsubaki

Many observers view the *oendan* as further proof of Japanese society's addiction to group activity and regulation. Some cheering groups charge membership fees and issue membership cards. Others, like that of the Giants, even assign seat numbers in nonreserved areas, and require members to come to the ballpark several hours early to practice their cheers. Slackers may lose their seating privileges.

Yet few *oendan* members have complained. As one fan said, "For the most part, the *oendan* organizations are an example of democracy at work. Anyone can join. You're free to form your own group if you want. And anyone can become a cheerleader, whether he is a wealthy businessman or a poor college student. It's simple. The noisiest rise to the top."

A Professor Oda, of Tsukuba University, has said the *oendan* serve an important psychological function: "Japanese work too hard. Traditionally, it has only been at *matsuri* (festival) time each year that we lose our inhibitions and let down our hair. These days, however, a trip to the baseball park has become a substitute for the *matsuri*. That's good. It means we're relaxing more."

Nowhere is a baseball game more of a *matsuri* than at sixty-thousand-seat Koshien Stadium, and nowhere are the fans more lustily supportive of their team. In 1985, when the Hanshin Tigers won their first pennant in twenty-one years, a wave of Tigermania swept the land, washing aside everything in its path. Thousands of Tiger supporters followed the team around the country on a special Tiger train, chartering several railcars exclusively for their use.

In setting a new attendance record for the club, the Tiger faithful sparked a mini-economic boom. They snapped up Tiger dolls, Tiger beer, Tiger underwear, and other memorabilia in a season-long frenzy of souvenir buying that, when combined with ticket sales and other related costs, amounted to nearly half a billion dollars' worth of revenue in the Osaka area alone.

So extraordinary were the exploits of the Tiger followers that in a year-end poll conducted by the leading daily newspaper *Yomiuri Shimbun,* Tiger fever was chosen as one of the top-ten news stories of 1985 in the regular domestic news category.

In 1987, the Tigers finished in last place, thirty-seven-and-a-half games out of first place. Yet, demand for tickets was so high that even the benches in the outfield stands were converted into reserved seats, sold by lottery months in advance.

    ⦿   ⦿   ⦿

> Man blooms as a flower of the earth.
> Baseball is a drama . . . it is life.
> Take the Tiger alive . . . catch the Whales,
> Swallow the Dragon . . . pull in the Carp,
> Knock down the Giant star.
> Fly away Yakult Swallows.
>
> from the Yakult Swallows song,
"Fly Away Yakult Swallows"

The power and spirit of the sun
Which shines on the field is in this breast
Living for baseball, full of dreams.
Nankai Hawks, let's go!
Aah . . . Flapping wings of gold in the sky.
The flag of victory unfurls.
Hawks! Hawks! Nankai Hawks.

from "The Nankai Hawks Song,"
lyrics by Takao Saeki

In the 1980s, attendance at pro-baseball games increased about 50 percent in Japan and a distinct change in the makeup of the crowds and their respective *oendan* became apparent. In the 1970s, Giants fans at Korakuen had been comfortably white-collar and upwardly mobile. Executives of the big multinational Japanese firms and upper-echelon government ministry officials occupied the exclusive infield seats. Lower-ranked company workers, precursors to the Japanese "yuppies," sat in the less expensive areas. Even those who filled the *oendan* sections in the outfield had a distinct, whiskey-and-water, businesslike air about them.

A decade later, however, one could notice an increased number of adolescent females, prenymphets from junior and senior high school, occupying the cheaper seats. There they would sit, screaming wildly, almost orgasmically, at the younger players on the field, oblivious to the score or game situation.

According to a survey taken in 1986, 35 percent of all Giants fans were secondary-school girls. "I couldn't believe it," said Reggie Smith. "The Giants would go into towns around Japan and the young girls would start screaming and falling down. You wave to them and say

'Hi,' and they pass out. It was like being a member of a rock band."

Fans in Osaka changed a bit too. Hanshin fans were once mostly artisans, craftsmen, and day laborers—earthy occupations typical of the industrial Kansai region. These vigorous enthusiasts would come to the game to let off steam after a hard day over the pickax and were not averse to dashing joyfully out onto the field to celebrate a home run.

By the mid-1980s, however, one began to notice younger fans in the stands—alienated youth, and high school dropouts bypassed in Japan's demanding educational system, who were quite often unemployed and trying to make themselves noticed in a society that had no place for them. Japanese sociologists dubbed them the "Wandering Generation," and attributed a certain rise in stadium violence to their presence at the ballpark.

At Koshien a series of incidents occurred where visiting players were struck by rocks, bottles, and other missiles. Once, in 1985, an umpire was carried off the field after an inebriated, angry young fan brained him with a bicycle chain. Frequently, games would end to an accompanying barrage of paper cups, eggs, steel pachinko balls, and whatever else fans had in hand.

One year, when a Giants-Tigers game was precipitously called because of rain, a detachment of several hundred angry *oendan*ers stormed the field to engage in hand-to-hand combat with the umpires. The next day, stadium authorities erected a barbed-wire fence in front of the outfield stands.

By contrast, Carp fans got noisier, but better behaved. Previously known for the danger they posed to the physical well-being of visiting teams—a group of them once smashed all the windows of the Yomiuri Giants' bus, causing Giants outfielder Isao Harimoto to take after them with a baseball bat—they began to acquire some semblance of civility. Perhaps it was all the pennants the team won, starting in 1975, that lent an air of respectability to

the town. Whatever the reason, they have stopped terror-
izing opposing players.

Yet, even with the increased rowdiness, Japan is still in
the minor leagues of fan violence when compared to the
U.S. No Japanese club has ever had to employ armed
guards and police dogs to keep order as Philadelphia did
in the 1980 World Series.

When the Hanshin Tigers won their 1985 pennant,
some fans celebrated by singing, dancing, and leaping
impulsively into the polluted canals that flow through
downtown Osaka. No one imitated the behavior of De-
troit Tigers fans who feted their team's World Series triumph in 1984 by overturning police cars and going on a
rampage that destroyed thousands of dollars of property
and caused the deaths of two people.

Said one Japanese magazine editor who, after a night
game at Yankee Stadium, experienced a terror-filled ride
by subway back to his Manhattan hotel, "It is hard to say
who is more dangerous—the muggers that roam the
streets at night, or the drunken fans inside the park who
like to beat people up. We're lucky in Japan. We don't
have guns or drugs. We don't have big race problems. We
have a tradition of law and order."

Sports Illustrated writer Bruce Anderson, after spending several days in August 1985 watching baseball Japanese style, said, "Perhaps there are isolated episodes, but
all in all there does not seem to be the mean-spiritedness
here that there is in the U.S. In Japan, it's more a spirit of
good, clean fun. It's very refreshing."

The height of "good, clean fun" Japanese style was perhaps reached by members of the Tiger *oendan* when they
highjacked a Seibu Railways train. That particular episode
occurred after the end of the sixth and final game of the
1985 Japan Series between Hanshin and Seibu at Lions
Stadium, which the Tigers won handily to wrap up their
Japan Championship. Several hundred delirious Tiger
supporters squeezed onto the last train from Tokorosawa

to Tokyo and continued their celebration all the way back into the city.

Not satisfied with having screamed themselves hoarse all afternoon, the *oendan,* under the vigorous orchestration of megaphone-bearing cheerleaders stationed in each car, sang individual cheers to all the players, coaches, and front-office people in the Hanshin organization (after the fashion of the song "A Hundred Bottles of Beer on the Wall"), all accompanied by much foot-stomping that literally had the train shaking on the tracks.

That finished, they started all over again—this time with chants deriding everyone on the Seibu and Yomiuri rosters.

Each time the train came to a halt at a station, the *oendan* chief called out his instructions: "Listen everyone. No one gets off this train. Repeat. No one. This is a Seibu line and everyone out there is a Seibu fan. So no one gets on either."

Those orders were unnecessary, because the entire train was so utterly jammed with people that it would have been impossible for anyone else to squeeze aboard. At one stop, a station official dropped his lantern and whistle and tried to force his way inside one of the coaches. After several unsuccessful attempts, he had to give up and let his colleagues send the train on its way.

After an hour's journey, the train finally reached the end of the line, whereupon the Tiger fans alit to do a rousing *banzai* cheer in front of the Lions corner—an open area selling Lions' souvenirs at the entrance to the Seibu Department Store. They capped it all off with several reverent bars of the Tiger song—just to rub it in.

As the group headed noisily for Tokyo Station and the three-and-a-half-hour ride back to Osaka, one person, who, by his own estimate, had been cheering for seven consecutive hours, was heard to remark, "I can't wait until we get on the bullet train. Then we can start all over again."

6

The Sandwich Man

When hit-and-run, runner on first, run to second, runner will yell to batter, batter must get by ball.

note from Japanese coach
to American player

When the runner hollers, the batter shouldn't swing.

translation of above

When I first started out as an interpreter, the manager wanted me to go out to the on-deck circle in one game to tell the American to hit-and-run. Well, I went out there and looked in my dictionary and under hit-and-run *it said something about an auto accident. I didn't know what to say. I just stood there, with everyone staring at me, feeling really embarrassed. I just turned around and walked off the field.*

baseball interpreter

There's only one thing wrong with my interpreter. He can't speak English.

American ballplayer

Every professional baseball team in Japan employs a full-time interpreter, a trained linguist to assist the club's foreign players both on and off the field. It is his job to faithfully translate the manager's instructions, to help the *gaijin* converse with their teammates, and, in general, to foster harmony, understanding, and a smooth flow of information among the parties concerned.

That's the ideal. The reality is a bit more complicated.

One American, for example, went through his first April in Japan swinging at the wrong pitches and agitating his manager greatly, all because his interpreter thought that *take* meant "swing away." Another American, Chuck Manuel, explained in a TV interview that he wasn't mad anymore over a beanball incident that had left him with a broken jaw. The translator then solemnly told the viewing audience that Manuel-*san* was no long insane. (Missing several games with the flu shortly after, Manuel was given a handwritten note by a team official. It read: "When you get a condition, be sure to keep your healthy.")

During a heart-to-heart talk one night, a former Hiroshima Carp interpreter confessed to his two foreign players that, since he really didn't understand what they said all of the time, he occasionally had to invent answers that would satisfy the coaches.

Such linguistic breakdowns are more common than one might suspect. They are partially the result of a formal foreign-language education system in Japan that overemphasizes reading and largely ignores practical conversation. Thus, there are Japanese students of English who can read Shakespeare, but have difficulty saying hello. They also find it hard to discern sounds which do not appear in their own language (such as *v, th, l,* and *r*).

When an American arrived fifteen minutes late to a contract negotiating session, he was told by his interpreter, "The general manager is very concerned about your late." The American apologized for his tardiness several times, and each time was told that the general manager "understood," but was "still very concerned about 'your late.' " The American had begun to worry he had committed a serious offense when the interpreter finally opened his dictionary and pointed to the word "rate" and the entry "exchange rate." At what exchange rate, the GM wanted to know, would he like to be paid?

Formal education is only part of the problem, however. Most American athletes pepper their speech with slang that a Tokyo University professor of linguistics would have trouble following. With foreign ballplayers using terms like *Uncle Charlie* (curve), *crow hop* (sort of a short, staccato step when fielding a ball), and *buzzards' luck* (hard luck), the wonder is any communication takes place at all. When an outfielder fresh from the New York Yankees organization wanted to know where to meet members of the opposite sex in Tokyo, he asked, "Where's all the good beef in this town?" His interpreter responded by telling him about the steakhouses in the city.

Furthermore, many foreign players have thick regional or ethnic accents that can be difficult to understand. When a pitcher from Tennessee replied, "Aahm tard," in response to a question about how he felt during the late innings of one game, his interpreter did not know what he was talking about. A designated hitter from Puerto Rico greeted an approaching newspaper reporter with, "Hi. Wha chu wan, man?" His team interpreter thought he was speaking Chinese.

Many baseball interpreters have been assigned to their jobs with little thought given to how much they knew about baseball. All that mattered was a background in English. The young interpreter on the 1988 Yokohama Taiyo Whales told Americans Jim Paciorek and Carlos Ponce, "I didn't even like baseball before I came here. The parent company just ordered me here because of my language ability." A Carp translator with a similar lack of interest in Japan's national sport was once the victim of an old practical joke. He was asked to go find the key to the batter's box and spent the better part of an hour looking for it.

Toyo Kunimitsu did a lot of things before a friend introduced him to the Lotte Orions. None of them had anything to do with sport. He was a bank teller, a CPA, a tour guide, and a translator of detective stories. He took the Lotte job in 1975, at age twenty-nine, because he was bored with sitting behind a desk and liked the idea of a three-month paid vacation in the off-season.

Kunimitsu had never played baseball and did not know any of its rules. In fact, the first time he touched a real hardball was when he joined Lotte. "My first day on the job an American asked me to bring him his (batting) tee," said Kunimitsu, "I asked him if he wanted it with lemon and sugar. When he started talking about whether it was okay to steal on his own, I thought I was dealing with a thief. I really didn't know about base stealing.

"There were other things. Americans would call a home run a *tater* and say things like 'Fuck this shit.' It was all very confusing in the beginning."

The fact that baseball in Japan has its own distinctive English-derived language only adds to the overall confusion. A curve is a *kabu,* a strike is a *sutoraikku. Endo ran* means "hit-and-run," and a 3–2 count has become *tsu-suree.*

Japanese say *dedo boru* (dead ball) for "hit by the pitch," *manaja* (manager) for "traveling secretary," *gemu setto* (game set) for "the game is over," and *ranningu homa* for "inside-the-park home run." *Suree banto* is another purely Japanese invention. "Americans can never understand it," said Kunimitsu, "because they say 'bunt on two strikes.' I wind up translating from English to English.

"The terms are so different. If I tell our new *gaijin* we

have a *naita,* which means 'night game,' scheduled for the next day, he may not even come to the ballpark. He might think *naita* means 'party' or something like that."

The skilled translator, of course, is the one who can come up with the word appropriate to the cultural context. But there are fundamental differences in Japanese and American thinking that make this very difficult.

"There is no such thing as a perfect Japanese-English bilingual," says Nippon Ham's Toshi Shimada, a Chinese-Japanese educated at Tokyo's American School in Japan and a man who is as a close to being a perfect Japanese-English bilingual as you can get. "There are some expressions that are extremely difficult to translate. *Kiai wo ireteiko* sort of means 'Show your fighting spirit.' A lot of managers will say that to a Japanese player to get him to play harder, and it works. But it's a Japanese concept and you just can't convey that meaning in English, so that an American will respond like a Japanese would."

Years ago, at Taiyo Whales team receptions, high officials from the mother company would come around and say *ganbatte* to the foreign ballplayer, which is a common Japanese greeting. Whales interpreter Tadahario Ushigome would translate it as "Do your best," because that is the definition in the dictionary, along with "hold out," "stick it out," and "bear up well."

The American, however, would invariably be offended and retort that he always did his best. This in turn would irritate the team official because the *gaijin* had not answered him with *domo* (thanks), as a polite Japanese player would have done. Ushigome eventually discovered if he used "Good luck" instead of "Do your best," then the American would automatically say "Thanks," and everyone would be happy.

Ushigome joined the Whales in 1962, fresh out of language school. He was the first interpreter in the organization's history. Prior to his arrival, the primary form of communication with foreign players on the team consisted of handwritten notes from the team president that nobody could understand.

At first, Ushigome was enthusiastic about his new position. "You get to travel and watch baseball," he said. "It's a great job." It didn't take long for his ardor to dim, however, and language turned out to be the least of his problems. All too often, he found himself in the middle of squabbles between Japanese and Americans. It proved a constant strain.

"There's always trouble," he said, like a veteran marriage counselor who had seen too many divorces. "Nothing but trouble." He adds:

> A lot of Japanese coaches expect the *gaijin* to adjust 100 percent to the Japanese way. A lot of the *gaijin* players have been following the same routine for fifteen to twenty years. They are veteran players, not kids. They're used to thinking for themselves and you can't change old habits overnight. But some coaches feel they have to coach even a ten-year major league veteran, especially if the general manager is watching.

Ushigome, a somber, soft-voiced man, was never punched by a coach, as was a hapless Pacific League interpreter when the American on his team failed to respond to batting practice instructions ("You're not telling him properly," yelled the enraged coach), nor was he ever fined and suspended as a Central League interpreter once was when his team's American players missed curfew. In addition, he has had countless experiences he would just as soon forget.

One of the worst was when a Japanese coach, a former outfielder, tried to tell Clete Boyer, an ex-Yankee and one of the all-time major league fielding greats, how to play third base. As Ushigome recalled:

Boyer was smart, he knew defense, and he learned the habits of the Japanese batters really fast, even though he had just joined the team. He had a lot of pride and he was so upset about this coach that he didn't want to stay in Japan.

So I went and suggested to the coach that he leave Boyer alone because as as fielder, he was the best there was. The coach got really angry at me. "Shut up!" he said. "This is Japan. You do things our way. You obey the coaches." He was convinced he knew everything. Coaches are like that in Japan.

So I had to have a long dinner with Boyer and explain Japanese customs and the fact that coaches have to overcoach and try to calm him down.

Boyer was nice about it. He didn't make an issue out of it, like another *gaijin* might have.

Nippon Ham's Shimada liked to say that if the language barrier ever disappeared, Japanese would still need help bridging the vast cultural abyss that separates them from Western thinking. One of the hardest things he ever had to do was convince Nippon Ham's manager, Keiji Osawa, that one of his *gaijin* should take the night off because his wife was having a baby. Such things simply were not done in Japan.

I was really surprised to see how much the American players care about their wives. This one guy's wife was pregnant. She went into the hospital to have the baby and there were some complications. So the guy said he couldn't play in the game that night because he had to stay with his wife.

Our manager, Osawa, was naturally upset. I was trying to explain to him the American way of thinking—the importance they place on their families—but he just could not understand how any player could miss a game for a reason like that. Finally Yato, our batting coach, who understands Americans, helped me out. He told

the manager that the *gaijin* would be worrying so
much he wouldn't be able to do good in the game anyway, so why not let him off. That kind of reasoning
worked.

Interpreters will tell you that the only thing that fully
matches Japanese intransigence is the unwillingness of
many American players to bend even a little to please
their hosts.

Toshiro Ashiki, interpreter for the Chunichi Dragons,
has tried hard to forget the petulant Willie Davis, who
would say, "Hey, you know who I am? I'm Willie Davis of
the major leagues. You can tell the others what to do. Not
me." Ashiki remembers all too well the night the Dragons
manager took Davis out of the starting lineup because he
thought Davis's thirty-seven-year-old legs could use a rest.

Davis was furious. "A major league manager would
have *asked* me if I wanted to sit down," he told Ashiki.
After sulking in the bullpen most of the evening, he
refused to go in the game in the late innings as a defensive
replacement. "The manager says I'm tired," he told
Ashiki. "So I guess I'm too tired to play defense."

Ashiki also remembers the time during a nationally
televised postgame interview, he had to ask Davis about
a game-winning home run the latter had smacked.

"What kind of ball did you hit?" he said, literally translating the TV announcer's question.

"I hit a baseball," replied Davis sarcastically.

Ashiki had started out as a pitcher for the Dragons in
the early 1950s. When arm trouble put an early end to his
career, he became the team's trainer and then was summarily given the job of translator when the team signed
up its first American, Bob Nieman.

"I had to learn English from scratch," he said, with a
hint of pride, "because I spent all my time in high school
playing ball. I studied textbook phrases like 'How are you
today?' but found that Americans didn't talk that way.

They'd all say, 'What the fuck's happenin', man?' I had no idea what they were talking about."

Ashiki, an animated, gregarious man with a playful sense of humor, confessed it took time before he could laugh about Americans. In the beginning, he could not understand their customs or manners. There were some nice people he met along the way, like Gene Martin and Gary Rajsich, but there were also some that he wasn't so sure about, like Davis and pitcher Bobby Castillo. After being kayoed in a game in 1987, Castillo angrily took off his spikes in the clubhouse at Korakuen, set them atop an ashtray stand, poured lighter fluid over them, and struck a match. Within minutes there was a visit by the Tokyo Metropolitan Fire Department.

In time, however, Ashiki began to appreciate certain things about Americans, like their directness. Americans came right out and said what was on their minds, while Japanese were always talking around in circles. You never knew what the hell they were thinking.

Moreover, in workouts, Americans always stressed a specific purpose, like hitting to the opposite field. Japanese just stressed practice. You chased fly balls until you were dripping with sweat. Then you were okay. It meant you had a great practice. He thought the American way more pragmatic.

If there was one general complaint you could make about Americans, he thought, it was that they complained too much. They would haggle over contract details and argue about even one day's meal money.

When you came right down to it, some Americans were, well, very cheap. A guy could be making a million dollars a year but would still throw a temper tantrum if the team didn't pay his electric bill. It happened all the time. He knew one player, a star on another team, who refused to suit up until the team took care of his utilities payments. A Japanese player would never do that, Ashiki thought. Even if he only made one-tenth the money.

If Yomiuri Giants interpreter Ichiro Tanuma ever decided to write a book about his experiences, it would make a good primer on aberrant behavior.

It was Tanuma's job not only to interpret but to somehow keep the *gaijin* on the team from tarnishing the super-clean Giants image. It proved to be an impossible task. Reggie Smith once showed up at a pregame practice with his uniform on backwards as a practical joke. Tanuma was ordered to straighten him out.

"What's the problem, Reggie?" he asked, sauntering up to Smith.

"You're my problem," Smith retorted. "You're always following me around. Why don't you get off the field?" Smith abruptly walked off into the outfield to shag flies.

Clyde Wright caused everyone else to pale in comparison. *Kurezi (Crazy) Raito* was always steaming mad whenever he was removed from a close game. On one such occasion, Tanuma walked off the field with him and patted Wright's shoulder soothingly, in commiseration.

"Take it easy, Clyde" he said. "It's all right.

With the TV cameras trained on them, Wright wheeled and grabbed Tanuma by the necktie, jerking him off his feet and nearly strangling him.

"Don't you *ever* touch me when I'm mad, boy," he snarled.

"That was kind of embarrassing," said Tanuma, "it being on television and all. But that's the nature of this job. You have to be a baby sitter and a therapist, among other things. Actually, Wright was an okay guy. I liked him . . . off the field. But when he put his uniform on, he was a different kind of person."

Equanimity is one of Tanuma's great features. A laconic, amiable man who was a travel agent in Miami before joining the team he had idolized from childhood, he remained oddly protective of his American charges over the years, often in the face of harsh criticism by the press and the front office.

> I think the Japanese expect too much. Reporters criticize the *gaijin*, saying they should try to be more a part of the team. That makes me mad. I think it's nonsense. Japanese don't really try to mix with the *gaijin*. They stay separate. Why should Americans have to do everything the Japanese way? Americans come here to play ball, so let them alone to do it. Why have them attending all the meetings and being together with the Japanese all the time? Stop trying to make Japanese out of them.

Luigi Nakajima is a dark-eyed Japanese-Italian, born and raised in Japan, who wears a perpetually harried look that reached its nadir when Yakult owner Matsuzono promoted him to chief of foreign affairs and dispatched him to the United States with the command: "Bring me back a big-name big leaguer or don't come back at all." (Nakajima brought back Bob Horner.) Nakajima is continually amazed at the number of ways there are for Japanese and Americans to irritate each other. His boyhood idol, Joe Pepitone, who left Japan after playing fourteen games in 1973, was his introduction to basic *gaijin* insensitivity. And a big, red-haired character from West Virginia named Charlie Manuel, with a talent for producing anarchy out of order, gave him advanced lessons.

He remembers the day a coach ordered Manuel to run ten extra sprints in a workout. Manuel replied with a very unequivocal, "Fuck no, I ain't." And walked off the field, leaving Nakajima to translate. Then there was the time Luigi reprimanded Manuel for being late. Manuel, six feet two inches tall and 190 pounds, lifted him off the ground by his lapels and asked if he would mind repeating what he just said.

But most of all, he recalls the time that Manuel suddenly decided to start calling the coaches by their first names as part of his own personal goodwill campaign. At the start of practice one afternoon, he walked up to coach Kanji Maruyama and said, "Hi, Kanji. How are you?"

Maruyama had a fit. A player addressing a coach with such familiarity in Japan is a sign of great disrespect and he called Nakajima over to complain about it. Nakajima tried to placate him. He explained that the custom in the United States is to call everyone by his first name. "Charlie is just trying to be friendly," he said.

Maruyama nodded. He was a broad-minded man and he understood. He proposed a compromise. He told Nakajima to tell Manuel that it would be fine to call him Kanji off the field, but on it, please show the proper respect and address him as Maruyama-*san*.

Nakajima relayed the coach's message to Manuel, who shrugged and said okay and the rest of the day passed uneventfully. But Manuel was stubborn. He strongly believed in his own way of doing things. He could not understand why he couldn't call someone by his first name if he wanted to. How could anyone reject such a display of friendship? After a night of mulling the situation, he determined that he couldn't give up so easily. And so, the very next day, arriving at the ballpark, the first thing he did was approach Maruyama to say, "Hi . . . Kanji."

Maruyama had another fit. Once again he sent for Nakajima. "Straighten that *gaijin* out!" he commanded.

Nakajima tried again to explain to his recalcitrant American how insulting his way of speaking was to Maruyama and how much face Maruyama lost in front of all the others being treated that way. If Manuel kept it up, Luigi said, then Maruyama's authority would be so diminished he would be unable to do his job. Discipline would suffer and the welfare of the team as a whole would be affected. It was Manuel's sacred duty as a Yakult Swallow to address the coaches by their last names.

"I don't care about that," Manuel shrugged. It didn't make any sense to him. He wanted to be friends with the coaches and, by god, he was going to call them by their first names whether they liked it or not. And no meddlesome interpreter was going to stop him.

So he kept it up. Partly out of pure stubbornness, perhaps, but he kept it up. Soon, Maruyama became convinced that Manuel was making fun of him. And because Nakajima could not make him stop, the coach turned his anger on the interpreter as well. For Nakajima, there was no solution, and for a while, feelings among the three were very unpleasant.

In the face of Manuel's obtuseness, Maruyama finally gave up. Eventually he and Manuel became good friends, but for a long time Nakajima could only suffer in silence. When it was all over, Manuel good-naturedly dubbed him the Sandwich Man, because he was always stuck in the middle.

Kunimitsu, who moved to the Dragons in 1988, viewed it as his job to keep his American players in good spirits. A short, bristly-haired man with a calm, unhurried manner, he said, "If the *gaijin* is depressed, I have to cheer him up. If he doesn't feel like running in the outfield, then I run with him and perhaps he does more as a result. You might say I'm a mental training coach."

Kunimitsu's worst experience came in 1979, not with imported players (he gave Leron Lee a "10" in deportment), but with a visiting tour of American major league All-Stars, including Rod Carew, Dave Parker, and Pete Rose, for whom he was asked to translate.

> The All-Stars were rather tacky and rude. I think they looked down on Japan. Once we were on a long bus ride to Tsumago City in Shizuoka. John Candelaria, the pitcher for the Pirates, had been drinking a lot of beer and had to urinate. So he urinated into a bucket and threw it out the window. I was shocked. The driver was

really angry. He wanted me to throw Candelaria off the bus, but finally agreed to let him stay when Candelaria said he would stop drinking beer.

I saw a lot of bad examples of spoiled Americans on that tour. But, in 1982, I worked with the Kansas City Royals on a tour of Japan and they were all very polite, very gentlemanly. They were very quiet, just like the kind of baseball they played—quiet and unexciting. The only problem I had with the Royals was that some of them wanted to go to a Turkish Bath[1] so I was asked to find a Turkish Bath that would admit black people, because a lot of them don't. It took a lot of time, but I finally found one.

Japanese interpreters have had a wide range of relationships with foreign players. One Carp linguist was fired for being too close to the Americans on his team. Front-office officials felt that he was too emotionally involved to be objective in his job, which required him to file sub-rosa reports on the nocturnal activities of the *gaijin*.

His successor operated under no such handicap. Said American Tim Ireland, who spent two years with him, "My performance in my first spring was so bad that my interpreter wouldn't even talk to me for a long while. When he finally did, he called me Filkins—which was the name of the other American on the team. I think he was ashamed to be associated with me."

Randy Bass and Rich Gale had their interpreter on the Hanshin Tigers replaced. "He wouldn't translate our feelings properly," said Bass. "The first time I went into contract negotiations with him, he told me I was demanding too much money.

---

1. A uniquely Japanese style of steam bath where female masseuses provide sexual services. The Turkish embassy complained so much about this misuse of the name that the Japanese government launched a campaign to select a new one. *Soapland* was chosen but the term *Turkish Bath* remained in the Japanese lexicon.

"If I didn't want to practice, I'd tell him, but instead of him relaying that to the manager he would say to me, 'Are you serious? You have to practice.' That kind of thing.

"He was like a spy for the front office. On the road, he would be there to make sure we got in by curfew. If we said something critical about the coaches, then he would go right to the front office and tell them."

The Tiger interpreter had only been doing his job, of course, and when the new man took his place, he was rewarded with a promotion to the post of PR director—much to the amusement of Bass and Gale.

One might ask why more foreigners don't study Japanese and thereby alleviate the need to rely on an interpreter all the time. In the entire history of Japanese baseball only a handful of Americans have taken it upon themselves to learn the language—Bucky Harris, Wally Yonamine, Bobby Marcano, and Leon Lee, among others.

Most cite time limitations—their average stay in Japan is too brief. Many others say the less you understand the better off you are, given the hypercritical attitude many of the coaches and writers assume toward the *gaijin*.

Kunimitsu, for example, once worked under a manager with a perverse sense of humor who would tell a foreigner who was doing poorly that he was a "salary thief," or say, "I bought your ticket home. Why don't you just go pack up your bags and go back to the U.S.

"Japanese pros are used to that," said Kunimitsu, "They're raised that way, but foreigners, especially Americans, aren't. So I couldn't translate that directly. I'd have to say 'The manager hopes your hitting improves' or something like that."

One American cited simple self-protection as a reason for not learning the language. "If you can't speak Japanese," he said, "then you can't put your foot in your mouth. Americans are always complaining about something. It's our national character. We're always saying the wrong thing, the undiplomatic thing, especially for Japan, like, 'That's the dumbest move I've ever seen,' or something like that. If the interpreter translated one-tenth of the things we say, we'd be fired immediately. So it's better we don't speak the lingo . . . you might say the interpreter is our best friend."

Indeed, some might say the most important function of an interpreter is not the translation of a foreigner's remarks, but the judicious laundering of them. "Some Americans players get mad if they find out I don't translate their feelings exactly," said Ashiki, "but I believe there are some things that you can't or should not translate exactly. If a *gaijin* says something like 'I don't give a fuck!' well, I'll say, 'I'll try harder' instead. It avoids trouble."

Diplomatic revisions by interpreters have saved the day on many an occasion. When a weary Clyde Wright was interviewed on television after pitching a 12-inning shutout for the Giants over the Dragons, his response to a question about how he felt was not what everyone wanted to hear. "Well," Wright drawled, "to tell the truth I really didn't care whether we won or lost. I just wanted to get the game over with so I could go home and get some sleep."

Tanuma's translation—"I did my best and I'm glad I was able to help the team"—spared Wright and the Giants front office a lot of embarrassment.

Tony Solaita, an American-Samoan who played for the Nippon Ham Fighters, was up in arms over brushback pitches in a game against the Lotte Orions and used his interpreter, Toshi Shimada, to raise the issue with the Orions catcher during pregame practice the following day.

"Listen you no-good son of a bitch," said Solaita, who was built like a Brinks armored truck and had a temper to match, "if you have a pitcher throw at my head again, I'll fucking kill you."

Shimada did not bat an eyelash as he translated: "Mr. Solaita asks that you please not throw at his head anymore. It makes his wife and children worry."

The catcher flashed an appropriate look of concern. He bowed slightly, then assured them it was all an accident and promised that such a terrible thing would never happen again.

Solaita nodded. The two shook hands and the meeting ended.

The catcher went away feeling somewhat sympathetic toward the *gaijin*. Solaita went away feeling that he had defended his honor. And Shimada went away satisfied that he had singlehandedly averted a major fight on the ball field in that evening's game.

Shimada's finest hour was the peacemaking role he played in a dispute between the Ham Fighters' manager, Keiji Osawa, and an American named Sam Ewing.

During a pregame meeting one day, Osawa fined Ewing's fellow *gaijin*, Bobby Mitchell, for bad defense the previous night. Ewing thought that grossly unfair, since Japanese players on the team had also made defensive misplays in the game and hadn't been fined. When the meeting was over, he told Osawa so in the runway near the dugout.

"You're horseshit!" he cried in English. Osawa retorted in Japanese, *"Nan da to kono yar? Baka yaro!"* ("What'd you say, you son of a bitch?")

Suddenly the two were screaming and yelling at each other as loud as they could, each in his native tongue, each not understanding exactly what the other was saying, although the general message was unmistakably clear.

Ewing, a hulking six feet three inches, grabbed Osawa, who was smaller but sturdily put together and rugged enough to fight back. Coaches rushed in to break it up before any damage could be done.

Shimada was beside himself with shock and worry. He

was only twenty-six and had just joined the organization. He had no idea Americans did such things.

Shimada was called into a closed-door meeting between the two combatants to translate. Ewing, still fuming, explained why he became angry: "Other players had screwed up too. Why pick only on Mitchell? It was a horse-shit thing to do." Shimada put this into Japanese and Osawa shot back, "I'm the manager of this team and if you don't like the way I manage then you can go home."

Realizing the direct approach wasn't working, Shimada softened his English translation to, "He says you might not like the way he does things, but please try to remember, that he's still the manager of this team."

Ewing relaxed slightly. "Tell him I apologize for shouting at him in front of all those people," he said. "I should have shouted at him here in private." Shimada relayed Ewing's remarks, omitting the last part of the sentence.

Osawa and Ewing went back and forth in this manner, Shimada discreetly modifying their statements, until finally, both men cooled down enough to shake hands. Ewing agreed to apologize in front of the team—something which very few Americans can bring themselves to do.

"Sam really didn't want to do it," said Shimada, "but I let him know that if he didn't, it would only make my job more difficult. Sam was a nice guy that way."

Nakajima, for one, feared that the tensions of being in the middle of so many confrontations would give him an ulcer. So he ultimately came to revise his philosophy toward his job and to forget about being a diplomat.

"I found it to be so simple," he said one afternoon during his fifteen-minute lunch break of curry rice in the Jingu clubhouse. "If the American told a coach to go to hell, or vice versa, then I just translated it that way without softening it: He says for you to go to hell. If they want to argue with each other, let them. I'd just be the translator. And you know what? I found my job got easier. Once both sides realized what I was doing they stopped using so many bad words."

It was early April. Cherry blossoms had exploded all over Tokyo, coloring the tree-lined pathways outside the stadium a glorious pink and white. Nakajima was in the process of breaking in yet another new pair of American players, and he spoke of a second change in his philosophy: He had stopped trying to cover for the *gaijin*. He told of the day an American outfielder on the team failed to show up for a 10:00 A.M. practice. At 10:15, Nakajima called his house, and there was no answer. He called again at 10:30 and at 10:45. At 11:00, the *gaijin* finally picked up the phone.

He groaned into the receiver and Luigi sensed immediately that he was either extremely hungover or still drunk.

"I know there is a practice today," the American mumbled, "but what can I do? I just can't make it. I was drinking until 5:00 A.M."

Luigi tried to persuade him to at least come to the ballpark. "If the trainer sees what condition you're in, and says you can't practice, maybe he can get permission from the manager for you to take off."

"I can't even walk, man. I just want to stay in bed all day today."

Luigi drew a breath. "Is it okay if I tell this to the manager?"

"Yeah, sure," came the muttered reply. "Go ahead. Do anything you want. Just let me go back to sleep." Then the player hung up.

Nakajima went to tell the manager, who became extremely angry and screamed *baka yaro* several times in the general direction of his *gaijin* outfielder's apartment. Then he levied a fine of fifty thousand yen.

"The American was thinking that I wouldn't do that,"

said Nakajima, chuckling lightly, "because I had always covered for him in the past. I would tell the team that he had a cold and that I had to take him to the hospital or something like that. That's the way I was before. But not this time.

"The next day, when the guy came to the park and found out what I'd done, he didn't even say a word to me. He just gave me a kind of dirty look.

"But that was his problem and I didn't want to be responsible anymore. I liked him a lot. But I've learned. I don't want to be in the middle anymore."

7

Blazer

All the managers manage differently here. I mean they manage Japanese style. And I do it more or less U.S. style. So I'm the one that's different, really.

It's really hard to maintain a sense of perspective because there is no one I can talk to who thinks like I do. It's a unique position to be in.

You know, sometimes I think to myself, I'm going half-crazy.

Don Blasingame
Ex-manager, Hanshin Tigers,
Nankai Hawks

Many Japanese will argue that a foreigner should never be allowed to manage a Japanese baseball team. The cultural requirements are too complex, they say, and the tissue of team unity too delicate to entrust to the heavy hand of the *gaijin*.

Among the handful of foreigners who have had a chance to manage in the Pacific or Central leagues, only Wally Yonamine, a *nisei* from Hawaii, ever won a pennant. Yonamine had special qualifications, however. At the time of his appointment to manage the Chunichi Dragons in 1972, he had been in Japan for twenty years, thirteen as a player, and he spoke fluent Japanese. In addition to his flag, won in 1974, he had two second-place finishes in his six-year managing career and liberal thinkers applauded his progressive methods.

Only two Caucasian managers have ever run Japanese teams and both spent much of their time embroiled in controversy. The first, Joe Lutz, a former Cleveland Indian coach, was hired to manage the Hiroshima Carp in 1975, after only one year's experience in Japan.

The idea of employing a white pilot was a radical one, especially in Hiroshima, a place where, as Nobuto Imaizumi, an assistant professor of Hiroshima University, once noted, "xenophobic tendencies are not absent."

Yoshinori Shigematsu, then the general manager of the Hiroshima Toyo Carp and the man whose decision it was to hire Lutz, seemed terror-stricken at the step he had taken. "Appointing Mr. Lutz as field manager was one of the greatest gambles I ever made in my life," he once told a reporter, "and I considered *seppuku* (suicide) in the event it didn't work. Well, I'm exaggerating. Still my decision was met with so much opposition from fans and some Carp executives that I knew there was no escaping my responsibility if things went wrong."

Lutz lasted less than a month. He resigned, claiming that the front office would not fully support him. Insiders said Lutz's real undoing was that he tried to change too much too soon. He tried to Americanize the players' eating and bathing habits and argued all too frequently with the umpires, embarrassing team officials. Said one observer, "He didn't seem to realize he was in a foreign country."

Fortunately for Mr. Shigematsu, the Carp won the pennant under new manager Takeshi Koba, who claimed inspiration from Lutz. However, no one in the Hiroshima organization ever mentioned the term *gaijin manager* again.

The second white pilot, Don Blasingame, had better qualifications for managing in Japan than Lutz. Although he was not nearly as adroit in the language as Yonamine, he had spent fourteen years in Japan as a player and coach and had a fundamental understanding of the Japanese psyche.

Blazer, as he was nicknamed, had been an All-Star second baseman for the St. Louis Cardinals. He had played for three seasons with the Nankai Hawks of Osaka at the end of his career and then stayed on for several more years as a coach under Hawks player-manager Katsuya Nomura, the stubby catcher who had hit more career home runs (657) than anyone else in the world except Oh, Aaron, Ruth, and Mays.

Blasingame and his wife Sara liked Japan. They had made a home in Kobe and had raised their four children there. It was a safe, drug-free environment and although Blazer had had offers from the Cardinals to manage in Triple-A ball, his position with the Hawks gave him more job security and more pay than he would have had anywhere else. Besides, Blazer thought that with the advent of free agency there were too many prima donnas in the major leagues for him to ever think of managing there. It was impossible to teach some of those players anything.

The Japanese liked Blasingame as much as he liked them. At five feet ten inches and 160 pounds, he was more to their liking than the Godzilla-sized *gaijin* they usually had to contend with. What's more, he was always very courteous and respectful toward his hosts. The Japanese were also impressed with his baseball knowledge. They had termed his philosophy of the game *shinkingu besuburu* (thinking baseball), and Hawk manager Nomura openly praised him. "Don is a good man," he said, "and a smart man. He helped me in many ways."

Thus, in 1979, when Blasingame was hired to manage the Central League Hanshin Tigers, there was nowhere near the anxiety that Lutz's signing had engendered in Hiroshima.

The Tigers, the second-oldest team in Japan and traditional rivals of the Tokyo Giants, had a large following that seemed to grow stronger every year. Their lusty, earthy fans were a direct contrast to the urbane cocktail crowd that frequented Giants games.

Yet, the team itself had fallen on hard times. The previous year, Hanshin had finished in last place, thirty-nine games under .500, the worst finish in the history of the franchise. The team was faction ridden. Many thought it the worst organization in all of Japanese pro baseball. It was said that at least twenty men had turned down the post of Tigers manager before it was finally offered to Blazer.

The president of the Tigers was an imposing man named Shojiro Ozu, who, like many other team officials in the Japanese game, had no baseball background. Acquaintances described him as a hard-headed railroad man. His primary claim to fame was that as an executive with Hanshin Railways, he had been able to suppress the labor unions.

He had a reputation for being penurious and purportedly once said it would be better for the Tigers not to win too many pennants so as to keep player salaries at an affordable level. Knowledgeable Americans at that time called Hanshin the Looney Tunes of the Central League.

All this was bad enough, but Blazer would be operating under a further handicap. He was, it was made clear, only temporary help. He would be used as a house-cleaning device to get rid of certain unwanted veteran players that a Japanese manager would feel uncomfortable trading and in two years he would be replaced by someone else— someone who would not be carrying an alien registration card.

Blazer accepted the job and its dubious restrictions on one condition: that he be granted final authority over all personnel, that no player change could be made without his permission. He had obtained what he thought was Ozu's verbal agreement in this regard, but as Blasingame would later come to regret, there was nothing to that effect in his contract.

Blasingame brought energy and enthusiasm to his new job. He cut down spring camp and practice sessions to about half of what other teams did. "I tried to pack more things into a shorter time span and avoid fatigue from too long a workout," he said. "Japanese players tend to give everything they have in practice, then get tired and lose concentration in the games—particularly in the second half of the season."

He also gave his batters more freedom at the plate, eliminated the use of starting pitchers in relief, and reduced the number of team meetings his players were used to having from about three a day to once or twice a week.

Blazer's minimalistic approach to managing immediately met with criticism that he was too lax. There was a certain set way of running a team in Japan—a managerial *kata* (form)—that demanded lots of hard training and lots of supervision, and Blazer's critics thought that his way was far too lax.

The two Americans on the Tigers thought the new system just right, a welcome relief from the Draconian regimes of past managers. But many of the Japanese players did not. Slugging star Masayuki Kakefu, among others, complained that the pregame routine was too light. He wanted harder warmup drills and more batting practice.

Blazer reluctantly acquiesced. "It was against my better judgement," he said, "But baseball is mental as well as physical. And if the players believe that they need that much work, then maybe they won't be able to play well without it."

Blazer mused that the Japanese ballplayer was just like the Japanese worker who would stay in the office for ten hours a day because he needed that feeling of having put in a hard day's work or whatever it was. Blazer even used to kid his friend Nomura about practicing so much. "Moose, you guys are hooked on that samurai bullshit," he would say. "You can't bear to leave the park." But Blazer could never accept the Japanese philosophy himself. He still thought the most important thing was not how much time was spent, but the quality of it.

Blazer presided over a remarkable turnaround. Pitcher Shigeru Kobayashi, a reedy, anorexic sidearm thrower acquired in the off-season in a trade with Yomiuri, won twenty-three games, his best total ever, including eight against the Giants. Other new players obtained in trades or brought up from the farm brought a new spirit and hustle to the team.

The Tigers stayed in contention until September and finished with a respectable record of 61–60–9, winning nineteen times in twenty-six games versus their Yomiuri rivals. Attendance rose 20 percent to over a million and a half, a new club record. In a season-ending survey, Blazer was given a 70-percent favorable rating by the fans.

Baseball experts seemed reluctant to give Blasingame any credit. "Blazer was lucky he had Kobayashi," said one columnist, ignoring the fact Kobayashi had gotten more rest under Blasingame than he had ever had with the Giants, where he was notorious for running out of gas in midsummer.

Critics attacked Blazer for playing "throwaway games." Unlike past Tiger managers, he refused to use his entire pitching staff in a short series with the arch rival Giants. Blazer's argument that baseball was a game of percentages was emotionally unsatisfying to those who thought that every Tigers-Giants game should have the intensity of the Russo-Japanese War.

A Japanese manager who had accomplished what Blazer did would have been a strong candidate for manager of the year. Yet Blazer finished far behind in that particular voting. Indeed, the 1979 season was barely over when many pundits began writing that 1980 would be his last year.

The criticism of Blazerball was nothing compared to the firestorm that awaited him the following spring, when, in less than a month, his favorable rating in fan surveys plummeted to 25 percent.

Blasingame had started that season using an American named Dave Hilton at second base. Hilton, a former San Diego Padre reserve, had played the previous two seasons for the Yakult Swallows. In 1978, he had helped the Swallows win a Japan Championship when he batted .317 and hit 19 home runs. He had also slammed a dramatic two-out ninth-inning home run to win Game 4 of the series versus the Hankyu Braves.

The following season, his average slid to .258 and his fielding suffered as well. Hilton pleaded injuries, but his manager, the imperious Tatsuro Hiroka, a man notoriously suspicious of American athletes, charged that Hilton was "taking Japanese baseball lightly" and had him released.

Hilton, an unassuming, deliberate young man of twenty-nine recalled his second year thusly:

> After my first season in 1978, I undertook a body-building program because I had lost a lot of weight during the previous season—from all the training I was forced to do. I arrived in camp twenty pounds heavier, all of it muscle—and Hiroka got angry at me. He said I was overweight, that I had been loafing, and he ordered me to reduce. A few days later, I developed a sore throwing arm and asked permission to ease up in fielding practice for a few days. Hiroka refused. He said I was getting a big head, that I was conceited, demanding special privileges. During the season, I injured my heel and was taking cortisone shots before each game. The

team doctor called Hiroka and said that the constant running and hour-long sessions of fielding ground balls every day were aggravating the condition. Hiroka got angry and hung up on him.

All my career, I considered myself a hard-working, unselfish individual who never caused trouble. Hiroka is the only manager I ever had who made me feel like a "bad boy," if you know what I mean.

Blazer defended his new acquisition by claiming Hilton had already proved he could play in Japan. What had happened in his second year was an aberration, fully understandable in view of the circumstances. "If the pitchers were going to find a weakness in Hilton's stance," he said, "they would have found it in the first two months of his first year. There are flaws in his fielding, but I like his hustle and his attitude. I think he can help this team."

The fans, and the ubiquitous press, however, did not agree. They considered Hilton second-hand goods. If Hiroka did not want him anymore, they reasoned, then there must be something wrong with him.

More to the point was the fact that Hilton's presence in the starting lineup left no room for a prize rookie named Akinobu Okada, a muscular, free-swinging infielder who had led the Big Six University League in home runs the year before. Blazer's decision to keep this unpolished jewel on the bench while using some recycled *gaijin* was more than many fans could bear.

From opening day on, they expressed their dissatisfaction in most unmistakable fashion. Whenever Hilton came to bat, an unnerving chant began in the stands: "Okada! Okada! Okada! Okada! Okada!" It would continue until the next batter came up.

Blazer attempted to explain himself to reporters. "Okada has great potential," he would say, "but using him right away would be just too much pressure for a rookie. What if Okada got off to a bad start and lost his confidence? Isn't it better to ease him in slowly by playing him in farm games and letting him pinch-hit occasionally in varsity games?"

Blazer conceded that Okada might be one of the best hitters on the team but no one would really know until he played every day. That, of course, would not happen until the veterans who had contributed so much the year before proved they could not do the job anymore. Everyone knew it was better to stay with players of proven competence.

It was a sound, logical argument, but Blazer's American reasoning was no match for Japanese emotion; for when Blazer was finished speaking, the writers would all nod their heads and say, "Yes, we understand, but when are you going to put Okada in the lineup?"

In Japan, the testing of a big-name rookie under fire is one of the great rituals of the game. It was a baseball rite of passage and an important gauge of an athlete's character. Blasingame was depriving them of that particular pleasure. Nearly every fan in Japan can tell you about the 1958 pro debut of a college sensation named Shigeo Nagashima: four embarrassing strikeouts against the great left-hander Masaichi Kaneda, who won four hundred games in his career. They can also tell you in glowing terms how Nagashima won the Central League batting title that very same year. It is one of the oft-told tales of Japanese baseball lore.

In the U.S., by contrast, because amateur baseball has such a limited following, most players must labor in obscurity until they establish themselves in the big leagues. It is rare for a rookie to be nationally known before playing his first major league game. Few Americans can tell you what Mickey Mantle, Wade Boggs, or Darryl Strawberry did in their first major league at-bats.

In a sense, Japanese baseball was show business. And Blasingame was beginning to realize that. If the fans were not satisfactorily entertained, they might begin throwing tomatoes, or worse.

The Tigers lost six of their first fifteen games as Hilton hit .207 and made several fielding miscues. The more he struck out, the more heated the Okada call became. Blasingame begged the fans to be patient. Even pennant winners and batting champions had slumps. But the fans had their own kind of quality control. They wanted perfection, at least where expensive *gaijin* were concerned.

Because of the shorter season and the more extensive media coverage, a single professional ball game took on more significance than it did in the U.S. In the major leagues the error made in April was forgotten in September. In Japan, it was remembered for years.

Reports of Hilton's imminent release and Blazer's firing appeared almost daily in the sports papers. "Blazer Destroying Hanshin!" one headline shrieked in huge red letters. "Blazer Killing Okada!" ran another. "What right does Blazer have to do this?" asked Akira Kunimatsu, a former Giants player, in his newspaper column, adding, "What Blazer is doing is unforgivable. He is ruining Okada's upbringing."

Anger toward Blasingame and Hilton intensified when regular third baseman Masayuki Kakefu was injured and Blazer still refused to start Okada—all because the Tigers were playing the Giants at Korakuen, and, as Blasingame said, "Fifty-thousand fans would be too much pressure for a rookie."

Blasingame tried to keep his distance from Hilton and Mike Reinbach, the second American on the team, a .300-hitting outfielder in his fifth year in Japan. He ate alone. He socialized with a different group of people. Still, there was talk of a *gaijin* conspiracy. On the road, reporters dutifully noted that Blazer stayed at the same luxury Western-style hotel as Hilton and Reinbach, while the Japanese players stayed in less glamorous communal-style accommodations, sleeping on *futons* and often fighting off the cockroaches.

Worst of all was an article in the weekly magazine *Shincho:*

> So why then does Blazer stick to using Hilton, whose fielding was so bad, while keeping Okada on the bench? Underneath it all, there is a strange smell. Hilton had told Blazer that if Hanshin would hire him, he would give him a part of his contract money. So Okada is a victim of this secret pact between Hilton and Blazer."

The *Shincho* presented not a scintilla of evidence to back up its allegation. And those who knew Blazer well were appalled that such a charge had been made. Friends described him as the original straight arrow—a man of the highest rectitude. Blazer himself angrily denied ever taking any commission from anyone. He had brought fifteen players to Japan in his days with the Hawks, he said, and he had never received a single yen from any of them. He would have sued were it not for the fact that it took years for the creaking, Japanese legal system to process cases.

Yet however reprehensible the *Shincho* attack might have been, no one in the Japanese press came to Blasingame's defense. It was not politic. Instead the vilification the sports dailies spewed on the Tigers' *gaijin* manager grew more feverish and the mood of the Tigers fans became even nastier. An angry postgame mob of Tigers supporters outside Tokyo's Korakuen Stadium surrounded a taxi carrying Blasingame, Hilton, and Hilton's wife Patty, who was several months pregnant at the time. The fans pounded the car with their fists and rocked it back and forth. "Go back to America!" they shouted. "Yankee Go Home!" *"Shinji mae!"* (Drop dead!)

A couple of nights later, outside the Swallows' Jingu Stadium, the taxi in which Blazer and Hilton were riding was almost overturned.

Blasingame also received death threats and hate mail.

Said one letter, "If you play Hilton one more time, I'll kill you and your family." Blasingame's wife Sara, the daughter of onetime Cardinals catcher Walker Cooper and a former flight attendant, was not unacquainted with the crazy things that people could do. But postcards threatening her husband's life so upset her she called in the police.

So vile was the atmosphere that both Blasingame's and Hilton's wives stopped going to the games. Anti-American emotions were high enough for the large international community living in Kobe, a few kilometers away from the Tigers' home park, to start feeling slightly uncomfortable.

Hilton and Okada remained silent through it all. Unaccustomed to the role of pariah and unable to fathom the depth of the fans' hatred of him, Hilton gritted his teeth and tried to block it out, with little success. The anxiety was corrosive and he found it difficult to sleep. "How can anyone play in these conditions?" he wondered aloud to friends.

Okada, for his part, seemed discomfited at being the center of all the fuss and by being asked by reporters after every single game how he felt about not playing. He was a somber, reticent youth, who would later distinguish himself in many ways: by hitting 39 homers and .340 when the Tigers won the pennant in 1985, by playing frequently with a hangover, and by being photographed on a late-night date with a transvestite, the pictures subsequently appearing in the mass-circulation magazine *Focus.*

Okada finally got his chance to start in late April, at third base, versus the Whales in Yokohama. He got three hits that evening, stayed in the starting lineup and did not stop hitting until the season ended. He finished with an average of .290 and 18 home runs. Hilton, still a target of the fans, continued to struggle. Finally, at the end of what was perhaps the worst month of Hilton's life, Blasingame, who did a lot of late-night floor pacing himself, benched him. "I did that as much for his own safety as for the fact that he wasn't hitting," said Blazer.

The alacrity with which the press jumped on Blazer was perhaps due to a deficiency in communication. Although he had always insisted that the language barrier was over-rated ("I work just fine through our first-base coach, our pitching coach, and our team interpreter, who all speak English well," he said), it was a definite roadblock where the veteran reporters covering the Tigers were con-cerned. They didn't like communicating through a third party. Since they could not talk to Blazer directly, they really could not assess him man-to-man as they had with previous Japanese managers.

Blasingame would occasionally go out drinking with the writers, interpreter in tow, but he complained they would always wind up getting drunk and start singing *karaoke*—a leading nocturnal passion in Japan. There was nothing they liked doing more, it seemed to Blazer, be-sides asking him about Okada. They could go on all night. But Blazer could not stand it and eventually he would have to leave.

Reporters intimidated by English or fed up with three-way conversations went to the batting coach, a man named Futoshi Nakanishi, or to team president Ozu and other sources in the front office for their information. As a result, there was more confusion (and suspicion) than usual.

Some reporters believed that Blasingame personally did not like Okada. When Blazer told a writer that Okada was lacking in experience, the man quoted him as saying that Okada was simply no good.

In the end, however, there was perhaps nothing Blazer could have done to quell the angry masses short of violat-ing his own principles and starting Okada from Day One.

⚾   ⚾   ⚾

Blasingame's long Nipponese nightmare was not quite over. There was one more scene left, this one scripted and directed by Mr. Ozu himself. Although Ozu had not interfered directly in Blazer's handling of the Okada-Hilton imbroglio, he had, unbeknownst to his manager, been moving quietly in the wings to find a new American to replace Hilton even before the season had started. Like most Tigers fans, he did not trust used goods either.

One May evening, with the Tigers' won-lost record finally at the .500 mark, Ozu called Blasingame to his hotel room. There he revealed his decision to release Hilton and sign a New York Mets reserve outfielder named Bruce Boisclair to a contract.

Blasingame immediately protested, claiming that Ozu had broken his earlier verbal promise to obtain Blazer's okay on all player changes. Blazer really did not object to Hilton's release, for he did not believe that Hilton would be able to come back and perform well, given the way the fans felt about him. However, he was bitterly opposed to the signing of Boisclair. He felt strongly that the last thing the team needed was a new American outfielder trying to adjust to Japan in the middle of the season. It would further strain the team's already damaged *wa*. If he used Boisclair there would be problems with the Japanese player he would have to take out of the lineup, not to mention the finicky Tigers fans. If he did not use Boisclair, then he would have problems with Mr. Ozu. He would be faced with yet another insoluble problem.

"What we really need is more pitching," Blasingame told Ozu, attempting to salvage the situation, "We don't know anything about Boisclair. We don't know how good he is or know what kind of guy he is or whether he's hurt or not. Besides, he's been out of baseball for a month."

"I already checked him out," Ozu replied.

"Where?" asked Blazer.

"His agent said he was okay."

Blasingame was incredulous. "Of course his agent said he was okay. What else would he tell you? You should have checked him out with a third party."

Ozu said that there had been no time because Boisclair's agent had told him that Boisclair had had a big offer
from another team. So if the Tigers wanted him, they
would have to move fast.

If Ozu believed that, Blazer thought, he was nuts and
Blazer had a bridge he wanted to sell him.

"They just badgered you into making a quick decision,"
he said. "I brought fifteen players to Japan. I think I know
better than anyone else what the Tigers need. That's my
job. I'm the manager, for Christ's sake. You'd think you
would consult me."

Ozu shrugged an apology.

"Our agreement was no changes without my approval."

"That's not the way I understand it," replied Ozu. "I'm
bringing him over."

"Well, if I go along with this," said Blasingame, "I'll lose
the respect of the players. I'd have to swallow my pride."

Ozu shrugged again.

Blasingame got up and left. Four days later, back in
Osaka, he submitted his resignation.

Before leaving Hiroshima, Blazer had had dinner with
a reporter who told him that a new coaching staff had
already been picked in anticipation of Blazer's exit, and
named names. When the new manager and coaches were
announced, he turned out to be right. It had seemingly all
been prearranged, without Blasingame's knowledge.

In the aftermath of Blazer's departure, President Ozu
declined to answer any questions from the press, telling
reporters, "I don't want to say anything bad about a man
who's leaving." Others were not so shy, however.

Columnist Okichi Terauchi, in his postmortem in the
Daily Sports, wrote, "Blazer was wrong in his use and
appraisal of Okada and he had to pay the price." Former
Giants catching star Masahiro Mori, later to manage
Seibu, wrote in his column, "Now that the language bar-
rier is gone, the level of understanding will deepen on the
Tigers. The things that Nakanishi notices, he can relay to

the Tigers in frequent meetings. Blazer neglected the bunt too much, opting for the big inning. But I think that was a mistake."

A *Nikkan Sports* editor lamented that the rational-minded American manager could not understand the Japanese way of thinking, while the Central League commissioner summed it all up with a heavy sigh, saying, "*Gaijin* managers are just not suitable for Japan."

Even the new Tiger manager, Nakanishi, the batting coach whom Blazer had personally hired and recommended as his eventual successor, told reporters, "It's too bad about Blazer, but, after all, only Japanese can understand the Japanese heart."

Few took the side of the departed American. A popular professional wrestler named Giant Baba, of all people, who also wrote about baseball, was one who spoke up for the *gaijin:* "Blazer improved the Tigers enormously. He deserves credit for that." An editorial in the *Asahi Shimbun* stated rather bluntly, "The front office has responsibilities in the matter too. You can't put a lid over garbage and expect to hide the smell." But it was left to Blazer himself to fire the biggest broadside on his behalf, as he did in one *sayonara* interview:

> A few writers have been fair but most are a disgrace to their profession. Some of them flat-out lied. What they did to Hilton was the most vicious campaign to get a guy out of baseball I've ever seen in my twenty-eight years in the game. No one hustled more. No one had a better attitude.
>
> How many Japanese players could hit well with everyone in the stadium screaming abuse? How many could field their positions properly with such hatred in the air?
>
> I said all along, I tried to play the best lineup. Any manager who doesn't do that is crazy. But they wouldn't listen. They tried to make it a personal thing between Hilton and Okada with me in the middle.

Japanese can hate Americans if they want to, but they have to admit that the situation on the Tigers is better than it was two years ago.

At the end of the year, the Tigers finished in fifth place with a record of 54–66–10. Boisclair, who had hit .249 with 8 home runs, was released. And Blazer was invited back to Japan to manage his old team, the Nankai Hawks, a club that had fallen into disarray since Nomura's departure and was suffering serious financial problems.

Blazer hired Wally Yonamine as his batting coach and imported Barney Schultz from the St. Louis organization to be his pitching coach. Their presence, combined with that of the two Americans playing for Nankai, Jim Tyrone and Carlos May, was enough to start the old *gaijin* conspiracy business all over again, albeit on a less hysterical scale than had been the case with Hanshin because the Pacific League perennially drew less attention than the Central.

Blazer's stint with Nankai did not turn out to be a success either, as he found himself unable to make trades or otherwise add new personnel. In his first season, the Hawks finished fifth, a slight improvement over their last-place showing of previous years, and Blazer suffered a mild heart attack, collapsing after a game the Hawks had lost to the Seibu Lions. At the end of the year, the front office had some new instructions for its *gaijin* manager aimed at closing what the press had begun referring to as the *Nichibei gyap* (Japanese-American gap).

They included the following: Speak Japanese more often. Preside over more coaches' meetings. While on the road, stay at the same hotel as the team. While on the field, think more sincerely about why attendance has fallen. Spend more of the off-season in Japan (Blazer usually left for his home in Missouri in early November and returned to Japan in mid-January).

Blazer consented to all the club's requests. In subsequent press conferences, he tried to use all the Japanese he knew. He stayed with the team in Japanese-style hotels and he tried his best to conduct more meetings.

It hardly mattered. Even Japanese citizenship would not have helped. The Hawks finished last this time and Blazer was asked to resign.

As Blazer and his family boarded a plane to leave Japan for good, an American TV news producer working in Tokyo was moved to remark, "This year has indeed been a black one for the United States. Three American coaches, two American players, and the Hawks wind up in last place. Will the reputation of American baseball ever recover?"

Blazer went on to become a scout and roving instructor, first in the Cardinals' farm system and then with the Phillies. Despite all that happened, he and his family retained their affection for Japan, as he told a magazine interviewer some years later:

> I have no real gripes. The Tiger fans, they were just overreacting about Okada. The Okada thing was frustrating but if I had to do it all over again, I would do the same. I had fun at Hanshin, all in all. I loved the popularity of the team, the noise. At Giants-Tigers games, it got so noisy you couldn't hear yourself think.
>
> I wish I had won more games for the Hawks because they really stood by me. But still, I'm one of only two Caucasian managers ever to manage in Japan. And I lasted much longer than the other one.
>
> I loved every minute of it. I really did. I wish it weren't over.

8

Giant Headache

*The media around the Giants clubhouse was
unbelievable. In the Yankee clubhouse, we always had just a handful of reporters. In Japan,
it seems like hundreds. I had my photo taken
more in two months in Japan than I did in my
entire lifetime in the major leagues. Rooting for
the Yankees was like rooting for General Mo-
tors. You didn't love them, but you respected
them. In Japan, it's pure love, everyone loves
them, no matter what they do.*

Roy White

Someone once compared the popularity of the Tokyo
Giants to that of the New York Yankees and Los Angeles
Dodgers combined. He rated them too lightly. Twenty-
four hours before they are scheduled to play, be it at their
home ground the Tokyo Dome or a remote field in the
countryside, fans, armed with riceball snacks and sleeping
bags, start queueing up for the few remaining tickets that
have not already been sold weeks in advance.

About 60 percent of all Japanese, it is generally believed, are Giants fans and the range of Giants fandom is
so wide the team's performance has been held responsible for everything from economic recession in Japan to
the national suicide rate.

Joining the Giants is like being admitted to West Point.
A player is expected to forget his individuality and fit the

Giants mold. That means a robotlike adherence to the rigid and standardized programs of the team, enduring constant browbeating by the coaches, and obeying curfews and other dogmatic rules that would try the souls of normal men. The Giants canon forbids, among other things, beards, mustaches, long hair, casual dress on the road (ties required at all times), visiting hostess bars, and talking to reporters without permission from the front office.

The presence of foreigners in such a restrictive atmosphere tends to create problems, especially since the team is so much in the public eye. Although *gaijin* players have been part of the Giants since 1936 when the Russian Victor Starfin pitched for them, many Giants fans will tell you their favorite era was the "pure-blooded period" from 1958 to 1974 when the team won thirteen pennants with no *gaijin* at all. First baseman Sadaharu Oh, who had a Chinese father, was born in Tokyo and therefore did not count as a foreigner according to league rules (even though he carried a Taiwanese passport and needed a reentry visa whenever he left Japan).

In 1975, weakened by the retirement of third baseman Shigeo Nagashima, its most popular star, the team was compelled to open its doors again, signing a major leaguer named Davey Johnson, and that, diehard fans will tell you, is when their heartaches really began.

Johnson was highly regarded. He was only thirty-two years old and was coming off a season in which he had hit .251 with 15 home runs for the Atlanta Braves. The year before that he had hit 43 home runs to break the single-season major league home run record for second basemen. He was as close to the Real Thing—a U.S. major league starter—as any Japanese team had gotten, and everyone expected big things from him.

However, Johnson could not immediately adjust to playing in a new and strange environment and failed miserably. He lost twenty-five pounds off his six-foot-one-inch frame (from 185 to 160) and suffered a broken bone in his shoulder that sidelined him for a month. He hit .197 with 13 home runs and the Giants finished last for the first time in the team's proud history.

Rookie manager Nagashima publicly defended his American, but privately he felt humiliated because it was he who had handpicked Johnson. Nagashima and Oh and Johnson had been prominently featured on the cover of the 1975 Giants calendar. In June, after Johnson had struck out eight times in a row, a Central League record, Nagashima began pinch-hitting for him. The writers began referring to him as *Dame* (no good) Johnson, and the fans began laughing at him. "Is this how the major leaguers play ball?" they asked.

Clete Boyer, the ex-Yankee who played for the Taiyo Whales that year, thought his fellow American had suffered brain lock. "Johnson looked like he was in a daze," said Boyer. "He didn't seem to know where he was or what he was doing."

Separated for much of the season from his wife and children, who were back in the U.S., he spent a lot of his time off the field alone. Acquaintances recalled seeing him on many a night sitting alone in a corner of the old Sanno Hotel Bar in Tokyo's Akasaka district, muttering to himself over his drink. "I swear, I would go to bed sometimes and hear bells," Johnson said later. "I thought I was losing it there for a while. It was really getting to me."

The following year, he vowed to redeem himself. He trained hard over the winter and became one of the few Americans ever to report for Japanese "voluntary training," in the arctic cold of late January. He worked diligently in camp and won the starting second baseman's job.

For the first three months of the regular season, he hit .281 with 8 home runs—playing with an injured nerve in his left thumb, which he had jammed sliding head-first into a base.

Manager Nagashima, however, had not forgotten about the disaster of the previous year. If Johnson went hitless in his first two at-bats, Nagashima would often remove him from the game and order him to take extra batting practice the next day, despite the bad hand.

His manager's quick hook affected Johnson's rhythm and concentration. It hurt his feelings as well.

> I felt I had to fight my own manager as well as the other team. It was almost as if Nagashima was taking revenge for what happened before.
>
> I was the type of hitter who'd get hits on my third or fourth at-bat, after I got used to the pitcher. But I wasn't getting that chance.
>
> I'd never been hit for in the major leagues, but Nagashima must have taken me out a hundred times; that's what it seemed like.
>
> It was goddamned frustrating. Sometimes I'd run out to my position at second base and some other player would be standing there. It was embarrassing.
>
> Nagashima was shitting on me. Baseball is a loud language and when you do something like that, it's tantamount to a public insult.
>
> In the States, the players naturally get mad. In Japan, however, it was just the opposite. They say if you get mad, then you have a "small heart." It was hard for me to control myself because I'm more sensitive than the average person.

The chill toward Johnson was palpable, as his American teammate, Clyde ("Crazy") Wright observed from the sidelines.

> They gave him no encouragement at all. It was the attitude, the way they talked to him. The whole mood.

If Davey struck out with the bases loaded, they'd get mad. He'd come back to the bench and there would be glum looks, scowls on all the coaches' faces. There was this cold uncomfortable silence on the bench. They didn't say, "Shake it off," or "Get them next time, Davey," like coaches normally would in the U.S. Nothing. Davey wasn't doing that bad. But they expected him to lead the league.

Johnson's hand got worse. None of the treatments prescribed by the team worked. The pain was so intense at times that he tried to beg off batting practice. Nagashima wouldn't hear of it. "You have to take BP," he said. "If you can't practice, then you can't play." Everyone knew that.

Johnson replied that if that was the attitude Nagashima was going to take then he would have to go to the States during the All-Star break and consult a specialist. Nagashima was incredulous. No one left his team in midyear. He accused Johnson of jaking it. He called him names. He absolutely refused him permission to go.

"I never jaked in my whole life," Johnson retorted. "But I'm going whether you allow it or not."

To defy Nagashima was no mean thing, for he was no ordinary hero. He was hands down the most beloved figure in Japan. Oh might have had more home runs, but Nagashima had six batting titles (to Oh's five), a lifetime average of .305 (to Oh's .301), and an uncanny ability to hit in the clutch, as attested to by his four Japan Series MVP awards and a dramatic home run in front of the emperor. He was also a full-blooded Japanese. In a country that prided itself on national purity and often seemed obsessed with the uniqueness of being Japanese, that counted for something too.

People would joke that charismatic Nagashima was the real head of state of Japan. Visitors to his house certainly got that impression. When Gary Carter, then of the Montreal Expos, visited Nagashima's home in the Tokyo suburb of Denen-Chofu in 1982, the first thing he saw displayed in the entranceway was a photo of Nagashima shaking hands with Canadian Prime Minister Pierre Trudeau. Carter was ushered into the living room and seated next to a photo of Nagashima with the pope.

Nagashima was not a samurai stoic. He was quick to talk, quick to laugh, and quick to anger. It was said that when his team played poorly, he would grab a baseball bat and start swinging at the trees in his backyard. By the end of his first season, reporters joked, there were no branches left.

So it was that in July of 1976, with his team losing its grip on first place in the face of the onrushing Hanshin Tigers and his infamous *gaijin* about to publicly embarrass him again by deserting the team, Nagashima's temper flared. It happened on the eve of the All-Star break, after the Giants' final game of the first half of the season. Johnson had emerged from the team shower, wearing only a towel around his waist, still dripping water, when Nagashima approached with Tanuma the interpreter and asked, "Are you really leaving?"

"Yes," said Johnson, "I'm going to see a specialist, Dr. Robert Kerlan in L.A. But I'll be back in three days. I promise."

Nagashima, certain Johnson would not return exploded, "Liar!" he roared, livid with fury, and yanked Johnson's towel off. "If you were a real man," he yelled, pointing between Johnson's legs, "if you had two balls like a real man, you wouldn't be going. But you're not a man. You're a woman."

Then he stormed out of the room.

"I almost punched him" Johnson told a friend later, "But I didn't do it because I realized he just wasn't capable of appreciating my thinking or my situation. So I picked up the towel, got dressed, and left."

Johnson was an educated man with a college degree in mathematics. He thought he understood Japanese psychology and that, presented with the facts of his situation, the Japanese would think and act in a rational manner. But that was not the case.

The Japanese sports press went into paroxysms of anger on hearing that Johnson was leaving. They had already seen samples of Clyde Wright's crazy behavior and so were in no mood to be sympathetic to a foreigner's cause. "Johnson's act is tantamount to desertion," one editorial asserted. "The Giants should ban all foreigners. They don't belong on the team."

Few people believed he had a medical problem serious enough to warrant his leaving. Those that did accused him of insulting Japanese doctors by seeking treatment in the U.S. The consensus was that he just wasn't man enough for Japan.

In Los Angeles two days later, Kerlan, a noted orthopedic surgeon, diagnosed Johnson's ailment as an inflamed neroma. He prescribed treatment and ordered that Johnson not take batting practice, "If you don't irritate it," he said, "it should improve."

Johnson was ready to return to Japan immediately but found that the Giants front office had neglected to arrange a new visa. Team executives did not believe he was coming back either. So he sat in a hotel room for two weeks, waiting for the necessary documents to be processed.

Upon arriving in Tokyo, Johnson met with Nagashima behind closed doors and proposed a deal. He said that if Nagashima would promise to leave him alone—to let him play his own game free from interference, then he would come through with the kind of batting performance Nagashima and the Giants fans had always wanted. Johnson guaranteed it.

"Don't bother me about batting practice, because I'm

not supposed to take any," Johnson said. "Don't pull me out of the game if I don't get a hit my first two times up. No more pinch hitters. Just get off my back."

Nagashima, perhaps in shock over actually seeing his wayward American in the flesh again, agreed, if somewhat reluctantly. Johnson had his promise, if that was what it would take.

"Strike out all you want," he said, "I won't do anything."

And thus did the next and final act of the drama begin.

On August 1, Johnson's first day back in uniform, he skipped BP completely and hit a grand slam home run to win the game. He hit 9 home runs in his next twelve games and by the end of August had helped put the team back in first place.

Johnson hit nine more home runs in September, including an eighth-inning shot in Hiroshima that won the contest and clinched the pennant by two games over the Tigers. Suddenly, improbably, he was a national hero. Everywhere he went he was mobbed. "I was more popular than Hirohito," he said later, paraphrasing John Lennon. "I had Japan in the palm of my hand."

And then, just as suddenly, he was in the doghouse again. An intense weeklong team workout in mid-October to prepare for the Japan Series with the Hankyu Braves set the stage for Johnson's tumble from grace, which Johnson described in a magazine interview:

> We were out there in a torrential rain, diving for batted balls in the mud and cold before hundreds of cameras, flashbulbs popping everywhere. We were supposed to be showing our "fighting spirit" to the fans. But I got sick instead. I caught the flu and got strep throat. So on the day of the first game, I told the Giants I didn't want to undergo a heavy pregame workout. I wanted to save myself for the game. But the coaches wouldn't

hear of it. This was the Japan Series. I had to practice.
So I ran and hit and fielded and dissipated my energy.
And I went 0-for-4 and struck out twice. The next day
I struck out again my first time up and Nagashima took
me out for a pinch hitter.

"That's it," I said to Nagashima, right then and there.
"You broke your promise to me. I worked hard for you
to get here and now you start the same old thing. Well,
forget it. I'm not coming back."

The Giants lost the Series to the Hankyu Braves in six
games. Johnson went hitless in thirteen at-bats, striking
out six times. When the Series was finished, Giants general
manager Roy Saeki called Johnson in to talk contract for
the following season. Johnson had finished with a batting
average of .268 and 26 home runs, he had been voted to
the Sportswriters Best 9, and had also won a Diamond
Glove, Japan's version of the Gold Glove. Saeki offered
eighty thousand dollars, a 20-percent cut.

"Nagashima made me take pregame practice when I
was sick," Johnson countered, still fuming over his Japan
Series treatment, "so I wound up playing ill. Then he
pinch-hit for me when it's only my second time at bat. He
really embarrassed me. Nagashima agreed not to mess
with me and then he did. That's wrong! I don't care where
you come from. I know that our cultures are different and
that the Oriental mind isn't logical sometimes, but it's still
wrong. So this is my deal.

"If Nagashima will apologize for what he did, and promise me once more he won't interfere with me again, I'll
come back to Japan next year and accept a 30-percent cut.
You can pay me more later if you think I have had a good
season. But Nagashima has to say he's sorry."

Saeki said he needed time to think. But of course, that
was the end for Johnson, because asking Nagashima to
apologize for the way he managed was like asking the

pope to apologize for being Catholic. Johnson returned to the U.S. without a contract or further word from Nagashima or Saeki.

Later that winter, the Giants, in a press release given major coverage by the *Asahi Shimbun* and other major dailies, announced they would not be renewing Johnson's contract. He had demanded a two-hundred-thousand-dollar raise and a multiyear deal, a spokesman said, and the Giants were not going to put up with any more unrealistic demands from egotistical foreigners. They had no choice but to put their foot down, to give Johnson his release and go look for another player.

Sadaharu Oh said it was too bad Johnson was so "naive." Other players made references to his "small heart." It was unfortunate he had to leave, they felt, but, well, you had to draw the line somewhere. You couldn't keep giving in. Giants pitching ace Tsuneo Horiuchi said bluntly, "We don't need any greedy *gaijin.*"

The epilogue was yet to come. Shortly after the release was announced, a Kintetsu Buffaloes representative telephoned Johnson at his Florida home to inquire if he were interested in becoming a Kintetsu Buffalo and, if so, how much money would he want?

Johnson, flabbergasted at the turn of events, replied, "I'll play for anything. I'll go back there for fifty thousand dollars. I'll hit 40 homers for you just to show the Giants how wrong they were."

A few days later, however, the representative called Johnson back to say the Buffaloes couldn't sign him after all because the Giants didn't want them to. It mattered not that Johnson had been released. If the be-all and end-all of Japanese baseball did not want him back in Japan, then that was the way it had to be. Sorry, but such was the power of the mighty *Kyojin-gun* (Giants troop)—a military term often used to refer to the team. (It was fitting, one anti-Giants columnist noted, that the word *gun* was pronounced "goon.")

Years later, even as manager of the New York Mets, Johnson still had not forgotten his encounter with Japan. "I'm still in a quandary over why things turned out as they did," he said sitting on the bench at Shea Stadium one sunlit June afternoon in 1986. Johnson had a paunch and sported a thick handlebar mustache that the Giants never would have allowed. But his feelings about the way he had been treated were as vivid and as bitter as ever.

I have never understood why the Giants did that to me. They made me out to be some kind of villain. All the way through, in fact, there was so much misunderstanding, so much distrust. I had a broken shoulder my first year. They thought I was faking it when I told them my shoulder hurt. To me the whole thing was a tragedy because I tried to do everything the Japanese did. I didn't ask for any special treatment like other *gaijin* did. I did all their conditioning. The only thing I had trouble with was sleeping on *tatami* (straw mat) floors; I couldn't handle that. I didn't like *sashimi* really, but the rest was nice.

I really wanted to play out my career in Japan and then be a coach there and help the younger Japanese in their minor leagues. In fact, I would still be there today if I had been treated differently.

But I guess the apology was too big a concession for Nagashima to make. I was personally crushed that I had to leave because I really liked the Japanese people. I had lots of good friends there and I liked everybody on the Giants team. Even today, it's painful for me to relive that experience, because there was so much hurt.

Johnson departed, but his teammate Crazy Wright stayed and that, for many Giants lovers, was perhaps the hardest burden to bear. Wright had proved to be a valuable pitching acquisition. He won eight games in 1976 after a late start and eleven games in 1977, helping the team to a second straight pennant. And he got along famously with Nagashima, who admired his combative attitude. Raito-*san* had *gattsu*, Nagashima would tell people.

Nagashima is super, Wright would say in return. He's one of the best men in baseball.

Yet Wright found himself constitutionally unable to obey the ten commandments the front office had delivered unto him. He simply could not help it. He stayed in Japan a total of two-and-a-half years and set a club record for fines. His transgressions included throwing a soda bottle through the window of the manager's office, demolishing a water cooler, breaking a photographer's camera, and urinating in a reporter's hat. He also participated in three fights—two on the field and one in a Tokyo disco named Byblos, where he and two other Americans, Chuck Manuel and Roger Repoz, took on the entire East German hockey team.

Wright found his hosts as bewildering as they found him, as he told another American in Japan.

> I lost two games in a row in the early part of the season and a Giants executive suggested that maybe I might want to consider sending my wife back to the States. I think they thought that sex was interfering with my pitching.
>
> If I gave up a home run to another American I would come back to the bench and invariably one of the coaches would say, *"Presento?"* (Was that a present?)
>
> One year I won four games in April and a Giants pitching coach told me that I was winning too much and that the other players would get angry.

Wright left in the middle of the 1978 season claiming he could not understand Japan.

Still, Wright enjoyed a weird sort of popularity, like professional wrestler Hulk Hogan later did in Japan. Some fans were entertained by his nose-to-nose confrontations with the umpires and his anarchistic attitude on the field. Once he approached a veteran umpire who had just received an award for officiating his 2,700th game, and said, "Congratulations. Let's see. That's 2,700 games, times ten mistakes a game. That equals 27,000 mistakes. That's some career."

Sometimes Wright would stick his face right in front of the TV cameras set up next to the Giants bench and break into song. Wright also seemed to have developed his own special rapport with his teammates, as he once related in a magazine interview:

There was not much clowning around like you'd see in the States. But they would fool around with me though. They were always pulling at the hair on my chest, things like that. Even in the dugout. Our right fielder Yanagida would go 0–3 and he'd run by me, reach inside my uniform, and pull some hair out. Then he'd put it down his chest and say, "Lucky, lucky." They don't have much hair of their own, so I guess they thought it was a big deal.

They'd fool around in the showers, too. I'd come in and they'd point between my legs and say, "*Ohki, desu ne*" (it's really big). I'd come out of the shower and I'd be standing there, drying myself off, and someone would run by and grab my thing and give it a little pull. They were just playing. Like I said, they didn't do that with each other. Just me, because I was American, and I was used to that sort of thing. Americans screw around like that all the time. I didn't mind. It was just their way of being friendly.

Sometimes they'd get a little rough, though. Suzuki, our running coach, came by and grabbed it one time so hard I thought I was going to die. God, I was mad. I flashed. I grabbed him and pushed him up against the wall outside the locker room and slapped him in the head. Kuroe, the coach, did it once too. I was standing there after coming out of the bath, bare-assed naked, and he came walking by and grabbed it. I thought he was going to pull it off. Jesus, I turned white. I was so mad. There was a bunch of grapes lying on the table and I picked them up, stuck them inside Kuroe's uniform, and smashed them all over his chest. That's how mad I was. But I calmed down. Kuroe calmed down. He apologized. And I did too. I shouldn't have lost my temper.

Chaos seemed to follow Wright everywhere he went. He struck out fellow American Chuck Manuel four times in a game and then teased him about it so much afterward, over several drinks at Wright's apartment, that Manuel busted him in the eye. Wright showed up at the park the next day with a noticeable shiner.

One night in April 1977, Wright unleashed a couple of pitches behind the head of a Hanshin Tigers batter. The Tiger manager rushed on the field and a bench-clearing tango ensued, during which most of Wright's teammates tried to pull him back to keep him from hurting someone.

The baseball viewing public found Raito's offense most rank. If you asked Takehiko Bessho, a former Giants pitcher, it stank to high heaven. "Wright is a despicable guy," he fulminated in his newspaper column. "The actions of the Tigers were understandable and natural in light of what Wright did. A bad man is a bad man."

Thereafter, Wright received numerous death threats from Hanshin Tigers fans. In Tigers games at Korakuen, he would hear people in the stands yelling insults in English: "Wright, you cocksucker!" "Fuck you, Wright." "Wright, you son of a bitch!" In Osaka, he would receive phone calls at his hotel room and a voice would say in broken English, "I kill you, Raito." He would get letters that said, "Raito you live in a pigsty. You go home, you crazy *gaijin.*"

Wright's demise came midway in the 1978 season, when he was involved in yet another on-field brouhaha, this time with teammate John Sipin. Sipin, a former San Diego second baseman, had twice during that season taken exception to deliveries apparently aimed at his person and had engaged the offending pitcher in hand-to-hand combat. After the second brawl, in which Wright had enthusiastically rushed to the aid of his teammate, Sipin was hit with a three-day suspension by his team and castigated by the press for his "barbaric" behavior. One sports-page editorial likened his conduct to that of a *yakuza* (Japanese gangster) while another called Sipin a throwback to the days of the U.S. military occupation when, to hear some Japanese tell it, American GIs regularly roamed the streets beating up on the local citizenry.

Wright, though not suspended, was similarly excoriated. Fuji TV's nightly baseball show reported that two out of three viewers deplored the actions of the two *gaijin*. A *Hochi Shimbun* columnist called them a "disgrace to the proud Giants heritage." "Neither Sipin nor Wright deserves to be with the Giants," wrote another columnist, beside himself with righteous indignation. "Kick them out and bring in better-behaved American players for the Giants."

Wright, his nerves frayed, his arm ailing, and his belly full of Japan, called it quits. "There's a double standard," he said, "It's always the *gaijin*'s fault, whenever there's trouble." Before he boarded the plane he was asked if he had any advice for his American replacement on the Giants.

"Yeah," said Wright, "don't come."

⊘　　⊘　　⊘

Giants fans, coaches, and front-office personnel breathed a collective sigh of relief when the gentlemanly Roy White came along in 1980. Finally here was a player worthy of the sainted Giants. White was one of the few *gaijin* players to study Japanese. Fans outside Korakuen Stadium would be treated to the unlikely sight of White, rushing to make batting practice on time, begging off autograph seekers in flawless Japanese: *"Isoide imasu. Jikan ga arimasen domo sumimasen"* (I'm sorry, but I'm in a hurry and I don't have time). He had even better manners than some of his Japanese teammates.

Showing signs of slowing down at the start of his third season, White was benched. But he kept his Eagle Scout mien. He waited, he delivered some key pinch hits, and in time he was back in the starting lineup for good. "I knew they wanted to give the younger players a look," said White, "But I also knew if I was patient, that I'd get my chance. And I did."

The acquisition of Reggie Smith in 1983 marked a return to those stormy days of yesteryear. Smith, a veteran of seven All-Star games and four World Series, was nearing the end of a long and rich career. He was a switch-hitting outfielder with a lifetime average of .287, and 314 home runs. He had played in Boston with Carl Yastrzemski in 1967, and in Los Angeles with Steve Garvey in the late seventies. He had ripped apart his shoulder making a throw from right field in 1980, but Dr. Frank Jobe, resurrector of Tommy John and Choji Murata, stapled it back together so Smith could play a year at first base in San Francisco under Frank Robinson, where he batted .284 and hit 18 home runs in 106 games.

Smith almost did not come to Japan. A Yomiuri representative had first contacted him in 1982, before he had signed with San Francisco. There had been several meetings, at the end of which Smith wondered why in the world anyone in his right mind would want to play for the Tokyo club.

The man had told Smith that the team already had a star, a young home run hitter named Tatsunori Hara, and

Smith's role would be just as a *suketto* (helper), a term commonly used to refer to foreign players. All he would have to do is play in eighty games and hit .270 with 20 home runs.

"What about money?" Smith asked. "How much are you going to pay me?"

The representative told him that the Giants could not discuss a figure until Smith had made a commitment to play for them. If the team made a legitimate offer and Smith turned it down, the man explained, it would be a great loss of face for the organization. Everything the Giants did was watched and if word leaked that Reggie Smith had rejected the pride of all Japanese baseball, it would be in all the papers and it would be a big loss of face to the club.

Smith replied that he could not understand people who thought that way. It would be an equal embarrassment for him if word got out that he had accepted a deal without knowing how much money he was going to make. So in the end, he told them he did not think he was ready for Japan, not just yet.

The following year, Yomiuri tried again, this time with a concrete offer for nearly a million dollars. It was more than twice what he had made in San Francisco and more than twice what any Japanese was getting. There would also be three cars thrown in, including a Mercedes. So he took it.

On the surface, Smith was not an ideal choice for any Japanese team. Jim Lefebvre, who had played in Japan and who knew Smith, had flatly predicted that Smith would not last half a season in Tokyo.

Smith was an intelligent, articulate man who had many interests outside of baseball. He had a pilot's license and could play seven different musical instruments. He was also proud, willful, outspoken, and very quick-tempered. His career had been punctuated by controversy, such as the time he called Boston a racist city and was publicly censured by Boston Mayor Kevin White. Some of Smith's former teammates described him as an agitator.

In L.A., he slammed a clubhouse cooler in anger during an argument with Dodger Derrel Thomas, opening a huge gash in his wrist that required sixty stitches. Two years later he went into the stands at Candlestick Park after a heckling fan.

Yet, the bottom line with Smith was that he was also a winner. He was capable of picking up a team and carrying it for weeks at a time. Dodger pitcher Don Sutton was once moved to say, "Everybody talks about how wonderful Steve Garvey is. But Reggie is the real leader of this team. As Reggie goes, so go the Dodgers. He doesn't smile at the right people, or say the right things. He tells the truth, even if it sometimes alienates people. He's a real person."

The enormous amount of money Yomiuri had paid to an aging (thirty-eight-year-old) athlete with a history of injuries generated the predictable amount of carping among Giant fans. They had even more to complain about when Smith arrived at the Giants' Miyazaki camp on the southern coast of Kyushu with his Afro hairdo and mustache. Never in the proud fifty-year history of the Giants had facial hair, or indeed, anything but a short military-style haircut, been permitted. Now Smith was trying to spoil that tradition.

When interviewed by a Japanese paper, Smith said that his mustache was something he had worn for fifteen years, that it had nothing to do with his ability to play baseball, and that he didn't intend to cut it off for anyone. He indeed understood that the Giants had their own way, but he also had his. And he said that he wouldn't play for any team if shaving off his mustache was one of the requirements.

In a private meeting with Smith, Giants owner Toru

Shoriki relented. "Hair like yours has never been allowed on the Giants before," he said, "but because of your stature and the time you spent in the major leagues . . . Well, we just want you to hit 40 home runs."

The entire spectrum of Yomiuri fandom uttered a collective groan. It was yet another crack in the temple of team purity first defiled by the hiring of Johnson.

In camp, Smith tried hard to be on his best behavior; he was cooperative with the press, accommodating to his teammates, and got along easily with Giants manager Motosi Fujita and Oh, who had retired to become the team's assistant manager.

The Giant coaches, however, were another matter. In all, there were eight coaches and each had more authority than most managers in the U.S. They worked harder than their American counterparts in the U.S. and it seemed to him they took their jobs more seriously. It was not long before they set their sights on Carl Reginald Smith.

Smith had been assigned to play the outfield. His arm had healed enough so that he could air out the ball once or twice a game if need be and Japan's ballparks were small enough so that a sidearm toss to an infielder would suffice on most relay plays.

A swarthy, square-jawed man named Isao Shibata was the outfield coach. He had been the center fielder, leadoff man, and top base stealer on the old "pure" Giants, as well as Japan's first switch-hitter. He was treated with much deference. Shibata was skeptical of Smith's abilities as an outfielder, despite the numerous Gold Gloves Smith had won in the U.S. One gray and particularly chilly afternoon, as the wind hissed in off the Pacific Ocean, he decided to put his new charge to the test.

Shibata stationed Smith alone in the outfield and began to hit fly balls to him—first to Smith's left, then to his right, back and forth, each one just out of Smith's reach. A number of reporters had gathered to watch. As Smith chased each ball down, there was a lot of joking and laughing between Shibata and the assembled press. Although Smith couldn't understand what they were saying, he strongly suspected that he was the object of everyone's mirth.

Shibata would hit the flies and Smith would run after them and every time he failed to catch up with a ball the writers would laugh some more. It seemed to Smith as if Shibata was doing this drill solely for their amusement.

Smith went along for a while, working up a sweat until one ball sailed high over his head and in trying to catch it he collided with the outfield fence.

There was more laughter and then suddenly Smith dropped his glove and walked off the field. "That's it," he called to Shibata, "That's the end. You'll never make me do this again. Call me when you want to hit some balls I can catch."

It was only the beginning of his descent into the maelstrom.

Smith's forte was power. A burly man at six feet one inch and 180 pounds, he had a ferocious swing with which he could propel the ball to the farthest reaches of any stadium in Japan. After he hit three huge home runs during the opening weekend of play, the opposition started walking him. In the first three weeks of the season, he was walked three times with the bases loaded (twice on four straight pitches).

He called the pitchers "gutless." Japanese baseball was just like Japanese society, he said. People were afraid of confrontation. They just laughed at him. Of course they were scared. They were scared witless. Challenging him was tantamount to suicide. They had no choice but to finesse him, if they pitched to him at all. So Smith continued to walk.

In late April, he hurt his knee sliding into third base and was not able to run hard again for several weeks. Limited to a pinch-hitting role, he became a target for bilious

Asahi Shimbun president Ryuhei Murayama throws out the first ball of the National High School Baseball Tournament, summer of 1915. Today it is the most popular amateur sporting event in Japan. The Asahi Shimbun originated the tourney and still sponsors it today. (*Asahi Shimbun*)

First High School of Tokyo baseball team, Japan's first baseball power, practices after school, late 1890s. (*Japanese Baseball Hall of Fame and Museum*)

Garbed in an ankle-length *Hakama*, an umpire peers over the catcher's shoulder in a collegiate game around 1920. By the turn of the century, college baseball was Japan's major sport, with large universities playing overseas. (*Japanese Baseball Hall of Fame and Museum*)

A poster advertising a team of United States major league All-Stars, featuring Babe Ruth, which toured in Japan in 1934. (*Japanese Baseball Hall of Fame and Museum*)

Caught in a downpour during the 1934 visit of United States All-Stars the Babe fields with an umbrella from a thoughtful fan. (*Yomiuri Shimbun*)

The 1935 Yomiuri Giants, Japan's first professional baseball team, in its first year of existence. The Giants toured the United States in 1935, playing Pacific Coast League teams and semi-pro squads. The Japanese numerals on their backs confused the Americans. (*Yomiuri Shimbun*)

Sachio Kinugasa, Japan's "Iron Man," and his wife meet former Prime Minister Yasuhiro Nakasone. (*Kyodo News Service*)

A poster produced by the Pacific League to promote the 1981 baseball season. It shows the six managers of the teams in the league dressed in the garb of feudal shoguns. At far right is Don Blasingame, then manager of the Nankai Hawks of Osaka. Blasingame was once an All-Star second baseman for the St. Louis Cardinals. (*Kyodo News Service*)

The right field stands at Koshien Stadium near Osaka. Barbed wire keeps overenthusiastic Hanshin Tiger fans off the field. (*Sports Nippon*)

Takenori Emoto, "Japan's Jim Bouton," ponders his future on the day his playing career abruptly ended. (*Daily Sports*)

Tokyo Giant star Tatsunori Hara, Japan's "male symbol" in 1981. (*Kyodo News Service*)

Perhaps the richest man in the world, Yoshiaki Tsutsumi, shakes hands with one of his prize possessions, the Seibu Lions first baseman Kazuhiro Kiyohara. (*Kyodo News Service*)

Choji Murata and his wife celebrate his baseball comeback in 1985 (*Sports Nippon*)

Former Minnesota Twin Charlie Manuel and his manager Yukio Nishimoto celebrate winning the 1980 Pacific League pennant. Manuel hit 48 home runs with 129 RBIs for the Kinetsu Buffaloes during the 1980 season. (*Kyodo News Service*)

happier days. Randy
ass (*left*), Rich Gale
enter), and Hanshin Ti-
r Yoshio Yoshida cele-
ate winning the 1985
pan championship.
Kyodo News Service)

Leron (*left*) and Leon Lee. (*Kyodo News Service*)

Warren Cromartie communicating cross-culturally with Taiyo Whales catcher
Yoshiharu Wakana. (*Kyodo News Service*)

Reggie Smith protesting in his own way.
(*Sankei Shimbun*)

The *gaijin* who spoke Japanese.
Three-time Triple Crown winner
Hiromitsu Ochiai in his Lotte Orion
days. (*Kyodo News Service*)

Seibu Lions "New Breed" center fielder Koji Akiyama cartwheels into home plate. (*Nikkan Sports*)

Dick Davis has a conference on the mound with opposing Seibu Lions pitcher Osamu Higashio. (*Nikkan Sports*)

Bob Horner meets the Japanese strike zone. (*Kyodo News Service*)

Poised above a Japanese invention—a block with spikes—a Seibu Lions catcher learns the correct way to crouch. (*Kyodo News Service*)

The wrath of Ueda. Hankyu Braves catcher Hiromasa Fujita learns what happens when you drop the ball in practice. (*Nikkan Sports*)

"Dirty Egawa" celebrates a Japan Series wir 1981. (*Kyodo News Service*)

newspaper editors. By June, after Smith had spent nearly two months on the bench, some sports dailies had begun referring to him in print as the "Million-Dollar Bench-warmer."

During the nightly nationwide telecasts of the Giants games, the TV cameras would zoom in on Smith, sitting on the bench next to his *gaijin* teammate Hector Cruz, who was also injured. The announcers would not say anything, but the unspoken message was clear: Here are the highly paid Americans relaxing on the bench, not contributing. If Smith and Cruz happened to be talking to each other, the camera would linger a bit longer than usual. This time the implied message was that Smith and Cruz were not contrite enough. A Japanese player in similar circumstances would be wearing a mask of infinite remorse that he could not help his teammates out. If Smith or Cruz actually smiled or, God forbid, laughed, well that was enough to elicit a click of disgust from one of the commentators, who might then pose that old question Giants fans were repeatedly asking themselves: Do the Giants really need foreigners?

When Smith was allowed to take his fiancée Rose on a road trip to Nagoya, people thought that he was getting away with murder because wives of Japanese players were normally relegated to homebody status. Inviting Rose along had been the idea of a front-office executive and Smith thought that perhaps the club was trying to make up to him for something that had happened the previous winter. He had taken Rose to see Shoriki at the Giants' hotel in Maui. There he was met by a team official in the lobby who told him that only Smith could go up to Shoriki's office on the top floor; that no women were allowed. He went up, but Rose's feelings were hurt and she had not forgotten about that day. So Smith felt that perhaps he had been allowed to take Rose on the road trip as a way of squaring things with her.

No one in the press knew that, however, and the very

next day, the *Nikkan Sports* saw fit to run a front-page photo of Reggie and Rose sitting together on the bullet train bound for Nagoya. The caption read, "As Always, Special Treatment."

The media would not let up. In one game, Smith was asked to pinch-hit and he stood in the on-deck circle taking practice swings. But when the batter at the plate doubled, Smith turned and headed back to the dugout. He pointed to first, shook his head, and said to Fujita, "It's no use letting me hit. They'll just walk me with first base open." Fujita agreed. It was the obvious move—unfortunately, it was not obvious to everyone.

The *Nikkan Gendai,* a mass-circulation evening tabloid with apoplectic tendencies, found Smith unbearably presumptuous and declared war on him in a back-cover story.

> What is this, acting big? Manager Fujita obeying Smith's instructions? What else can this be but the *gaijin* major league complex? And Smith is taking full advantage of it.

The paper quoted a Japanese college professor who said Smith's behavior reflected American attitudes of superiority toward Japanese in general.

> The Americans are making fools of the Japanese and baseball is only one example. They think of the Japanese as "yellow," and as "acting like monkeys." So naturally a baseball player like Smith says, "Sure. Give me two hundred million yen and I'll do a little dance for baseball. . . ."
>
> *Gaijin* cut into lines at Tokyo Disneyland and the Japanese let them. They look the other way at such lawless behavior. It's a fact of life they let Westerners run over them. . . .
>
> Nakasone and Reagan might call each other "Ron and Yasu." But deep inside, Reagan must only be thinking

he is gaining some advantage by allowing that. That group thinks of people with colored skin as yellow monkeys with tongues sticking out. Japanese are being held cheaply all the way from the prime minister's office to the world of baseball.

Granted, neither the *Nikkan Sports* nor the *Nikkan Gendai* were on the same level as, say, the *New York Times* or the *Asahi Shimbun.* But the older, "serious" dailies, like the *Asahi,* gave minimal coverage to sports— two pages a day in the thirty-page daily issue, presenting their articles in a dryly factual, objective manner befitting their gray, somewhat intellectual image. They did not always give their readers what they wanted or needed.

If one walked into any bar in Tokyo at the end of the day, what people were all talking about over their beer and *sake* was baseball in general, the Giants in particular, and more specifically, at this time, Reggie Smith. What the hell was going on with him, they wanted to know?

So, it was the sports dailies and the evening tabloids that told them. These papers had emerged after the war, aimed at the nascent middle class, and were enormously well received. The fourteen daily sports papers, including regional editions, had combined sales of over 10 million, while the evening tabloids like the *Nikkan Gendai* and the *Yukan Fuji* had circulations of about a million each.

"Newspapers like the *Asahi* try to educate their readers," said one tabloid editor. "Papers like ours tell people what to think." And what the *Gendai* believed people should think was very unequivocal in Smith's case. It printed a follow-up story with the big blaring red headline: "Fire Smith." The paranoid contents are paraphrased below.

Smith must be thinking that there is no other business as good as this: receiving 200 million yen for sitting on the bench and occasionally pinch-hitting. The coaches smile at him and say, "Thank you." And Smith walks around with a big, self-important "I'm a major leaguer" look on his face.

Isn't this all because of the *gaijin* complex that the Japanese have, letting an old broken-down wreck like Smith act as important as he does? Because of this the whole of Japan is being held cheaply by the rest of the world.

It is still not too late. Fire him and send him back to America as soon as possible. For if we do that then all nations will look at our country with different eyes and change their way of dealing with us. This is not just a problem of the Giants and Reggie Smith. This is not just a problem of pro baseball. This is a problem of Japan.

In late June, Smith finally returned to the starting lineup full-time, his knee healed, but he continued to make headlines. He hit several long home runs, one of them an enormous blast over the center field wall in Yokohama that knocked the opposing pitcher out of the game and caused him to break into tears. But pressing to make up for lost time, he struck out all too often. He fanned six of seven times against a tricky Carp lefthander named Yutaka Ono alone. Now the sports press was calling him "the Giant Human Fan," after Gary Thomasson.

He began to complain about the umpires. "There is a strike zone for the Japanese," he said, "and another one for the *gaijin*. That is clear. Ours is a lot bigger. I took a pitch that was so far inside it was impossible to hit and the umpire called it strike three. I got angry and he stood there smiling, enjoying himself, because he caused the big former major leaguer to be upset—so he can say, 'If the great Reggie Smith is so good, why can't he hit in Japan?' "

The umpires denied they were picking on him but Smith was adamant. He was so agitated by them that in one game he went up to the plate without his batting gloves, holding his bat limply, down by his belt, and intentionally struck out.

"You're not trying," Oh said.

"Every time I complain about the umpires, people like you say hard luck," Smith retorted. "I thought I'd try something else to state my case."

In Hiroshima he hit a home run off the back screen and another over the back wall in right field, completely out of the park. His third time up, the umpire called him out on a third strike that Smith described as half a foot inside. In a rage, he smashed his dressing room locker with a baseball bat.

There were other harassments.

It was his habit to use the labyrinthine Tokyo subway system to get to the park every day. Going by cab invariably risked being caught in one of the city's massive traffic jams. But always the fans were there. He once told a reporter:

> In a sense, I felt I earned my money in Japan by giving up my privacy. They surround you, like you're some kind of freak. They pull on you. Poke at you. Pull your hair. They don't do that to the Japanese players. I'm waiting for a train and I feel a hand slipping through my shirt, sneaking across my chest. Someone else is sticking me in the behind with the pole of one of those Yomiuri Giants flags. I broke the pole.
>
> I know that to the fans I am bigger than the Japanese players and that I'm a rarity, but they don't understand how degrading that is. I'm not a freak.

After the Carp series, Smith had accused the Giants of spying on him during his off-days. "I bought some lithographs," he said, "and by the time I got back to the hotel, team officials knew where I'd been, what I'd bought, and even how much I'd paid for it. On the road, when I'd try to take the train by myself, they'd have someone follow me. I'm a grown man, for Christ's sake. They seem afraid to have me go anywhere alone."

Sullen and lethargic in a pregame batting practice at Koshien, Smith was benched by Oh who expressed concern over his "mental condition." Other American ballplayers in Japan began to wonder if Smith wasn't losing it.

At Jingu Stadium in early August, he decided on an impulse that he would have a "backwards day" to symbolize how badly things had been going for him. In the Giants locker room, with Hara and other teammates giggling and providing assistance, he put his pants on backwards, then his jersey and his cap. Then he reversed his shoes, right to left. He even had his underwear turned around.

Smith walked out on the field and started running—backwards. The assembled crowd of press, players, and coaches looked on in disbelief. Some laughed, but others just stared, mouths agape. The Giants coaches were not amused, nor were they enlightened. There was no place for spontaneous American-style lunacy in an organization like theirs. "You can't take batting practice that way," Shibata barked, "you're embarrassing the team."

"Then I'll take batting practice in my mind," Smith retorted. That evening, back in regular uniform, with only his imaginary batting practice as a warm-up, he hit a three-run homer and a double.

The muggy Japanese summer had arrived, revivifying his aged bones. He had shortened his swing and tried to go after the first hittable pitch, whether it was a strike or not. He began striking out less and hitting the ball hard more often.

But there remained still more hoops for Smith to jump through. Now as the pennant race narrowed down to two teams, the Giants and the Carp, Carp pitchers started throwing brushback pitches at him. They had determined that the high inside pitch was his weak point, because he stood so close to the plate.

The Carp had surged to two-and-a-half games behind the Giants and came into Tokyo for an important two-game series in the middle of August. On a torrid Saturday night, before a standing-room-only crowd at Korakuen Stadium, Carp starter Manabu Kitabeppu faced Smith in the first inning and threw consecutive high-and-tight pitches that sent Smith reeling backwards. As he regained his balance on the second pitch, he used the tip of his bat to flip dirt in the eyes of the Carp catcher Tatsukawa.

Both teams dashed onto the field for some Japanese style scuffling and shoving, with no punches thrown. The umpires quickly broke it up before any serious damage could be done.

When the smoke had cleared, plate umpire Hiroya Tomizawa, as was usual, announced a ruling to the fans over the stadium PA system. His verdict was that Smith was entirely to blame. Smith's conduct, Tomizawa told the crowd, was not that of a gentleman and therefore the chief umpire would officially warn Smith that if he repeated such conduct in the future, he would be ejected from the game.

Tomizawa then turned the mike off and addressed Smith, who was standing off to the side of home plate waiting to resume his at-bat. "If you want to fight," Tomizawa said in English, "do it after the game."

Smith was phlegmatic. "If I had wanted to fight," he replied dryly, "the catcher would already be lying on the ground."

What annoyed Smith even more than the brushbacks was the jockeying he had been hearing from the Hiroshima bench. Carp subs had been chiding him when he came to bat. *"Gaijin! Gaijin!"* they would cry, hooting and laughing and yelling what seemed to him to be insults in Japanese.

It absolutely infuriated him. Some of the players were

not even good enough to play Class A ball in the U.S., he thought, and here they had the gall to make fun of a man such as himself. At one point in the game, he turned to the Hiroshima bench and yelled, "Fuck you!"

The Giants won the game 3–2 that night in the twelfth inning on Hector Cruz's game-winning hit. Late the next afternoon, as the sun set behind right field, coloring the sky a fiery reddish-orange, Smith collared Hiroshima's team interpreter and approached the Carp bench. "This beanball business has got to stop," he said. "And so have your insults. If you want to fight, then we'll all fight. I'll take all of you on if I have to. And that will be too bad, because then somebody is going to get seriously hurt. So you have to decide, do you want to fight or do you want to play baseball."

The air crackled with tension. The players sat there, frozen in silence, until Smith walked away. It seemed that nobody wanted to accept his challenge. During that evening's game the Carp bench was subdued. The moment of reckoning came when Smith stepped up to bat in the seventh inning with the tying and go-ahead runners on base. The situation and the count called for an inside pitch, but the Carp pitcher threw outside instead. Smith reached out and pulled the ball into the left field stands for a three-run homer and a 4–3 Giants win.

A newspaper headline the next morning said it all: "Smith Typhoon Sinks Carp."

The victory moved the Giants four-and-a-half games ahead of the Carp. Far more important was the psychological impact of the win. It seemed to break the Carp's spirit. They never got any closer and the Giants went on to win by six games.

After that, everyone seemed to back off. It was as if Smith had taken all Japan could dish out and there was no more left. Fewer pitches seemed to come for his head.

And he found himself complaining less about the strike zone.

He hit 20 home runs in the second half of the season, including three homers in the pennant-clinching game against Yakult and a bases-loaded homer in the final game of the year. He finished with 28 homers in 261 at-bats, 72 RBIs, and a batting average of .284. Tatsunori Hara, who won the MVP, finished with 31 homers and 103 RBIs in nearly twice as many at-bats.

By season's end, the press was respectfully referring to Smith as "Professor Baseball." Shoriki was stating publicly that if it had not been for Reggie Smith, the Giants would not have won the pennant. He added that Smith had been a bargain at one million dollars.

Smith had gone through all the stages most foreigners go through in Japan: condescension, shock, frustration, resignation, and determination. And he had prevailed.

Smith's second year, in which Oh became Giants manager, was, unfortunately, not any easier for Smith. He complained in private that he could not turn on even a Japanese fastball anymore, and that the base runners completely ignored his throwing arm. Certain Carp base runners would even taunt him. They would round first on a single to right field and take second base easily, laughing as they did.

It was not because he was out of shape. For Smith staying in condition had never been a problem. And he was not big on night life. "I'm not like most ballplayers," he would say, "I'm not interested in going out to bars with everybody else and getting drunk and biting my glass in half. That's not my idea of a good time, and so I'm not one of the boys, you see. When we go on a road trip, I like to visit parks and art galleries and museums. In the States, anyway, people thought me strange because those are 'white pastimes' if you know what I mean. Black people are not *supposed* to do them."

The racial prejudice he found in Japan bothered him no end. When he stood in the outfield and heard Tiger fans insult his race, he found it very difficult to maintain his composure.

"The fans in the outfield stands at Koshien Stadium were the worst," he said. "They throw things at you: batteries, *sake* bottles, stones; and yell insults like 'nigger.' I'm standing there in the outfield thinking to myself, 'I came nine thousand miles to hear this kind of insult? I felt I was going backwards because even fans in the U.S. don't yell that anymore."

He tried to maintain a sense of humor about it all, because most Japanese could not pronounce the word properly. It came out something like "nee-gah-roo," but in his second year, Smith stopped laughing—perhaps because his skills were leaving him and he was more vulnerable. The verbal attacks were beginning to irritate him. The more the Tiger fans saw they were getting under his skin, of course, the more they did it.

And so it happened that one day during a Giants-Tigers series, he spotted one of the more vociferous Tigers fans in the crowd milling outside the park and, according to one eyewitness, walked up to the man and decked him.

The very next day he emerged from a Korakuen subway exit with his sixteen-year-old son Reggie Junior to find fifty to one hundred belligerent Tiger supporters in their black and yellow Tiger *happi* coats waiting for him. There were more insults, some jostling, and suddenly his son was down on the ground. Smith uncorked a left hook to the jaw of the nearest man, a twenty-one-year-old fan named Masahiro Suzuki. Smith and his son made it to the safety of the stadium, but Suzuki filed assault charges and Smith was detained after the game and questioned at a nearby police station.

The police eventually cleared Smith of the charges and publicly admonished Tigers fans to try to keep a leash on their emotions. But to Giants lovers, the incident was yet another damaging blow to the gentlemanly image of the club.

Smith finished the year at .255 with 17 home runs and was given his release. He had wanted to stay on as a Giants instructor, but in the end it proved impossible. Smith knew baseball. No one denied him that. In his two years in Japan he had tried to pass on some of his knowledge of the game in a quiet, indirect way.

At the park, Tatsunori Hara (whom Smith considered his best friend on the team) and outfielder Kenji Awaguchi, among others, would approach him with questions about hitting in carefully practiced English. And Smith would willingly answer.

In the early part of his second year, he had also stood next to Oh in the dugout at Oh's request and dispensed his opinions about aspects of the game. It was something he had done with Tommy Lasorda on the L.A. Dodgers. But his presence next to Oh upset Shibata, who thought the role of primary advisor belonged to him. So Smith backed off. And in the end he just went home.

◉   ◉   ◉

The signing of Warren Cromartie marked yet another chapter in the continuing quest to find the Perfect *Gaijin.* Cromartie had played in Montreal for several years alongside Gary Carter, Andre Dawson, and Steve Rogers. He had been a .280 career hitter with moderate power, a player who could do a lot of different things well. In 1983, at the age of thirty, he had filed for free agency and turned down an offer from the San Francisco Giants to take a better one from the Yomiuri Giants—a three-year deal worth a reported six hundred thousand dollars a year.

Cromartie turned out to be the best American hitter the Giants had ever had. After an initial period of adjustment, when Oh had to bench him for poor hitting, Cromartie gained his bearings and went on to average .300 and 30 homers a year for the next four years. His best year was 1986, when he hit .363, second in the league, with 37 home runs. He helped the Giants win a pennant in 1987, when he hit 28 home runs and batted .300.

Cromartie also became one of the more popular foreign players in Japan. He was a free spirit who blew bubble gum at bat and who would raise his fist in a showy "*gattsu pozu* (guts pose)" whenever he hit a home run—a mannerism some of his teammates picked up. Assuming his position in the outfield the next inning, he would then lead the bleachers in rousing choruses of *banzai!*

In the years since Johnson and Wright, Giants fans had gotten used to American faces in the sacred orange and black of Kyojin, and many of them found Cromartie entertaining—although there were plenty of the type that did not.

Cromartie's low point was the time he punched a Dragons pitcher for whacking him in the back with a fastball. "I had to do it," said Cromartie, drawing on his experience in Japan. "The guy didn't tip his hat, the way Japanese are supposed to."

Dragons fans were not appeased by Cromartie's subsequent suspension and fine by his team. The next time the Giants played in Nagoya, Cromartie needed police protection to make it safely from the train station to the hotel and to the ballpark and back. As he alit from the bus in front of the stadium three hours before game time, a crowd of hecklers was waiting for him. An old woman screamed at him in accented English, "Yankee go *homu!*" Inside the packed stadium, 240 security guards were on hand to keep the peace. Fans held up a crudely painted banner that said in huge black letters, "Mother fucking Cro!"

On the bench before the game, Oh turned to Cromartie and allowed that he was more popular than rock star Madonna, who was then touring Japan.

One act that endeared Cromartie to Giants fans was in 1986 when he got up out of a hospital bed, where he had spent the night recovering from a beaning, to hit a pinch-hit grand slam home run that kept the Giants in a late-season pennant race. Everyone warmly praised Cromartie's courage. Why, some people even said he had as much guts as a Japanese.

When Cromartie crossed home plate into the waiting arms of his jubilant teammates after that blast, he saw genuine tears of joy in many of their eyes. "For the first time, I finally felt accepted," he said, "that I was a real member of the team."

Cromartie was known in Japan for his abiding, un-abashed affection for Oh and named a son born in Tokyo in 1985 after him—Cody Oh Cromartie.

"Oh has a heart of gold," Cromartie would say of his manager. "There's not a selfish bone in his body."

There were many things Cromartie liked about Oh. He admired the patient way Oh would sign stack after stack of Japanese-style eight-by-ten-inch autograph cards each day at the park and the way he always had a kind word and a smile for everyone. He also thought that Oh knew as much about batting as anyone he had ever met. From his prac-tice with a sword, Oh knew how to position the bat, how to balance the body, how to twist the wrist. If Cromartie had a slump, it was always Oh he turned to—"the best batting coach in the world," as Cromartie called him.

At the same time, Cromartie felt that Oh held back too much. When Hara was in a slump, every ex-Giant within hailing distance of a taxi would come out to the park and try to correct his form. And Oh would let it happen. He wondered why Oh did not just take charge and kick ev-eryone out. But then again, he and Smith knew the real reason.

The forced resignation of Nagashima in 1980, which was brought about because the Giants had won only two pennants and no Japan Series in his six years at the helm, was not a popular move. There was still a strong Naga-shima faction on the team. Cromartie also knew that many of the Giants players did not care for Oh simply because he was not a pure-blooded Japanese. Cromartie thought Oh sensed this and perhaps that was why he was not more authoritative and why he often seemed to let his coaches guide his moves.

Oh employed the standard offensive system in Japan, called *kidoryoku yakyu* (mechanical baseball), in which runners were advanced base by base, through bunting and hitting to the opposite field. Whereas many U.S. man-agers would let their players alone, at least until the later innings of a game, Oh told his players what to do on every single pitch from the first inning on. He would even make Hara bunt.

Like many other Japanese managers, Oh also relied on his intuition. He would change players on a whim, employ pinch hitters in the early stages of a game, and he was superstitious. He used talismans. He sprinkled salt. He believed in dragons. He made moves that even Japanese fans couldn't figure out.

He would take a starting pitcher out with a lead and two out in the fifth inning. Or he would warm up a pitcher in the bullpen for half an hour then bring him in to face one batter.

Criticism of Oh by the fans, the press, and former Giants coaches was more intense than that of any other manager in the history of the Giants. It had taken Oh four years to win his first pennant (1987), and even then the Giants had fallen in six games to the Seibu Lions in the Japan Series.

Japanese were always impatient where the Giants were concerned. But in Oh's case, their voices were more stri-dent than usual. "Oh Screws Up!" was a frequent headline in the news.

Cromartie knew that Oh was not a particularly good

manager, even though he was intelligent enough to be one. Cromartie knew that Oh knew it too. Once the two had dinner together, at an old Tokyo restaurant in a private room behind sliding paper doors. There, sitting on *tatami* floors at a black lacquered table sipping cold *sake*, Oh confided in his American star. "Cro, great players don't always make great managers," he would say. "Even Ted Williams was not a good manager, right?" Cromartie replied, "Yes, you're right." And Oh took comfort from that. Cromartie knew that Oh did not really like his job, that he was staying only out of a feeling of loyalty to Shoriki. That's the way Oh was. And Cromartie respected him all the more because of it. (Oh once had a choice of taking a ball signed by Lou Gehrig and another one signed by Babe Ruth. Oh took the Gehrig ball because Gehrig had never played for any other team but the Yankees.)

Oh, it seemed, was always suffering from stress. The pressure of running the Giants and the constant niggling of the press and sniping by even his own players was getting to him. He took vitamin shots and other medicines to calm his nerves.

There were also reports of domestic strife. A big family argument had occurred on a street in Harajuku, Tokyo's fashion center, during which, it was reported, one of Oh's three daughter hit him with her purse and screamed, *"Dai kirai!"* (I hate you!) A Japanese publication wrote that people would visit Oh's house in the suburbs and when no coffee was served, Oh would say, "I guess my wife's not here," and he would get up to go make the coffee and serve it himself. On one such occasion, a reporter spied Oh's wife sitting alone in the kitchen, angrily mixing a drink for herself.

Reporters would joke that the only one in Japan who truly, unconditionally supported Oh was his mother, who lived with Oh and his family. She would come to home games every day, a kindly faced elderly woman who was always dressed in a kimono and sat on the first base side behind her son in the dugout. Each day she would pray for her son at the wooden Buddhist altar in their home, setting out an offering of rice, salad, water, and some *sake*. And each evening before she retired, she would pray to the soul of Oh's departed father and report the news of the day's game.

At the time, Oh was a middle-aged man, his hair flecked with gray, his once-handsome face grown puffed and weary from the pressures of his job. One of his few respites was the daily ride to the stadium in the chauffeur-driven limousine, provided by the team. He would sit there clad in his usual attire of polo shirt and golf slacks, broad, powerful shoulders leaning against the back seat, listening to rock music on the car stereo—a favorite was Rod Stewart. As the car jerked and halted through Tokyo's smoggy traffic, he would sometimes find himself singing along with the lyrics: "I am sailing, I am sailing, . . ." Sadaharu Oh and Rod Stewart, two superstars in tandem.

Cromartie often said that the one thing he wanted in Japan was to help win a pennant for Oh and in 1987 he did just that. One of his big hits that year came late in the season—a dramatic two-out, two-strike, bottom-of-the-ninth-inning home run that gave the Giants a come-from-behind win over the second-place Carp.

On the day the Giants clinched the flag, Oh cried for joy in front of his players. And no one celebrated harder than Warren Cromartie. Beer in one hand, cigar in the other, wearing a *hachimaki* (headband) stamped with the word *victory*, he led his teammates in a *Banzai* salute to their manager.

⚾   ⚾   ⚾

The Giants have always had more than a passing interest in their relationship with the media. When Reggie

Smith began a long series of interviews with the magazine *Weekly Post* in which he was critical of how the Giants overtrained and often brutalized their young players, the Giants front office applied pressure on the magazine's editors to dilute Smith's message in translation. The editors willingly complied, fearing the likely loss of access to other Giants players if they didn't. When Smith found out, he angrily ceased the interviews.

As media interest in baseball and the Giants continued to rise, over the years it became more and more difficult for Yomiuri executives to control those who covered the team. Moreover, a host of new mass-market photojournalism magazines had sprung up during the 1980s with names like *Focus* and *Friday,* which pursued celebrities and sports stars in search of compromising photos.

They represented the worst of Japanese journalism, employing reprehensible tactics to get their stories. A baseball star was walking down the street one night in Roppongi and as he stopped at a traffic signal, a famous porno film actress walked up beside him and grabbed his arm. A magazine photographer then dashed in front of them to take their picture together. The photo of their "date" was published in a magazine with a circulation of a million and a half.

Not every publication was so irresponsible. But to the Giants' upper management, anyone not connected in some way with Yomiuri's media machine—which included Nippon Television Network, the *Yomiuri Shimbun* (with a circulation of eight million), and the daily sports paper *Hochi Shimbun,* with sales of nearly a million—was in the enemy camp.

In 1986, a former *Yomiuri* reporter named Wakabayashi was appointed to the post of press relations director. "I'm here to guide the media," he was quoted as saying, a remarkable statement from a man who had spent his life chasing scoops. The new policy he implemented was even more remarkable for a team owned by the world's largest-selling newspaper—one openly dedicated to freedom of speech.

Henceforth, no publication could interview anyone on the Giants without first obtaining the formal permission of the front office. To obtain that permission, the publication had to submit a list of questions it wanted to ask to Wakabayashi and his assistants, and when the article was finished it also had to be submitted for approval. (A sum of several hundred dollars was also required as an interview fee, to be given to the player.)

Shoriki's staff sifted daily through the mass of newspapers, sports dailies, and magazines that comprised Japan's enormous and energetic print media in search of stories about the Giants. Those that criticized the organization were scolded and usually denied further access. *Yomiuri* reporters by contrast produced only favorable copy about the team. It was an unusual way to practice journalism, but in Japan company loyalty always comes first.

The control Yomiuri exerted sometimes approached the ridiculous. The story is told of the time a former Japanese world boxing champion visited the Giants camp in Miyazaki and said hello to a Giants player he knew personally.

"I can't talk to you," said the player.

"But I only said hello," replied the startled boxer.

"You have to get permission from the team before I can talk to you."

The censorious ways of the Giants bothered Warren Cromartie, who liked media attention but found he hardly ever got written about. So when he signed a new two-year contract in 1987 (for nearly 3 million dollars), he had a clause inserted which gave him the freedom to talk to anyone he wished in the media.

In a number of interviews that season, he spoke candidly of his feelings about Japanese baseball—for example, "There's only one player on the Giants who could start in the major leagues"—and occasionally he criticized team policy. Among other things, he thought it a bit much to send the regular shortstop down to the farm team as punishment for committing a game-losing error.

Giants PR officials complained but Cromartie would just wave his contract. So they did the next-best thing which was to blacklist the writer who had assembled many of the Cromartie pieces and urge other teams in the Central League to follow suit. As a Giants spokesman explained to an editor at *Number,* a leading sports publication, it just wouldn't do to have *gaijin* speaking their *honne* (real feelings).

Periodically, the public gains a glimpse of just how powerful the Giants can be in protecting their image. Such was the case in 1987 when certain facts about the Giants young outfielder Sadaaki Yoshimura came to light. He had hit .343, .328, and .312 in his first three seasons. He had power, he could run, and the only cloud on his horizon was a bad shoulder which affected his throwing, the result of an injury he had suffered in practice in 1986, or so the Giants had informed the press.

In September of 1987, however, a story appeared in the monthly magazine *Gendai* claiming that Yoshimura had hurt himself in a drunk-driving incident which had been covered up with the help of Tokyo police. The author of the article wrote that Yomiuri had drawn on the close ties it had had with the National Police Agency ever since Matsutaro Shoriki, the founder of the team, held a high position in government overseeing the NPA. When the reporter went to the police station which had handled the matter to make inquiries, he said the first thing he was asked was, "What are you? A Hanshin Tigers fan?"

The story seemed to be true, since no one in Yomiuri refuted it. A Giants spokesman merely said, "The incident is closed and we have no further comment."

The alleged police cover-up should have been a major

news item, but it went virtually unmentioned in the sports dailies. As one reporter explained, "The Japan Series was coming up and the Giants were playing Seibu and we knew that if we wrote about the Yoshimura problem, the Giants would deny us access. We had no choice."

℗   ℗   ℗

In June of 1988, Cromartie, with 10 home runs, got hit by a pitch that broke his hand in two places and effectively finished him for the season. His replacement was a twenty-three-year-old Giants farmhand named Lu Mingtsu—a hard-swinging Taiwanese slugger whom the Japanese called Meishi Ro. Ro hit 7 home runs in his first eleven games and all of a sudden people forgot about Cromartie.

The Giants also had another new American, million-dollar pitcher Bill Gullickson who become the first player in Japanese baseball to be granted a three-day paternity leave to be with his wife during labor.

"Gully," as the six-foot-three-inch, 220-pound Gullickson was known, went on to compile a record of 14–9 with a 3.10 ERA and 124 strikeouts. His and Ro's success left the Giants in the unusual position of having three good foreigners while league rules permitted only two per varsity squad.

Talk in the Giants camp turned to revising the limit—not necessarily to allow more Americans but to permit more Chinese *gaijin* like Ro, whose salary was, at that time, only one-twentieth of Cromartie's.

9

The Gaijin
Who Spoke Japanese,
Dirty Egawa, and the
New-Breed Heroes

It is said that in Japan one must have a sensei *(teacher, master). Indeed, to be dependent on a* sensei *is considered the correct and proper way. If one does not have that kind of arrangement, it is very difficult to live in Japanese society.*

Ochiai is the exception. He is the kind of man who is strongest when he is alone. He doesn't need a sensei.

That is very rare.

Mitsuyoshi Okazaki
Magazine Editor

There are lots of different ways of doing things, not just the way of a previous generation. I have my own way and I can't stand people telling me what to do.

The problem is that people in this country think being individualistic is antisocial behavior. And that won't change for a long time. It's the national disease of Japan.

Hiromitsu Ochiai

He was the premier Japanese baseball player of the 1980s. Yet he hardly ever practiced, he laughed at the term *fighting spirit,* and said he played baseball only for the money. He was also appallingly immodest. Four times he predicted he would win the Triple Crown and three times he did just that. Although he was a purebred native of Akita, a rice-farming area of northern Honshu, he was so different from what people expected a star in Japan to be that they called him The *Gaijin* Who Spoke Japanese.

Everything about Hiromitsu Ochiai, a sleepy-eyed third baseman who had played for Lotte and Chunichi, baffled the Japanese, even his childhood. Most ballplayers in Japan reach the top only after years of harsh training and suffering that starts in Little League. But Ochiai, by all accounts, had a very low tolerance for self-denial.

The youngest of five children whose father was a small-town civil servant, young Ochiai was spoiled, biographers said, by a doting grandfather who catered to his every whim. As a boy, he went to an estimated one hundred movies a year. (He saw *My Fair Lady* seven times and was able to recite whole lines from it in English.) In high school, he spent more time at the local theater than he did playing baseball. Seven times he quit the school baseball team because he did not like the practices—but was always coaxed back before the next game because nobody else could pitch and hit cleanup the way he did.

At Toyo University, he balked at performing duties that freshman players were traditionally required to do—washing the underwear and scrubbing the backs of the senior players in the team bath, giving them massages, lighting their cigarettes, and other such tasks designed to inculcate humility. He quit in disgust in less than a year. "If I'd wanted to be a nightclub hostess," he said, "I'd have gone to work on the Ginza."

For the next five years, he played for Toshiba Fuchu in a Japanese industrial league and in 1978, at age twenty-six, he was drafted by the Lotte Orions—where he ran into trouble again. Lotte coaches did not care for his unorthodox right-handed batting form, in which he aimed his bat toward the first base dugout like a Shinto priest performing a blessing and then stepped firmly in the bucket when he swung. Then Lotte manager Kazuhiro Yamaichi took one look and said, "That guy will never make it as a pro."

This time Ochiai did not quit, however. When he finally got his chance to play regularly in 1981, he hit .326 to win the batting crown. It seemed Ochiai's hands were so fast that it did not really matter where the placed his feet or how he held his bat.

Two years later, he started predicting and winning Triple Crowns. In 1983, he won it with a .325 average, 32 home runs, and 99 RBIs. In 1985 and 1986, he won back-to-back Triple Crowns with the numbers .367, 52, 146; and .360, 50, 116.

To Ochiai, predicting a title was a way of demonstrating confidence, as well as being honest, but to most Japanese, it was a sign of overwhelming arrogance—as was his attitude toward practicing. After his first Triple Crown year, he refused to attend voluntary training in January. In camp, he would seldom swing a bat in earnest until the exhibition games were over, and during the season, while his teammates went through long and hard pregame workouts that left them soaked with sweat, Ochiai would lounge on the sidelines. "Ten swings is all I need," he would say nonchalantly. "Then a good massage and I'm ready to play." By his tenth year, his broad-shouldered five-foot-ten-inch, 170-pound frame sported an impressive potbelly.

Reporters loved Ochiai because he was so unequivocal. "The history of Japanese baseball," he once told an interviewer, "is the history of pitchers throwing until their arms fall off for the team. It's crazy. Like dying for your country—doing a *banzai* (yelling "Long live the Emperor!") with your last breath. That mentality is why Japan lost the war. . . . *Spirit, effort,* those are words that I absolutely can not stand."

Sadaharu Oh among others was not a big fan of Ochiai. Oh was famous for the crippling hours he put in on the training ground, even up to the year he retired. He was suspicious of people who said they did not need to practice and he once participated in a magazine interview with Ochiai in which he said he was afraid Ochiai's way would mislead the youth of the nation.

Ochiai responded that he had practiced hard in his semipro days. He had built up his basic body strength and had developed his technique. But that was then. And this was now. It was not necessary to knock himself out in pregame workouts every day to do his job well. Americans did things their own way. Why couldn't he?

Ochiai rattled the *shoji* in other ways. He openly blamed Oh and former Giants great Nagashima for the wretched state of player salaries, which were about one-fifth of the major leagues on the average. They were like obedient children, he said, always taking what was offered them, so as not to disrupt team harmony. As a result, the players of Ochiai's era had to suffer.

Eager to rectify the imbalance, Ochiai demanded Brobdingnagian raises after each of his big years and bewailed the fact that American players in Japan were always paid much more than Japanese. At his peak, Ochiai made only half as much money as the top foreigner.

Ochiai's wife was even blunter. "Maybe Hiromitsu can bleach his hair blond and put on blue contact lenses," she said sarcastically. "Then maybe he'll get the salary he deserves."

Ochiai said that if *doryoku* (effort) was Oh's motto, then his would be, "Enjoy yourself and get rich." He had good reason to be money conscious. Tokyo land prices had quadrupled in the mid-1980s. He had to spend an entire year's salary to buy an ordinary two-bedroom house for him and his wife and new baby to live in.

Ochiai had liked the Lotte manager during his big Triple Crown years, the affable Kazuhisa Inao. Inao had been a friend and had let Ochiai do pretty much as he pleased. When Inao was dismissed at the end of the 1986 season, however, and the job of manager was given to a gung-ho veteran Orion infielder named Michiyo Aritoh, Ochiai's days were numbered. Aritoh knew that Ochiai would never subject himself to the type of blood-and-guts regimen that he was planning to impose, so he had a trade arranged. Ochiai was sent to the Central League Chunichi Dragons, where he showed that at least part of his heart was that of a traditional Japanese.

When Ochiai finished 1987 with a batting average of .331, 28 homers, and 85 RBIs, despite having to adjust to a new league and play with an injured wrist for much of the season (by now he had moved to first base), he declared that he did not deserve a raise because he had not fulfilled his cocky preseason prediction of another Triple Crown. Instead, he went straight to the Dragons' fall camp in Hammamatsu.

There, in a forest clearing amidst the browns and golds of autumn, was baseball's leading iconoclast running sprints and fielding ground balls like a raw rookie in rigorous daily sessions that lasted until the onset of winter.

"It's the least I can do," he said matter-of-factly, "after the kind of season that I had."

                                       ⊗   ⊗   ⊗

Ochiai once said that the contemporary he admired most was a moon-faced Giants pitcher named Suguru Egawa. It was a telling remark because Egawa aroused more emotion among Japanese than any other player of that era—even Ochiai himself. Egawa's behavior so

tweaked the baseball establishment that he was nicknamed variously "Dirty Egawa," "The Giant Devil," and
"The Enemy of the People" over the course of his career.

Egawa had graduated from Hosei University in 1977
where he had set several pitching records. He had an
explosive fastball, a big sweeping curve, and the poise of
a fifteen-year veteran. Baseball executives were drooling
over him but he shocked everyone when he turned down
a record contract bonus offer from the Lions, the team
that had won the sole rights to negotiate with him for a
year in the 1977 draft, and vowed he would only play for
his beloved Giants.

Egawa spent the next twelve months playing semipro
ball in the U.S. and the day before the 1978 draft, he
signed a contract with Yomiuri, claiming a loophole in the
Japanese baseball rules to the effect that 365 days had
passed, the "year" officially ended, and that he was therefore a free agent. Twenty-four hours later, the Hanshin
Tigers drew the right to negotiate with him and a battle
between the two clubs began.

When the professional baseball executive committee
ruled the Yomiuri contract illegal, the Giants threatened
to withdraw from the Central League and form their own
baseball association. Since the Giants drew so many fans,
the threat was viewed with much alarm by other team
owners.

Egawa remained adamant that he would play for no
one but the Giants. Finally, commissioner Toshi Kaneko
was forced to bend. Whether because Kaneko feared the
power of the Giants or because he, like almost everyone
else in the country, was an avowed Giants fan, he urged
the Tigers to sign Egawa and trade him to the Giants for
one of their top pitchers. This was in direct violation of a
rule prohibiting the trade or sale of first-year draftees.

The trade was thus made, but the uproar that ensued
forced Kaneko to resign and the Giants to suspend Egawa

for two months for conduct detrimental to the sport. It also caused the circulation of the *Yomiuri Shimbun* to drop and prompted one reporter to remark, "There have been two despicable events in the news this year . . . the Guyana Mass Murder-Suicides and the Egawa Affair."

What particularly galled journalists covering Egawa was his surly attitude. At the start of his first press conference as a Giant, he addressed the noisy crowd of reporters by saying, "Now, now, everyone. Don't get excited." In Japan, twenty-four-year-olds are simply not supposed to talk that way.

Egawa went on to become the best pitcher in either league. In 1981, he led the league in wins (20–5), ERA (2.29), and strikeouts (221). At his peak, Americans said, he was as good as Nolan Ryan. In one All-Star game he struck out eight men in a row.

Yet, it was several years before he was deemed acceptable enough by sponsors to endorse products on television. Although he was voted MVP in 1981 by the nation's sportswriters' association, he was denied the Sawamura Award, Japan's version of the Cy Young Award that's chosen by a select panel of senior editors. They voted to give the prize instead to Egawa's teammate Takashi Nishimoto whose record was 18–12, 2.58, and 126 strikeouts. They made it clear that "personal character" had been a key factor in their decision.

Younger fans liked Egawa for his renegade ways. At six feet one inch and 200 pounds, he was always overweight. He ridiculed venerated traditions like *yamagomori* (spiritual retreat to the mountains), which he said was "nonsense." He dawdled in practice when the coaches were not watching, never throwing anywhere near the 100 to 150 pitches a day other Giants pitchers did, and he skipped starts if his arm bothered him. "Life is more important than baseball," he would frequently say.

Egawa buffs liked to tell the story of the time in 1985

when a player named Nakai, a reserve Giants outfielder, appeared on the practice field wearing a Dodgers jacket. Giants manager Oh told him to take it off. "Don't you have pride in the Giants uniform?" he asked. Nakai took the jacket off, but Egawa picked it up and put it on. Grinning, he paraded in front of Oh. For such insolence, he was always out of favor with the older generation.

He was more than just a sports figure. He was the ace pitcher on Japan's "national team" and he was constantly in the public eye. The older generation thought his impudence set a bad example for the nation and that he symbolized the deterioration of modern Japan. Said Kozo Abe, an editor at the *Yukan Fuji:*

Manners have changed in Japan. Younger people are rude. They brush by you and don't even say "excuse me." Beautiful young women occupy two seats on the subway. People are becoming selfish and their attitude is, "What can you do for me?"

Japanese are imitating the worst part of the American way and many say that the turning point was the arrival of Egawa. The fact that Egawa challenged the draft is secondary to his arrogant attitude.

The worst thing about Egawa is that he didn't always do his best. If his arm hurt, he wouldn't pitch. He always calculated how many wins he could get so he could negotiate his contract upward. He gave 70 percent just like many *sarariman,* who put in long hours but sit at their desks daydreaming. Egawa is just like them.

In Japan, I guess you could say that how you win is more important than just winning. He had a great fastball, but he didn't throw it enough. He threw too many change-ups and slow curves. He should have thrown it all the time to lift us out of our doldrums, to help us forget our meaningless existence. Great players should make you shed tears. His responsibility was to us, the fans, not to himself.

What we the fans wanted him to do was something
ordinary salary workers couldn't. Something beautiful
and moving. He should have inspired us to greater
heights. But he didn't.

He didn't feel *giri* (duty to the team) or *ninjo* (heart,
kindness for his teammates). That was his tragedy. For
him baseball was just pure economics.

In his later years Egawa had a habit of losing steam after
throwing a hundred pitches in a game and for that he was
scornfully referred to as the hundred-pitch arm. Few of
his critics ever wondered if they were asking too much.

"No one demanded him to pitch every two or three
days like Inao and the other pitchers of old," said Yoshiaki
Arimoto of the *Sports Nippon*, "but he would sometimes
go a week or more without pitching and if he lost a big
game, he would just shrug and say so what. His lack of
spirit betrayed the fans' expectations."

For many people, Egawa's final act of evil was his retirement in 1987, when he was only thirty-two years old. He
had just come off a 13–5 season with an ERA of 3.51
(giving him a career record of 135–72, 3.02), but he
pleaded a sore arm and called it quits.

Egawa claimed that he had long been pitching in pain,
but that no one on the Giants would believe him. He
would warm up in the bullpen to test his aching shoulder
and Oh would say, "Your arm looks okay. How come you
can't pitch?"

Egawa had consulted soothsayers, doctors, and acupuncturists, but nothing worked. He claimed that receiving acupuncture treatment had irreparably damaged his
arm (a statement which was immediately challenged by
the Japan Acupuncturists Association). But whatever the
reason, he said his arm was no good anymore. He had had
enough.

The Giants owner, Shoriki, was reportedly seething.

Minoru Murayama, a former pitching star, said, "He should pitch until his arm falls off. He can't just quit like that. There is more to think about than just himself." Egawa was just "greedy," observed one editorialist, noting that by becoming a TV commentator he would double his present income.

Egawa's defenders, though in the minority, applauded his guts. Kazuo Chujo, a columnist for the Yomiuri's rival paper, the *Asahi,* was downright jubilant:

> Pitcher Suguru Egawa has left the Yomiuri Giants and I salute him for his courage. . . .
> The Giants pride themselves on their long tradition of military-style iron discipline. And the team is indeed run much more like some moralistic, educational organ than a pro baseball club.
> In this "army" of religiously disciplined men, Egawa was a heretic and an iconoclast. Amply endowed with unusual talent, he chose to pace himself as he pleased, and let the team down in crucial games from time to time. And in the end, he rebelled against this "army."
> As a rule, Giants players don't quit. To submit a note of resignation is considered a terrible insult to the team's owner and executives. But nobody and nothing could keep Egawa on the team once his mind was made up.
> Nine years ago, the front office had resorted to hardly honorable means to get Egawa at all costs. Because of this history, the Giants' executives apparently took it for granted that Egawa wouldn't dare be so ungrateful and egocentric as to insist on quitting. Manager Oh tried to talk him out of it, as if the team's very survival depended on him.
> But Egawa stuck to his decision. he reiterated that his pitching shoulder was already too far gone. But there had to be other reasons why he wanted out. One of them, I suspect, was that he obviously didn't fit the mold of the Giants-style "army life."

I admire and even envy his strong will. His defiance
of dubious "virtues" is refreshing and welcome in this
society.

Egawa and Ochiai were called the precursors to a new
generation of Japanese known as *shinjin-rui* (new breed),
which emerged in the latter part of the 1980s. The term
was used to describe young Japanese who openly rejected
their parents' values of obligation, self-sacrifice, and deference to their superiors.

Japan had undergone a tremendous metamorphosis
from a ravaged, vanquished nation that extolled the virtues of poverty to an incredibly wealthy industrial
power—a country with the number-two GNP, the fourth-
largest navy, and the longest life expectancy in the world,
as well as the leading edge in fashion and architecture.

At the end of the decade, Japan also had more singles
in their twenties than anywhere else in the world. Tokyo
was filled with attractive, well-dressed, sophisticated
young people who vacationed in Hawaii and Paris and for
whom materialism had become as much a philosophy of
life as spirit had been for their fathers.

The older generation barely recognized its progeny.
Japanese men of a decade before had worn dark blue
suits, black horn-rimmed spectacles, kept their hair
cropped short, and drank Kirin beer from large bottles.
They admired business leaders, aspired to advancement
in their corporations, and controlled their emotions with
samurai stoicism. They also voted for the Liberal Democratic Party, rooted passionately for the Tokyo Giants, and
thought that a woman's place was in the home.

The New Breed wore name-brand fashions, gold neck-
laces, and carried Luis Vuitton bags. They permed their
hair, drank imported canned beer, and used designer
telephones. They admired musicians and glib comedians
and thought that real money came from financial specula-

tion and not from product sales. Their favorite buzz word was *zai-tech* (the money game).

New-Breed women moved into the work place and invited men out on dates. Virginity was out. Divorce was in. And so was makeup for males. Most everyone still supported the Liberal Democratic Party and the Giants, but it had also become fashionable to poke fun at them now and then.

New-Breed TV also made its Japan debut. A young crop of announcers, always breathlessly excited, began to replace the gray, somber news anchors of many years. Sports news programs switched their emphasis to humor, showing slow-motion replays of a silly error, an outfielder getting hit on the head by a fly ball, a young couple locked in a passionate embrace in a darkened corner of the bleachers. In general, the New Breed found life a lot more hilarious than their parents ever had. Even a *gaijin* batter punching a pitcher was cause for merriment, at least on the nightly news.

A favorite target of the cameras was an American relief pitcher named Brad ("The Animal") Lesley, a former Cincinnati Red and Milwaukee Brewer who played with the Hankyu Braves for two years starting in 1986.

Lesley was clearly the most unusual player Japan had ever seen. He had shoulder-length hair and a huge mustache and he would go through an assortment of wild gyrations and flamboyant gestures after every pitch. He would put the hex on opposing batters and when he nailed down the final out of a win, he would violently punch his catcher in the shoulder.

The Animal would tell reporters his nickname was a tribute to certain off-the-field acts like the time he pushed a car off a cliff in Alaska because it was blocking his exit from a cliffside restaurant parking lot. "The owner was inside the restaurant," the Animal said. "And I went in and asked him in a nice way to move it, but he refused to leave his table. He had an attitude problem, you know. So I went back outside, reached in, and released his handbrake, and then rolled his car over the cliff and into the ocean."

Lesley was a gross caricature of what many Japanese perceived an American to be. If he was upsetting team *wa*, however, nobody was complaining. The Braves set a new attendance record in the Animal's first year. The team held Animal look-alike and act-alike contests for kids, and the stands were always filled. As one fan put it, "Going to see Animal-*san* play was like going to the circus."

Animal developed arm trouble in his second year and was released, but he parlayed his Animal character into a new career in comedy on Japanese TV.

The sporting heroes of the New Breed were Ochiai and Egawa and Shigeo Nagashima's son, Kazushige, who signed with the Yakult Swallows in 1988 for 80-million yen, despite a college career in which he hit only .225, though with 11 home runs. Nagashima Junior, as he was dubbed, had his father's luminous good looks, broad shoulders, and vitality—if not his talent. That seemed to be enough for his fans.

He had 1 home run and an average of .164 by the midway point of his rookie season—having spent most of his time on the bench—and yet he barely missed leading all players in the All-Star balloting for his third-base position. When the Swallows' regular third baseman, American Doug DeCinces, hit a dramatic ninth-inning *sayonara* home run to beat the Giants in a game in June that year, TV viewers did not see him cross home plate because all the cameras in the stadium were focused on young Mr. Nagashima, who was leaping for joy on the Swallows bench.

The New Breed also idolized the young stars of the Seibu Lions, like a jaunty lefthanded pitcher named

Kimiyasu Kudo, who drew a heart by his name whenever he signed his autograph and who caused a minor scandal in the 1986 Japan Series when he pitched a game with the top two buttoms of his uniform open—such beef-cake was a violation of pro baseball's unofficial dress code.

A six-foot-four-inch, 170-pound right-handed pitcher named Hisanabu Watanabe was another favorite. The girls liked him for his long legs and unusual taste in clothes, which ran to black leather pants, knee-high boots, red blazers, and floppy hats. Then there was a bushy-haired center fielder named Koji Akiyama, who hit 124 home runs in his first three years as a regular and who did occasional cartwheels as he crossed home plate, his black curly hair flying.

The most-loved Lion, however, was tall and angular first baseman Kazuhiro Kiyohara, who hit .304 with 31 home runs in 1986 as an eighteen-year-old rookie. Kiyohara signed for 80-million yen, which was then the highest bonus in the history of Japanese baseball. He was so popular in his first few years on the team that whenever he returned from a road trip, his tiny room in the Seibu dormitory would be filled with presents from worshiping fans.

Kiyohara cried easily. He and Giants pitching star Masumi Kuwata had been teammates on the Osaka PL Gakuen nine, which won the national high school championship in 1985. Kiyohara had desperately longed to play for the Tokyo Giants and wept openly when they chose Kuwata instead of him in the draft.

In the final inning of the 1987 Japan Series with Seibu one out away from defeating Yomiuri, Kiyohara was so overcome with emotion at what was about to happen that he broke into tears once more, temporarily interrupting the game.

Anyone who doubted that the standards for player behavior had changed somewhat had only to watch the Lions celebrate their 1987 championship—an event which was shown in all its bizarre, rambunctious detail on the evening news.

Until then, most victory celebrations in Japan were relatively sedate affairs in which the participants would douse each other with beer for a while and then go home. The young Lions had a style all their own, however. They swilled beer and spit it out, à la Sid Vicious, all over each other as well as the raincoat-clad members of the press covering the scene. Kudo kissed the third baseman and team captain, Hiromichi Ishige, flush on the lips, and cried "I *rabu* you" (I love you) in accented English. "I *needo* you" replied Ishige and kissed Kudo back, as teammates emptied bottles of beer into their trousers.

Kiyohara, who had donned a rubber Ronald Reagan mask, and Akiyama picked up the second baseman and dumped him headfirst into a large wooden barrel filled with sake. Then they picked up a second barrel of sake and poured its contents over a TV cameraman. Next, Kiyohara pushed Akiyama's face into a chocolate cake. The anchorwoman for one of the evening news shows was clearly shocked. She looked up from her script, mouth agape, and gasped, "Can these people really be Japanese?"

Lions fans loved it. Said Midori Matsui, a young translator, "There is none of this seniority business on the team. Kiyohara is the youngest player on the club and yet he says what he wants. The Giants players are too goody-goody. They do everything the right way. They're not at all interesting."

Their manager, Masaaki Mori, smiled tolerantly and said, "I think it's natural that players should show their own individuality—as long as they practice the way they are supposed to."

＠　　　＠　　　＠

Though many young Japanese resented being labeled as hard-working and harmonious people, they were not the burning sybaritic individualists they would like to believe they were.

They would still get up in the morning, affix the company pin to their suits, and join the ranks of faceless *sarariman* on Japan's incredibly packed commuter trains. They would sing the company song when they arrived at work and do the company's morning exercises, and when five o'clock came, very few had the nerve to get up and leave. They would sit there and wait, even if there was no work to do, because that's what everyone else did and it was bad form to leave on time. There was too much pressure from their superiors to do otherwise.

Perhaps they did not feel loyal to the company as their fathers had, but still, they went through the same routine because, quite simply, they had no choice. Government surveys continued to show the Japanese worked longer than any other nationality in the world, with the exception perhaps of the Koreans.

And while younger Japanese may acted less shy and less insular than their parents, when they traveled to a place like Paris, for example, they would still fly Japan Air Lines on a group tour, stay in Japanese hotels, eat in Japanese restaurants, and shop at the Paris branch of the Takashimaya department store. If there was any contact with the French, it was purely accidental. One writer summed up New Breedism by cracking, "They practice their individualism as a group."

Nonfiction writer Naoki Inose went so far as to say, "The New-Breed Japanese is a myth. It is just a word the mass media has thought up. The emphasis on the group and on making the Great Effort is still there. Only the semantics are different. Japan will never change."

Sports commentators talked a lot about the new era of individualism, but the reality was that everyone still trained the same way. Not one player in Japan, young or old, emulated Ochiai. It was revealing that the only achievement of the players union in 1989 was to eliminate the presence of coaches at preseason voluntary training. In other words, to make voluntary training noncompulsory. The routine went on as usual. The players worked as hard as always. They just did it on their own. But Seibu, among others has instituted strict fines and other penalties for those who report to camp on February 1 not in *peak* physical condition (ready to run 10 miles without collapsing).

There were lots of young players who thought the whole idea of spirit silly and who laughed to themselves when managers told them that they would come to "understand the heart of the ball" by doing the one thousand fungo drill (in which one fielded ground balls until the point of exhaustion). Nevertheless, they would all go out and to a man endure that punishing drill every spring. They did not want anyone to think they were incapable of doing it.

The ultimate irony, perhaps, was that the Seibu Lions, the putative bastion of New Breedism, practiced harder than any other team in baseball and were more tightly controlled than any organization except the Giants. In 1988, when Seibu revised its "educational program" for its younger players, Kiyohara received a new set of rules, including instructions on taking better care of his teeth, his eyes, and his weight.

"We still don't practice as much as we should," complained their manager, Masaaki Mori after winning a third straight Japan championship in 1988. "We don't work as hard as Olympic medal winners, for example. I want my players to practice even more thoroughly in the off-season. I don't want them to think of themselves as stars."

Many young Japanese applauded when a Meiji University pitching star, Kazuhiro Takeda, quit the team in 1987 in defiance of manager Kichiro Shimaoka's dictatorial ways. Then they watched dumbfounded and dismayed as Takeda did a complete turnabout several days later and begged his manager's forgiveness. He shaved his head as penance and went off to a Zen temple where he listened to the wind and mortified his flesh. But he was never reinstated. The lesson had to be taught.

☯   ☯   ☯

The most popular manager of the late 1980s among young Japanese was the choleric Sennichi Hoshino, who took over the Chunichi Dragons in 1987 and guided them to a pennant the following year. At age forty-two, he was a fascinating blend of the old and the new. He let his players grow beards. Yet, he talked incessantly of fighting spirit, which he claimed was never, ever out of date and he was not above cuffing the younger members of the team if he thought they needed it.

Sports fans picked up their newspapers one morning in the summer of 1987 to see a photo of a Dragons coach slapping a young outfielder named Hikono for having made a base-running mistake. In the next game Hikono was a ball of fire. He had three hits and scored four runs and the Dragons coach was given a lot of credit for "waking him up." Hoshino said later, "We should have hit him earlier. He would have been a much better player by now."

Hoshino was a former Dragons pitcher and the pit bull of the Japanese game. He made *kenka yakyu* (fighting baseball) his club motto, and was involved in a number of scuffles.

In one, he punched a Carp infielder for tagging a Dragons baserunner in the face. Hoshino was kicked out of the game, fined one-hundred-thousand yen, and given an official warning. (The next day Tetsuji Kawakami, a close friend of Hoshino, wrote another of his columns on the evils of violence, but it was interesting to note that he made no mention of the "sanctity of the ground" or the "holiness of the ballpark," nor did he accuse Hoshino of "taking Japanese baseball lightly and making fun of the Japanese," as he had on previous occasions when Americans were involved.)

Off the field, Hoshino was just as fearless. Hoshino watchers liked to tell the story of the time in Hiroshima he ran into an old friend, a former ballplayer, who was eating dinner in a Chinese restaurant with two *yakuza* (Japanese gangsters).

"What the hell are you doing?" he screamed. "You shouldn't be eating with this kind of people."

One of the gangsters angrily stood up, but Hoshino, shoved him right back down again. "We've got a public image to uphold," he said to the man. "Please understand that."

On another occasion, according to a sports reporter, one of the Dragons players got himself in colossal trouble by fooling around with the girlfriend of a Nagoya *yakuza*. Hoshino personally took the player by the hand to the home of the gang's boss where Hoshino got down on his hands and knees to make a formal apology. The boss, a fierce-looking older man, gave him a long wilting stare, then finally said: "Okay, Sennichi, I'll let it go this time, for you."

For a time, talking Hoshino Dolls, extolling the virtues of fighting spirit, heart, and guts, were a hot item in the stores. Hoshino taught his young fans that there were lots of things about the Japanese character worth keeping.

10

The Emperor's Team

If you want Sundays off, don't be a manager in my company.

Yoshiaki Tsutsumi

To take the train out from Tokyo to Seibu Stadium, home of the Seibu Lions, winners of more Japan Series than any other team in the 1980s, is to encounter first-hand Japanese expertise at making money. Depending on one's point of view, the Seibu operation is a piece of planning genius that maximizes profits, or a Machiavellian scheme to relieve baseball fans of all their money.

The park, a sparkling modern structure resembling Royals Stadium in Kansas City, is located several kilometers outside the capital in the suburb of Tokorozawa, surrounded by green rolling hills and pine trees. Because of chronic traffic jams, the most practical way of getting there from the city center is by a Seibu Railways line which conveniently originates in the basement of the Ikebukuro Seibu department store on the northern edge of the metropolis. Ads for Lions games and game results are posted all over the store, as well as on the Seibu train.

The one-hundred-meter walk from Tokorozawa station to the stadium entrance is a gauntlet of concession stands peddling bats, balls, T-shirts, caps, and other souvenirs bearing the Seibu mark. The gaudy Seibu Amusement Park sits next to the stadium, as does a Seibu golf driving range, tennis court, swimming pool, artificial ski jump, bicycle racetrack, and model Unesco village.

The ballpark itself boasts 37,000 wide seats, plus a comfortable grassy slope in the outfield where several thousand more fans can lounge. Miniskirted waitresses stationed in the expensive infield box seats area serve cocktails at the lift of a finger. A Chinese restaurant located behind the park on the third-base side serves mandarin duck and other delicacies. A euphonious female voice announces batters and provides information on the upcoming games.

Stadium attendants retrieve all foul balls, as is customary in Japan, but do so with more panache than their counterparts at other parks who often bark, "Give it back!" At Seibu, they politely doff their caps, bow, and chirp, "We hope you weren't hurt." Then they present a small gift in return for the ball.

Every Seibu league pennant win and Japan Championship victory is followed by a massive celebratory sale at the group's fifteen hundred department stores throughout the nation. In 1987, Seibu held a three-day bargain sale at its stores in which clothing, furniture, and foodstuffs were sold at discounts of up to 40 percent. It brought in reported total sales of 5 billion yen, or roughly $35 million.

The driving force behind the Lions money machine is their owner, Yoshiaki Tsutsumi, one of four brothers who preside over the powerful Seibu Group, a gargantuan complex of department stores, hotels, railroads, supermarkets, and real estate that is worth trillions of yen. In addition to the Seibu Lions, he oversees the Seibu Railways Group, Japan's largest landowner, whose assets in 1988 included twenty-seven resorts, twenty-five golf courses, ski slopes, train lines, and the Prince Hotel chain, which boasted fifty-six hotels with over 13,000 rooms. A power broker who hobnobs with prime ministers, he was, according to a survey conducted by *Forbes* magazine in 1987, worth $21 billion, which made him the richest man in the world.

Tsutsumi oversees his empire by helicopter and buys chunks of high-priced Japanese land the way other people buy the morning newspaper. He is also Japan's first sports entrepreneur. He founded the Japan Hockey League in the mid-1960s, owns two successful JHL franchises, and is the only baseball franchise owner in Japan to run his team like an American big league operation—in other words, like a business. Other teams are run by large corporations, primarily for public relations benefits. Though the Tokyo Giants earn billions of yen a year, they are essentially a tax write-off for the *Yomiuri Shimbun*. They don't own but rather rent their home stadium, which controls all the ballpark food, drink, and parking concessions.

But if most owners look at their teams and see free PR and reflected glory, Tsutsumi looks and sees only yen signs. He demands the Lions be a self-sustaining, profit-making operation, and paradoxically, has probably had less interest in the game of baseball itself than any other owner in modern history, on either side of the Pacific.

When the Seibu Lions won their first ever Japan Series one magnificent afternoon in the fall of 1982, Tsutsumi was conspicuously absent. He was at a hockey game, and an exhibition hockey game at that. Hockey, he claims, is his first love.

It was an exciting sixth and final game in Nagoya. Riot police were out in force to control angry Chunichi Dragons fans who, after an earlier loss, had rained rocks and bottles on the field, forcing the Lions to take shelter in their dugout.

But Tsutsumi was not interested in the drama at Nagoya. He left his seat at the Tokyo hockey arena only briefly to view the final out on TV. It was bizarre behavior in a country where baseball is tantamount to being a national religion, but Tsutsumi is by no means an ordinary man.

The Seibu Group was founded by Yasujiro Tsutsumi, who rose from a small farming family in the Kansai area to the chairmanship of the lower house of the Diet, or parliament, becoming a tycoon in the process. When, in the late 1930s, Japan embarked on its ill-fated path to militarism, Yasujiro, or "Pistol" as he was known to his friends, got his start selling inexpensive resort villas to the newly emerging middle class.

Later, in the postwar poverty of Japan, he bought land cheaply from the estates of tax-impoverished former imperial princes, building on their spacious forested grounds a chain of elegant resort "Prince Hotels." By judicious use of the imperial emblem, which as one Japanese author said, "gave his hotels snob appeal," he was able to attract the new urban-moneyed class that evolved in Japan in the 1950s and 60s.

The Seibu Group then mushroomed dramatically, expanding along its railway lines by building department stores, housing developments, and new supermarkets around the stations. Seibu bus lines tied them all together.

Before Pistol died in 1964, he divided his wealth among his sons. The stores went to eldest son Seiji, who turned them into models of fashion and style, led by the ultrachic Parco store in the Tokyo ward of Shibuya. The land went to Yoshiaki, who had been born to Pistol's mistress and who was reportedly not on the best of terms with his half brother. Within two decades, he had put together Japan's largest real estate empire.

Even as a young man, Yoshiaki Tsutsumi was a visionary who, his admirers said, could see ten years into the future. His graduate thesis at Waseda University was on the tourism industry. In it he described how to build a pool with artificial waves on a beach at Oiso, south of Tokyo. At the time, many people thought him *baka* (stupid). Today, the

Seibu outdoor pool at Oiso Long Beach draws hundreds of thousands of visitors each summer who want to be at the fashionable seashore, but not in Japan's polluted coastal waters.

It was with such foresight that Tsutsumi set his sights on the business of baseball. People laughed at his folly in buying the Lions of Fukuoka—then owned by Crown Lighter Corporation and perhaps the worst franchise in Japan's pro baseball leagues—and moving them to the Tokyo area which already had five teams. But once again, Tsutsumi proved that he could read the future. In Tokorosawa, a Tokyo suburb, he built what was, at the time, the most modern athletic facility in all of Asia. The millions of baseball fans in Tokyo loved it and admissions soared.

Having created the perfect setting to make money out of sport, Tsutsumi set out to create the perfect money-making baseball machine.

His team was run in a pure Japanese fashion: The man at the top created the image and the people below carried it out. Tsutsumi hired good people to run his team and then let them do their jobs, declining to involve himself in the day-to-day affairs of running a ball club. His ready bankroll snared "name" players from the United States. Steve Ontiveros signed for three-and-a-half years in 1980—the first million-dollar contract in Japanese baseball history. A San Francisco Giants reserve outfielder named Terry Whitfield and George Vukovich from the Cleveland Indians got even more. Seibu scouts also reeled in a pitcher from Taiwan named Kuo Tai-yuan, or Kaku Tai-gen as he was known in Japan, whose ninety-six-mile-an-hour fastball was the swiftest in all of Asia, and a number of prospects in Japan, often outside organized baseball that other teams did not even know about. Young Seibu players were sent to the States every year for training.

Tsutsumi's people also found a way of circumventing

the annual baseball draft, the traditional way of acquiring players whereby teams chose graduating high school and college stars and those good enough to leave semipro ball. Each team has six picks, with the pick order decided by lottery. The teams draw to get the negotiating rights to a player, which are in effect for a year.

Seibu's method was diabolically simple. If a desired player could not be obtained in the draft, the organization simply hired him to go work in the Prince Hotels chain and play for the Prince Hotels amateur team. A player could thus hone his skills on the Prince Hotels nine until he was passed over in subsequent drafts, then sign a contract with the Lions. Team captain Hiromichi Ishige was originally an employee of Seibu Prince Hotels and he envisioned a future with that organization outside baseball. Pitcher Kimiyasu Kudo signed up because his father was given a job with the Prince chain.

If it was slightly unethical, Tsutsumi had his connections and a succession of baseball commissioners remained silent.

After losing twenty-one straight games to open their first season in Tokorozawa in 1979, the Lions grew stronger and started winning pennants in 1982. By the late 1980s, Seibu had clearly become the class of Japanese pro ball. Seibu attendance also rose to over a million and a half annually and the Lions led the Pacific League in attendance for seven straight years, until the Nippon Ham Fighters drew two million in 1988, in their first season in the new and therefore novel Tokyo Dome. It was said that tickets to Lions home games were apportioned out to Seibu business associates. If they declined to buy, they found it became difficult to do business with Seibu.

Though many of the top men in baseball are not owners in the sense of controlling majority shares in the parent company, they still have been granted vast powers and the title *ohna* by the board of directors. One of them, Shunjiro Kuma of the Hanshin Tigers, took a page from George Steinbrenner's book when he publicly ridiculed the team's star third baseman Masayuki Kakefu after the latter was caught driving drunk—a half a fifth of whiskey in his system. At a team reception, he labeled Kakefu a "defective product," and announced the team was looking for a new "Mr. Tiger."

But the enigmatic and powerful Tsutsumi, who never attends owners' meetings, is above such things. He has other ways to exercise his power.

Tsutsumi's office is located in a white, twelve-story building in the chic Harajuku area of Tokyo. Visitors are shown to a waiting room where a young female employee serves tea while bowing deeply on her knees.

It is reported that his workers are terrified of him. Said one employee, typically, "He's like the emperor." Taro Nawa, a journalist and longtime friend, told an *Asahi Evening News* interviewer, "If his orders aren't carried out as soon as possible, there will be thunder."

A filmmaker once produced a TV documentary about Tsutsumi. His shooting was so tightly controlled that when "the emperor" twisted his ankle in a tennis game, Tsutsumi's bodyguards were quick to stop the cameras. When the project was finished, the director said, "I felt I did a PR piece for Seibu and Tsutsumi."

Of course, obedience and efficiency are Japanese business trademarks, but at Seibu they are practically corporate mantras.

There was the time Tsutsumi decided to tour Japan via Seibu Railways in a special Seibu railway car. At every station, workers stood at rigid attention on the platform as Tsutsumi's train whooshed by, the great man himself waving from the conductor's car.

Then there was the time that he was courting the highly regarded baseball manager Toshiharu Ueda, who had temporarily resigned as pilot of the Hankyu Braves.

Ueda had suggested that the balls being used in the Pacific League that season were not lively enough to suit him. By the end of the week, all of the balls owned by the Seibu Lions had been changed to more responsive ones.

Late one season when the Lions were 17 games ahead of the rest of the League, the team's field manager complained that attendance was slipping. Tsutsumi issued an order and the very next day an SRO crowd filled the stadium.

Ted McAneely, a Canadian and former Edmonton Oiler who once played hockey for a Seibu team, told of the time his boss wanted to evaluate some new young talent on his hockey teams. He called the Seibu and Kokudo managers at three o'clock in the afternoon and ordered a game to be played the following morning. MacAneely was stunned at the results. "I walked into the Kokudo arena in Tokyo at a quarter past nine the next day and the place was absolutely packed with company workers who had come to cheer the teams on. It was incredible.

"I'm sure many of them, our cheergirls included, didn't even understand hockey," he said, suppressing a smile. "But that didn't matter. Their attitude was 'this is our job, our company team and we're going to support them.' "

Similar devotion has been seen on the baseball side. Seibu employees are expected to show loyalty by buying tickets and showing up at the ballpark as often as possible. Departmental managers make certain that Seibu employees turn out in abundant numbers to cheer the team on.

Seibu's *oendan* chiefs have even been known to take attendance before a game to see if everyone in the group is there. The sub-*oendan* chiefs have been heard sounding off in front of their respective sections: "Group A all present and accounted for!" "Group B all present and accounted for!"

"It's like being in the military," said one cynical sportswriter working for Seibu. "You know what happens to those who don't come. Your standing in the company goes down."

        ⓘ   ⓘ   ⓘ

Tsutsumi is a dour perfectionist, who works constantly and is besieged by the phone wherever he goes, even on the golf course. He is a very frank person, who dislikes neckties and has been known to say in meetings, "Let's get naked," meaning, "take off jackets, shirts, and ties."

He once told a reporter, "I have no friends. They only try to take advantage of you."

A trim, athletic man, he sleeps six hours a night, golfs to relieve stress, and is frugal to the point of neurosis. He lives in a modest two-story house in Tokyo, collects no art, and according to one report, patches the soles of his shoes with black tape. He expects his staff to work overtime with no extra pay.

The story is told of the time Tsutsumi sat down for morning coffee at the Seibu Prince Hotel in Kōchi, opened a packet of sugar, and poured some into his coffee. Most of the contents of the eight-gram packet emptied easily into his cup, but about two grams remained lodged inside. From this Tsutsumi concluded that there was too much sugar in the packet. He called his hotel manager and ordered some changes made. By the next day, all the sugar packets in all the hotels in the Seibu Prince Hotels chain held just six grams.

As a child, Tsutsumi had a classical Japanese education, which included Zen, judo, and rising at the first light of dawn to study on a cold floor. He once described the considerable impact his father had on him in a magazine interview.

    My father used to get up at four o'clock in the morning and work and discover my mistakes. He would call me and say *baka!*

I developed a kind of neurosis about the telephone. Whenever I heard the phone ringing, I got so nervous my palms started sweating. Even now when I hear the phone ring while eating dinner, for example, I start. All my nerves stand on end. And I lose my appetite.

On the value of studying the martial arts, he said:

You have to be able to present your views forcefully in meetings. And if you're not strong, it's hard to do that. I'm not talking about a fistfight, but there is some table pounding and yelling. So in order to make cool judgments, you have to have a certain confidence and composure. That was my father's idea, anyway.

My father used to punch me a lot, whenever I did something he didn't like. And I could let him do it. Even in school when I was strong. He used to hit me even after I got out of college, the last time was when I was twenty-seven. . . .

I think that was a valuable thing.

Tsutsumi's corporate philosophy has been dubbed "Seibu Familyism." His employees are all expected to be well-mannered, to refrain from drinking, smoking, and gambling, and to respect their parents. Tsutsumi has checks conducted to see that all of his male employees are on good terms with their fathers.

He once told an interviewer, "If I received a wedding invitation from a Seibu employee with his own name on it instead of his parents', I wouldn't go."

He has said that his managers should not take time off while working on a given project. That means no summer vacation, no days off, not even Sundays. "They should always be thinking about the company," he said. "If they leave, it's too hard to pick up where they left off when they come back."

The Tsutsumi-Seibu philosophy is, of course, reflected

in the way his baseball team is run. In addition to bans on smoking, drinking, gambling, long hair, beards, and mustaches, players are not allowed to hang laundry or bedding from the team dormitory windows because it would lower the club's image. Said one player, "Living in the dormitory is like living in a sanitarium."

They are also forbidden to make endorsements because Tsutsumi feels such activity would take their minds off their game. Seibu players are expected to appear at all ritual group functions in their gray double-breasted team suits, as well as to carry their official Seibu namecards with them at all times. Suits and ties on the road are mandatory, even in the hottest weather.

"One cannot build a strong team just on technique alone," said the boss. "You have to assemble players who have the right human qualities. One needs spirit before technique."

After the Lions defeated the Tokyo Giants in the 1987 Japan Series, Seibu's illustrious leader explained how they did it: "The Giants are stronger than our team," he was quoted as saying, "but they are so busy doing commercials and appearing on TV that they don't practice as much as they should. I think that's why they make defensive mistakes. They are supposed to be professional ballplayers, not TV stars."

It was quite a statement, given that the Giants already practiced twice as hard as any American big-league team.

Once a year, in a closed practice session, the Seibu players are put through a session of close-order drills to keep their general sense of discipline in tune. Everyone is expected to do this, from the oldest veteran and the highest-paid star right down to the lowest, rawest rookie. And everybody has meekly complied, even those burning models of New-Breed Individualism, Kudo, Kiyohara, and Akiyama.

A Japanese reporter once remarked to a Seibu outfielder named Yasushi Tao, "Seibu is just like the army, isn't it?"

"No," replied Tao. "It's just like an average Japanese company."

⊘　　　⊘　　　⊘

Seibu's managers have naturally mirrored the Tsutsumi philosophy. The most famous perhaps was Tatsuro Hiroka, the cold, imperious perfectionist who believed in constant practice and dedication to baseball to the exclusion of everything else.

His practice routine was so taxing that even Japanese players, who were certainly not immune to hard work, hated him. He would call special practices at noon, in mid-August, before a night game scheduled to begin at six. His team would fly into a city, hot and wilted, then head straight to the park for a three-hour workout. Said Steve Ontiveros, an American who played under him:

> The routine was really tough. Extremely tough. There was never any time to spend with my family. I would leave my apartment around noon each day and get back home after midnight. It was a very big problem between me and my wife that we had so little time together.

Added teammate Terry Whitfield who once played for the Dodgers:

> It was a bit difficult to get used to some aspects of Hiroka's system. For example, the eleven o'clock road curfew. After the game was over, there would be our postgame meeting and we would eat our dinner. So it's already eleven o'clock. There's no time. I feel that as adults, as grown men, we should be able to have some time of our own, but that's not Seibu's way. I'm a grown

man and I am old enough to know what to eat and when to go to bed. I don't like being treated like a child.

On road trips, our lunch consisted of rice, bean milk, and some soup. By the time we arrived at the ballpark, we were hungry again—there's nothing wrong with the idea of natural foods, but it just wasn't enough for Steve and me. We had to start sneaking sandwiches on the side to keep from starving to death.

Hiroka, it was said, knew as much about the game of baseball as anybody alive—in Japan or America. He constantly studied the game and was more sophisticated about the strategy and the mechanics of the game than any of his contemporaries. It seemed he knew just when to change pitchers, to put in the right pinch hitter. He had a knack for making the right move at the right time. In tight pressure situations he did not make mistakes. He kept his cool. In one big game, he surprised everyone by starting Seibu's late-inning relief ace.

Furthermore, he was an excellent teacher. He could take a look at a player's fielding, throwing, or batting and immediately see what was wrong and help him rectify his errors. From spring camp on, he always took time aside to work with players on their defensive plays and positioning and stances. He provided considerably more instruction than players normally got in the U.S.

But his regime was also one of constant negativism. Upon losing a game, he would openly chastise his players, citing by name to the press players he thought had played poorly. Behind closed doors, it was even worse. After every game, win or lose, there would be a meeting in which Hiroka, or Mori, his head coach, would go over each mistake that was made and assess penalties and fines. There was hardly any praise, complained the players—just criticism, even when the team won big.

The bottom line, however, was that he was successful. His teams were known for their skill in execution; they seldom beat themselves. They worked on every possible situation that could arise. Said Roy White, who watched Hiroka's teams play when he was in Japan, "His teams were thoroughly prepared in every aspect of the game. It was like watching a well-oiled, smoothly working machine in operation. They were good at using the delayed steal and the push bunt—small things that gave them the edge."

Being a foreigner on Hiroka's teams was particularly trying. Hiroka was suspicious, almost paranoid, about American players. "It's nothing personal," he once told American Chuck Manuel. "I just don't like American ballplayers. I tolerate them because that's what the front office wants. . . . But Americans are only in Japan because they are no longer wanted in the U.S."

Hiroka would ridicule Ontiveros and Whitfield in public and remind them, by way of the media, that neither was indispensable to the team. (Although, for several years, both players were just that. Ontiveros hit over .300 every year he played in Japan, while Whitfield was always among the home run leaders.)

In an exhibition game in late February one year, Hiroka yanked Ontiveros off the field for not running hard on an easy ground ball to the infield and benched him the next day. Ontiveros, who had hit .300 with 25 home runs the previous season, protested he had been leery of pulling a muscle in the cold weather, but Hiroka was having no excuses. "Steve is taking Japanese baseball lightly," he told a reporter. "How can you use a player like that?" On another occasion, Hiroka referred to Terry Whitfield as a "clown" because of Whitfield's exuberant, hat-tipping, crowd-pleasing style of play. (He would doff his cap and bow to the crowd after hitting a home run.) Fed up with the abuse, Whitfield, who had averaged 33 home runs a year in Japan, went back to the States when his contract expired. He turned down a big offer from Seibu to take a three-year, one-million dollar deal with the Dodgers.

Ontiveros was released at the end of the 1985 season, after hitting .320 with 16 home runs.

Ontiveros, upon leaving, had this to say about Hiroka:

> I once had a manager who was like Hiroka. His name was Preston Gomez and he was our manager on the Chicago Cubs when I was playing there. His personality was about the same. He was very cool, aloof, and a real disciplinarian. And he never praised anybody. He had a curfew and tight, tiring training schedules. He made you feel as if you were playing in Little League. Well, Gomez lasted about four months, because the players just refused to go along with his system. But then, that's the way Americans are . . . especially after free agency.
>
> It took some time to get used to Hiroka's system and also to realize that he criticized the Japanese too. He was just not the type of guy to hand out a lot of praise. He was like a machine. But I admired his dedication. He was 100-percent baseball. Some other guys might not like that, but I do and I give credit to him for his commitment.

Hiroka was a stiff, unyielding man who seldom smiled, never questioned an arbiter's call, and believed that ballplayers should be seen and not heard. He once told a magazine interviewer that he valued Seibu's clean image and that his dream (in addition to toppling the Giants) was to create a team where parents would feel comfortable leaving their sons. Hiroka and Tsutsumi had a falling out of sorts, or at least that is what reporters speculated when Hiroka announced his resignation at the end of the 1985 season. Hiroka wanted power in the front office, it was said, in addition to his manager's job, but Tsutsumi wouldn't give it to him.

At any rate, few people believed Hiroka when he pleaded ill health (chronic gout) on quitting Seibu. Tsutsumi did not appear to be among them, especially when

Hiroka paid a farewell visit to his boss, who had invited TV cameras in to record the scene.

"I'm sorry, I can't manage anymore with this body," said Hiroka.

"You look fine to me," said Tsutsumi, smiling a shade wickedly.

Hiroka, perhaps for the first time in his life, blushed.

Hiroka was replaced by his head coach and liege Masaaki Mori, who had been a catcher on the famous Giants. And although Mori was somewhat looser and more gregarious than his predecessor, his practices were just as long—and he was always conscious of Tsutsumi's presence.

Nearing the end of the 1987 season, the Lions had an eight-game lead with eleven games left to play. Mori visited with his boss, reporting that the team had almost clinched the pennant. Tsutsumi had once again invited the TV cameras.

"It looks good," said Tsutsumi, "but is there a chance you could still lose the pennant?"

"It's possible," replied Mori, laughing, "but it isn't very probable."

"As long as it's possible then we can't relax yet, can we," said Tsutsumi.

Mori stopped laughing. His smile faded and he replied with as much sincerity as he could muster at that point, "You're absolutely right."

⚾   ⚾   ⚾

By the late 1980s, Seibu had become the dominant team in baseball, but other teams still got the lion's share of attention. In the sixteen years following the Giants' streak of nine straight Japan Championships, the Lions won five Japan Series and six pennants, compared to the one Japan title and five flags won by the Giants. Yet Seibu season attendance was only half of that of the Giants, who could draw 3 million with their eyes closed, and less than other Central League teams who benefited from playing the Giants.

In terms of the media, the Lions also had weak-sister status. The best Seibu could do was national exposure of their games on weekend afternoons and local UHF in the evening, while the Giants continued to occupy prime-time TV—on their own station, NTV (Nippon Television Network Corporation)—every single night while at home and on other channels when on the road.

Although interest in sports in general and pro baseball in particular increased exponentially in the wealthy new Japan of the 1980s, few TV stations were willing to run a non-Giant baseball game in prime time. Some things simply were not done. Fan preference surveys revealed that only 10 percent of the baseball-watching population liked the Lions (a figure far behind the 60 percent for the Giants and the 25 percent for the Tigers).

Such was the brainstem appeal of the nation's oldest team. As Don Blasingame once said, "You could take the groundskeepers at any stadium in Japan, put them in Giants uniforms, play a game at 3:00 A.M. in midwinter, and the place would be packed. It's just the idea of the Giants."

The "idea" of the Giants has been propagated by the massive and capable media machine owned by the team's parent company, the Yomiuri Shimbun. No other organization in baseball, anywhere, can match it, including as it does the *Yomiuri Shimbun,* which is the world's largest selling daily, the *Huchi,* a leading sports daily, and a major TV network, NTV. All work together to keep the Giants relentlessly in the public eye.

Communications professor Fumio Eto of Seikei University likened their efforts to brainwashing. "If you are exposed to the Giants every day," he said, "sooner or later you are going to feel as if you have to see them every day.

It is this mentality that advertising takes advantage of. And it is a particular weakness of the Japanese."

But social pressure also plays a part.

The Seibu Lions should stand as a shining example of how to build a baseball franchise. If the Lions had been an American team, they might well have captured the fancy of the U.S. public. But in Japan they were still regarded as the new family in the neighborhood even after three Japan championships in a row. Order and tradition seemed to require it.

Said Hidesuke Matsuo, founder and onetime editor of *Number,* Japan's leading sports magazine, "The Japanese people don't like to stand out or be different. They like to be the same as everyone else. And since everyone else is a Giants fan, it's only natural to root for that team.

"Japanese don't want to see the hierarchy changed, and it's got nothing to do with logic or reason. They go by emotion. Japanese people have a low level of security. They are uncomfortable with challenges to the system. Hitotsubashi will never surpass Tokyo University as Japan's top university. The imperial household will always be there, as will the Liberal Democratic Party. And so will Yomiuri. It's a fact of life."

Still, there have been signs of change. It used to be that if a Japanese was not a Giants fan, he was practically considered unpatriotic. However, according to a survey taken in 1986, about 25 percent of the baseball-viewing population considered themselves "Anti-Giants." Many of these are fans of the Hanshin Tigers of Osaka, with other pockets of resistance in Hiroshima, Nagoya, and Tokorosawa. But when the Giants invade these areas, fully half of the ballpark crowd is rooting madly for the home team to lose. As one business executive snootily declared, "Those who are not Giants fans are rated low in Japanese society."

By the decade's end the Tokyo Dome for a Giants game

was as fashionable a place to be seen as Tokyo's Roppongi district, and a fitting tribute to the ability of the Japanese to "converge," as one writer put it.

To say "I'm a Kyojin fan," many Japanese still believed, gave them status—in an exclusive club, with nationwide membership.

There were, it seemed, limits to what even Tsutsumi could do.

11

The Schoolboys
of Summer

*Koshien is a page of history. It burns some-
where inside every man's heart. I never made it
there, and I always feel that it was an opportunity lost. I always think, what if . . .*

Shigeo Nagashima
former infielder, Tokyo Giants

*High school baseball is an education of the
heart, the ground is a classroom of purity, a
gymnasium of morality; that is its essential
meaning.*

Suishu Tobita (1886–1965)
former manager, Waseda University

*I saw high school games in Japan and after the
game the players would line up and take off
their caps and the manager would go down the
line and hit every third or fourth player because of some mistake or other that the guy
made—hit him on top of the head with his
hand. Really dictatorial.*

Davey Johnson
former infielder, Tokyo Giants

*I always wanted to piss in the "sacred" dirt of
Koshien.*

(name withheld)
ex-outfielder, Hanshin Tigers

Meet Makiko Kawamura, wife, mother, and successful clothes designer. She lives in the fashionable Tokyo suburb of Denenchofu with her husband and young daughter, drives a BMW, and commutes to a gleaming new office in the chic Harajuku district. Each summer, she vacations at a posh lakeside resort near Mount Fuji. While there, she spends the entire time in her room watching high school baseball on TV, from morning to night.

Mrs. Kawamura is a devotee of the annual National High School Baseball Summer Championship Tournament, and there are millions of Japanese just like her. In fact, for two solid weeks, starting with the second Friday in August, the eyes and ears of virtually the entire nation are turned to aging Koshien Stadium, near Osaka, where the top schoolboy teams in the country battle for national supremacy.

Evidence of this peculiar addiction is impossible for any sentient person to miss. Taxicabs patrol the street with the play-by-play blaring on the radio. Department store windows display inning-by-inning line scores. Even activity at Tokyo's normally bustling stock exchanges grows quiet as traders slip off to follow the action.

In fact, so many television sets around the land—in coffee shops, households, and factories alike—are tuned to the continuous 9:00 A.M. to 6:00 P.M. coverage of the games that electricity consumption, already high from the use of air conditioning, reaches alarming levels.

Professional baseball may be Japan's front-running sport, but this schoolboy tournament is unquestionably the country's single biggest sporting event; a bona fide national fixation, like America's Super Bowl and World Series all rolled into one. As Makiko Kawamura put it, "Even people who don't like baseball watch it. It's the thing to do."

The competition is a single-elimination affair involving forty-nine teams called from nearly four thousand participating schools in regional preliminaries. It draws as many as sixty thousand fans a day. Sponsored by the *Asahi Shimbun,* the annual midsummer extravaganza occupies a particularly warm spot in the Japanese heart because of a long and special tradition. By the time the first professional Japanese team was formed in 1934, the high school tourney was already twenty years old and amateur baseball had been played for over half a century. Masaru Ikei, a Keio University professor and author of many *Besuboru* books, said, "Perhaps the biggest difference between Japanese and American baseball is that the U.S. game was a pro sport long before it was ever played in high school and college, while in Japan, it was just the opposite. Amateur baseball is a big part of our sports heritage."

A visit to the tourney, known simply as *Koshien* to most Japanese, offers a rousing spectacle of sound and color that is worthy of the Olympics, starting with the opening ceremony when hundreds of shaven-headed youths march lockstep into the stadium, regional flags held proudly aloft, and make a fierce vow to uphold the spirit of sport. Banner-waving supporters bused in from home-towns all over the country fill the stands and cheer their favorites on. Miniskirted pom-pom girls with *pasa rosa* faces assist them in their cause, as do student brass bands, playing spirited renditions of "Popeye the Sailor Man" and other stirring fight songs with mind-numbing persistence.

On the field in furnacelike temperatures, contestants in baggy uniforms play with such untrammeled intensity that the losers unashamedly break into tears. Games feature a profusion of maniacal head-first slides, batters streaking wildly to first base on ordinary walks, and the opposing teams dashing madly on and off the field between innings.

Rival cheer groups, yelling through plastic megaphones, wage a vocal battle almost as intense as the one on the field. At midday, temperatures are so searingly hot that majorettes' batons and the players' metal bats become too hot to handle if left in the sun.

Olympian standards of decorum are also on display. Dubious umpiring calls go unchallenged. Hit batsmen receive an apologetic bow from the offending pitcher and the sacrifice bunt is laid down at every conceivable opportunity. At the end of each contest, the participants immediately dash to home plate, where they line up, remove their caps and bow deeply to one another. In the postgame interview area under the grandstand, amidst a logjam of reporters and TV camera crews, the sweat-soaked athletes answer questions with the ramrod deference of military academy plebes. As one school official said, "Such behavior is part of the children's education."

To many Japanese, Koshien is more than an athletic contest; it is a celebration of the purity and spirit of Japanese youth. Said one TV commentator, "The total devotion of these players to the game is refreshing. The tourney is evidence that old values have not yet been swept away by the wave of internationalization that has hit Japan."

Whereas amateur sports in most countries are played for recreation, Japanese emphasize the educational and moral aspects of school athletics. They view baseball as a part of the school curriculum, a means of developing discipline and of instilling sincerity in students in the pursuit of their life goals. The emphasis on purity is so great that former professional ballplayers have long been forbidden by Japan's Amateur Sports Federation to coach high school athletes. Nearly all school uniforms are white or off-white to symbolize that purity.

The National High School Baseball Summer Championship Tournament was originated in 1915 by the *Asahi Shimbun*, which only a couple of years earlier had participated in a movement to have baseball banned. In an

editorial written for the inaugural tourney, the paper explained why high school baseball was, after all, good for
the Japanese: (1) It teaches the players to be unified, to
play as a unit on both offense and defense; (2) It is good
exercise for the arms, legs, and whole body; (3) It teaches
a player to use his brain to formulate strategy; (4) It
teaches a player to be quick-witted, to act in a split second, but also to be prudent for a prolonged period of time;
and (5) It teaches a player to be cooperative.

In terms of PR, establishing the tourney was the best
investment the *Asahi* ever made. That first tournament
involved only ten teams. It was played in the Osaka suburb of Toyonaka in a park that seated less than fifteen
thousand. But the games quickly caught on; their popularity mushroomed so fast that larger accommodations were
soon required. One contest had to be cancelled when the
crowd overflowed onto the field.

In 1922, work was begun on a park to be built in nearby
Koshien which would rival anything in the U.S. major
leagues. Its seating capacity of fifty thousand (later ex-
panded to sixty thousand) would make it the largest athletic facility in all of Asia.

So vast were its dimensions—330 feet down the lines
and 410 feet to the center field fence—that many feared
it would be too big for baseball. In fact, twice during
construction, engineers halted work to conduct test
games. They resumed building only when they were assured that people seated in the distant centerfield stands
would actually be able to see the ball in play.

When Koshien Stadium was finally completed in 1924,
the first fans inside were awestruck. The single grandstand stretched fifty rows back and a huge iron roof tow-
ered over the infield seats. It was promptly nicknamed
"The Iron Umbrella."

That same year also saw another leading daily, the
Mainichi Shimbun, establish a tournament of its own—a

ten-day spring invitational which would also become popular, although somewhat less so than its summer cousin, because fewer teams were involved. Since then, two tournaments have been held annually at Koshien, except for a four-year break during World War II when the movement of students was banned. During that period the stadium grounds were reserved for grenade-throwing practice, while the Iron Umbrella was torn down and used in the manufacture of Zero fighter planes.

Koshien survived a firebombing in August 1945 to resume its role as the Mecca of High School Baseball. The Hanshin Tigers, who also used the park, were forced to go on a three-week road trip each summer so the tourney could be played. For a time it was the Osaka headquarters of U.S. Army forces.

Despite the postwar surge of professional baseball, high school baseball, particularly the summer gamefest, retained its magical pull. The 1988 tourney drew about 820,000 and the spring invitational over half that.

More than once, officials moved some early-round games to nearby Nishinomiya Stadium in an effort to ease congestion outside Koshien. Nishinomiya, however, remained virtually empty while Koshien continued to overflow with fans. Such was the allure of Japan's favorite ballpark.

Japanese writers tend to wax maudlin where high school baseball is concerned. They have eulogized the sport as an "ode to fighting spirit"; the tourney as the "ultimate crucible of youth"; and Koshien Stadium itself as a "temple of purity." Suishu Tobita, the famed Waseda manager cum baseball guru, was among the many who have proclaimed the ground at Koshien "sacred."

Masahiro Shinoda, a movie director and noted Koshienophile, has declared that an almost religious feeling pervades these games. In that sense, he said, Koshien was holy ground and the young players were "Japanese gods."

"That may be going too far," a tournament official, Kazuyuki Matsui, told the *New York Times* in 1987, "but I think that fans do see this as a pure and sincere form of the sport."

Indeed, the long history of Koshien is brimming with heroic tales of players overcoming adversity with stoutness of heart, as if inspired by the paeans written about the games. The apotheosis of Koshien stars was Takehiko Bessho, a right-handed hurler who pitched his final of the 1941 tournament with a broken left arm bound in a sling. Losing 2–1, Bessho, by necessity, made all his fielding plays barehanded and had his catcher roll the ball back to him after each delivery. Said Bessho, who was headed for wartime duty in the Japanese army, "I want to play as much baseball as I can before I die."

There was also Sadaharu Oh, pitching Waseda High School to victory in 1957 despite a painful ruptured blister on his pitching hand. When a teammate expressed concern about the blood dripping from his fingers during a midgame meeting on the mound, Oh begged him to keep quiet. "Don't tell our manager," he pleaded. "I've got to stay in the game."

Another stoic hero was Koji Ohta, the blue-eyed product of a Russian-Japanese marriage, who led little-known Misawa High School Number 9 into the final day of the 1969 summer tourney by pitching four consecutive complete games. In the final game, before one of the largest daytime audiences in Japanese TV history, he hurled eighteen consecutive scoreless innings, in a 0–0 game that was called on account of darkness. The next day, workaholic Japan ground to a halt once more to watch Ohta lose 4–2 in a continuance.

The loss hardly mattered. In defeat, Ohta became a national hero. His shy good looks sent teenage girls into a dither and he was the subject of numerous TV documentaries and one book before he had even graduated from high school. Like many Koshien aces, Ohta burned his arm out young. After a spotty pro career, which saw him washed up by age twenty-seven, he became a TV commentator. But, even today, fans remember him with affection and respect.

Ohta's performance sent interest in the high school tournament rocketing to new highs. So did the deeds of a baby-faced, sloe-eyed pitcher named Daisuke Araki who was a national idol even before his voice began to change. Araki took Waseda High to three straight near-misses in the summer tourneys (1980 through 1982), the first when he was only fifteen. In 1986, as a professional just up from the Yakult Swallows farm team, Araki won but one game, but he was the overwhelming choice of the fans as starting pitcher in the All-Star series.

The batting star of the 1985 games, PL Gakuen's Kazuhiro Kiyohara, who hit four home runs (two in the final) became a household name overnight. He was trailed for months afterward by a pack of magazine reporters who recorded his every move in copious detail—from what he ate for breakfast to which comic books he read in study hall.

Koshien is a highly symbolic event for the Japanese. It takes place during the *obon* holidays, the Buddhist festival of paying respect to departed souls, a time when workers take leave to return to their hometowns. Mitsuyoshi Okazaki, an editor at *Bungei Shunju,* has written: "With the massive postwar shift of the Japanese population from rural to urban industrial areas, the Koshien tourney has become one of the few remaining ways Japanese have of displaying regional loyalties. To many people, especially those in big cities, Koshien evokes nostalgia for their youth and for a time that doesn't exist anymore."

One can see ample evidence of regional ties in the myriad support groups queueing up outside the park before each game. A large proportion are elderly people, clad in colorful *happi* coats festooned with logos and badges showing their school affiliation. The stands are filled with beaming parents, and of course, little brothers and sisters cheering their elder siblings. One columnist has called Koshien a "universal Japanese experience."

Newspaper editorials also stress the visceral attraction of the "specter of inevitable defeat which looms over the games." "Just think of it," gushed one writer, "Nearly four thousand teams around the nation, remorselessly pared down. For half of the teams that play each day there is no tomorrow. That's desperation at its finest. The players try so hard that many say they can't remember hitting or catching a ball."

"Koshien is about suffering and loss," said a radio talk show host one evening. "One empathizes with the losers instead of cheering the winners, because all their effort has gone for naught. It is doubly poignant since the end of the tourney signifies the end of summer in Japan, the change of seasons. It symbolizes something irrevocably lost. There's a kind of melancholy to it all."

Those playing high school baseball are committed to a system so austere it would tax a samurai's resolve. At most schools in Japan, players are expected to practice every single day of the year, before and after school, rain or shine, except for a brief respite at the New Year. During summer and winter vacations, they are sequestered at special baseball camps where the program might include marathon all-night workouts and other excruciating exercises designed to hone fighting spirit. Teams in the frigid regions of Hokkaido and the Japan Alps often practice in the snow using an orange ball for better visibility.

A young magazine editor described what it was like when he played on his high school team:

> We used to have this drill at the end of practice every night. It was a race involving all the first- and second-year students on the team. Everyone would have to dash from one foul line in the outfield to the other and

only the first-place finisher was allowed to go home.
We'd keep repeating this until there was only one person left.

We'd also have to do sit (meditating), or stand in place
and hold our arms outstretched for thirty minutes, or
we'd have to stand on our toes and a senior classman
would put his foot underneath the soles. If we touched
his foot with ours, we'd get scolded.

If you could put up with all this, then you got to give
the orders when you became a third-year student. If
you couldn't, it was believed that you could never develop fighting spirit either in sports or in life.

Our coaches would say that there was beauty in suffering. They would physically punish slow learners.

Training extends off the field as well. On most teams,
the junior members must perform such edifying tasks as
scrubbing floors or cleaning toilets. GI haircuts are de
riguer—a way of showing that nothing is more important
than the team, even one's appearance.

School officials emphasize self-discipline and self-reflection. Collective responsibility is a general rule and
woe betide the player who gets into a fight or otherwise
sullies the name of the school. The entire team may be
suspended from play as punishment. When the student
manager of Tokyo's Keio High baseball squad was caught
stealing a pair of little girl's undergarments from the
locker room of a primary school, the Keio principal withdrew the entire team from the regional tourney.

Corporal punishment is another colorful feature of high
school baseball, as it is of Japanese education as a whole.
TV viewers watching a regional game in the summer of
1983 were startled to see a manager go to the mound and
slap his pitcher for giving up a couple of runs. "Pull yourself together," he growled. Later the youngster thanked
the coach in front of the TV cameras for having brought
him back to his senses. "Being hit by my manager made

me realize the situation we were in," said the grateful slappee, "so I was able to throw my best for the rest of the game."

During the 1987 games, the manager of the team from the Saga Prefectural High School of Technology and Engineering discovered several of his players up late at night talking in the kitchen of the *ryokan* (inn) where the team was staying. He whacked each of them over the head with the grip end of an aluminum bat, cutting the scalps of two of them.

As a result of the late-night whacking, the team played listlessly the next day and was eliminated from the tourney. Saga Manager Yasuhiko Kugimoto, forty-five, apologized for his actions, but said he could not hold his temper because the boys were so noisy.

The Saga High principal thought it all a bit much. He delivered an apology to the Japan High School Baseball Federation and suspended Kugimoto for a year. But Saga's captain and ace pitcher who was among the whackees, was mortified. "I don't blame the manager," he told reporters, "Because I was the one who was really bad. And my parents agreed with that. I just feel sorry that this happened. It's all our fault."

⚾   ⚾   ⚾

On a hillside in the southern part of Osaka stands a cluster of undistinguished buildings that form the campus of PL Gakuen, acknowledged king of high school baseball. PL has been to Koshien twenty-five times and has won six championships in its thirty-five-year history, more times than any other school in history. Knowledgeable Americans have compared it to a Texas high school baseball power. Perhaps the University of Texas would be more like it.

PL was founded in 1954 by the Church of Perfect Liberty, one of the many nondenominational religious groups that sprang up in Japan after the war. It is a coeducational school with a student body of approximately eight hundred, sixty of whom live in the baseball team dormitory, a three-storied structure next to the main PL practice field, which has, not coincidentally, exactly the same dimensions as Koshien Stadium.

The select sixty who are scouted by PL coaches in junior high school compete for one of the fifteen first-team spots.

Year round, these players follow the same monklike routine, arising at 4:30 A.M. for prayers and study, followed by four hours of practice in the afternoon.

After evening meditation, the players fall out for voluntary training which may continue past the 11:00 lights-out curfew with shadow (make believe) pitching and batting drills in the dark.

When PL's stern-faced manager Junji Nakamura peers through his steel-framed glasses and tells reporters, "I don't force my players to practice that much. It's up to them," everyone chuckles.

PL plays nearly two hundred games a year, from March to December.

At the center of student athletics in Japan—some would say Japanese civilization—is the *senpai-kohai* relationship, whereby underclassmen *(kohai)* perform services for their upperclassmen *(senpai)*, who lend advice and guidance in return.

A journalist named William R. May has written, "Some *senpai* believe that they are responsible for the *kohai*'s spiritual development, not in a religious sense, but within the Japanese belief that they possess a unique Japanese spirit that needs to be disciplined, refined, and polished."

At PL, every senior ballplayer is assigned a *kohai* to wash his underwear, assist him in late-night practice, and otherwise do his bidding, all of which leaves the *kohai* with little time for training or study of his own.

Few complain. To these players, baseball represents a

way of circumventing Japan's infamous "examination
hell" education system which forces junior and senior
high school students to study seven days a week, almost
year-round, both in and out of the classroom, so as to pass
stiff university entrance exams. Qualifying for admission
to a prestigious university guarantees entry to one of
Japan's top companies and a good position for life.

Playing in a Koshien tournament, however, can be a
virtual ticket to success in that national recognition and
stardom can be instantly achieved. Over half of the players on Japanese pro rosters have been scouted at Koshien
tournaments. Even those who don't gain lucrative professional contracts can still wind up as well-paid employees
of corporations that maintain teams in Japan's industrial
leagues. Just the fact that a man has appeared in Koshien
means he will be honored for life in Japanese society. (It
is also said that an appearance in the Koshien quarterfi-
nals is enough to guarantee a youth admission to certain
big-name private universities, whether or not he passes
their entrance examination).

"Some mothers force their sons to play high school
baseball because they think the discipline will straighten
them out," said a baseball writer who wished to remain
anonymous. "But others want the prestige of Koshien.
Some mothers will even screw the coach, if it means getting their sons on the ball club. It's rare, but it happens."

PL graduates are particularly valued by companies because competition within the team is so tough that PL
players are considered to have much more energy than
those of other high schools. Said the father of one third-
year player at PL, "In the two-and-a-half years that my
son has been there, I haven't seen him for more than a
total of one month. But I know it's good for him, because
he will be able to advance in life."

The baseball budget at PL is said to be in the neighborhood of 10 million yen a year, ten times that of ordinary

schools. But then, being a Koshien regular has its own rewards. What PL expends it gets back many times over in donations, enhanced prestige, and increased applications. Said one newspaper reporter, "You have to think of PL's baseball expenses as being in the same category as the national advertising budget for Hitachi or Panasonic or some other big Japanese firm. It's big business."

Hiroshima Carp cleanup batter Takehiko Kobayakawa is one of many PL players in the pro ranks. He was recruited from a Hiroshima junior high school by a PL scout when he was fifteen. He was brought to Osaka to live in the school dorm, his family remaining in Hiroshima. All expenses were paid by the school.

Kobayakawa once described what his studies were like at PL: "I slept in class," he said. He wasn't the only one. A survey taken in 1984 at a high school baseball power in Tokyo revealed that nearly two-thirds of the players never did any homework. (When a journalist asked graduating phenom Tatsunori Hara what his major would be in college, Hara reportedly replied, "Major . . . what's that?")

But Kobayakawa's somnabulence in class didn't hurt him. Upon graduating from PL, he entered Hosei, a top baseball university, where he starred for four years and was then drafted by the Carp, who paid him a huge signing bonus. Hara, who went to Tokai, got an even bigger one from the Giants.

There are lots of schools like PL in Japan. There are also lots of the other kind. Yokohama Shogyo Koko has been to Koshien several times (albeit without winning a championship). Their manager, a cordial, friendly bookkeeping teacher named Fumio Furuya, is an enlightened despot. He does not require his boys to shave their heads or live in a dormitory. He has never hit any of his players and his practices last only two hours a day—though the team works out nearly every day of the year. Furuya's unique system of training encourages first-year students to razz the third-year students in practice. Y-Ko, as it is called, plays seventy games a year and has tight academic eligibility requirements.

Then there are institutions like Rakusei Koko, a Catholic high school nestled in a corner of Kyoto, the ancient capital of Japan, not far from the sleepy waters of the Kamo River. Rakusei, with a student body of eight hundred, is highly ranked academically and regularly sends graduates to the top universities in Japan.

The baseball budget there is minuscule. The twenty-two players on the team share a tiny field with the soccer squad. They practice, using patched and restitched balls, an average of two hours a day from January to December, except during exam periods. The pitchers throw in practice an average of two hundred pitches a day, three days out of four. Their schedule calls for forty games a year.

Rakusei manager Fumio Nishino, a warm-faced man in his late forties, eschews the one-thousand-fungo drill, all-night sessions, and other forms of brutality. His players are models of deportment—when visitors come to the field, they immediately stop whatever they are doing, remove their caps, and cry out, *"Irrashai!"* (Welcome!)

But Rakusei has never been to Koshien.

The closest manager Nishino ever came was a 1–0 loss in the regional finals of 1987. That was the year he had a big right-handed pitcher with a blazing fastball, a wide-breaking curve, and an ERA of under 1.00.

"My players cried after the game," said Nishino. "And so did I. It had always been my dream to go to Koshien, but it is very difficult. It is very rare that a small baseball club like ours can ever make it."

There have been compensations, however. Scouts from the mighty Tokyo Giants came around to recruit the 1987 ace but the boy said he was not interested in turning pro. "I'm going to Todai," he declared, referring to Japan's most elite university.

Such moments made Nishino proud he was a Rakusei man.

◈   ◈   ◈

Game time. PL Gakuen's first-round opponent in the 1987 summer tournament is Chuo High from Gumma—a lesser light on the teen baseball scene. Outside the stadium, under a hazy blue sky and withering noon heat, the PL players await the signal to enter. Some are stretching, others are running in place. Everyone looks confident, like Mike Tyson waiting to enter the ring.

Nearby, the PL cheering section, several hundred students strong and supplemented by the forty-five members of the baseball squad who did not earn a spot on the first team, is going through its own pregame warmups: fifteen minutes of calisthenics, then fifteen minutes of yelling practice. Wearing black school uniforms and white headbands on their shaven skulls inscribed with the Rising Sun and the word *hissho* (desperate victory), they look as formidable as the ballplayers and in fact have practiced almost as hard. Those chosen for the PL *oendan* have passed tryouts in which they were required to yell for several consecutive hours.

Koshien is serious business. The *oendan* of one school from the chilly climes of northern Hokkaido prepared for an appearance in Koshien by practicing for several days inside a vinyl tent where the temperature was 101 degrees.

Reminders of the importance of spirit are seen everywhere. In the souvenir stands by the main and rear gates, hawkers peddle baseballs with the word *konjo* (spirit) painted on them with a fine calligraphy brush, as well as banners urging *nekyu* (Passionate Baseball) and flags carrying Suishu Tobita's famous motto, *ikkyu nyukon* (total concentration). The air is filled with the acrid odor of smoked fish from vending stalls under the stands.

The game starts slowly for PL. By the end of the fifth inning, Chuo is leading, 2–1. Everyone in the PL *oendan* is cheering lustily and with soldierly precision, as the PL band plays prewar military songs and Meiji Era music. Still the head cheerleader looks worried.

"You're not cheering loud enough," he yells. "You there, back row, third from right. Show some spirit."

He shoots his hands in the air in karate chopping motions, exhorting them to greater heights. The roar increases. It is almost painful to listen to.

"I still can't hear you!" he screams. "Give me more!"

Some reporters in the area clap their hands over their ears.

Miniskirted majorettes prance in the aisles, kicking their legs high. Photographers surreptitiously station themselves at the base of the stands, their cameras angled at the girls' crotches. Certain magazines in Japan will pay several hundred dollars for the right kind of picture. Pubescent cheesecake is a favorite of the Japanese male.

"They're all virgins," explains one of the photographers, offhandedly. "At least I think they are. That's part of the appeal."

The federation had complained about such photos. It has asked the magazines concerned to respect the innocence and purity of the affair and not publish "indecent" pictures. No one seemed to pay attention.

"These games aren't as pure as everyone would like to think," said a big, bearded, deep-voiced man in his midthirties named Masayuki Tamaki, who has written several successful books on baseball. "There are high school baseball groupies, you know. It was harder in the days when all the teams stayed in communal-style Japanese *ryokan*. There was no privacy. Nowadays, many stay in regular hotel rooms. There are always girls milling around outside. These guys are big heroes. All a player has to do is wave from his window and someone will come up.

"Hotel proprietors say they find all sorts of interesting

things in the lavatory trash cans up by the players' rooms. Cigarette butts, beer cans. Even used condoms."

In the first row of the cheering section, the junior students make tea for the seniors. "That's another part of their education," says Tamaki. "They're studying to be adults and work in a corporation." He laughs.

Tamaki is an iconoclast—the Ochiai of Japanese sports journalism—who, among other things, writes satires on Japan's ongoing obsession with adolescent baseball. Once he was quoted in a magazine as saying that ballplayers at Koshien looked like prison inmates with their bowed heads and shaven skulls. The high school federation complained to the magazine's editor-in-chief.

Fifty rows up, the PL flag bearer holds the school flag aloft. The flag and the pole weigh fifteen pounds, yet he will stand at attention the entire nine innings. He has "spirit."

The cheering never stops. On offense, it is *kattobase* (slam it out). On defense, the yell changes to *gambare* (do your best). The energy level is astounding. The tempo picks up as PL comes to bat in the bottom of the sixth inning. The students are screaming so hard the cords in their necks stand out like steel cables. Their faces are purple, contorted in pain. Sweat flies from their brows. It is scorching hot: ninety-nine degrees at 2:30.

It is also polluted, Osaka being surrounded by a plethora of factories. Outside the stadium stands a permanent sign which reads, "Beware of Photochemical Smog." A student in the crowd collapses from the heat. Under the grandstand in the first-aid room, several people are being treated for heatstroke. Most of the press corps are down in the coffee shop under the stadium watching the game on TV in air-conditioned comfort.

A walk to the PL leadoff batter in the sixth is followed by the inevitable bunt, which is misplayed, leaving two runners on base. Many students in the *oendan* are clutching *mamori* (good luck charms), eyes closed, praying for a hit as they yell. The next batter steps up to the plate. He lines a single into left center field. A gift from the gods. The tying run crosses the plate.

"It gives me the creeps," says Tamaki.

The score is still tied in the PL half of the eighth as the first batter steps in. He screams at the pitcher—an animal-like "Aarrgh!"—to demonstrate that the time has come to get serious about the game. The cheering is more intense than ever—reverberating through the stadium—and so is the praying. The batter singles. So does the next man (on a bunt). And the next. A run comes in. Then another. Then two more. Then still another. Suddenly the game has turned into a rout.

Over on the Chuo side of the field, the large contingent of hometown supporters—local residents, town officials, mothers, and fathers, all wearing straw hats to ward off the heat—are despondent. Going to Koshien is about the biggest honor a school can bring to its town. It ranks with sending someone to Todai, or sending a man to the moon. Many Chuo supporters made the eight-hour trip to Osaka the night before on one of the many special trains Japan Railways rigs up. But now, their dreams of an upset at an end, they will have to turn around and go right back home again, barely before the two-week tournament has even started.

Most of the Chuo students and cheering section members are openly sobbing, oblivious to the NHK cameras zooming in on them. For them, it is a great tragedy. But the viewers at home will love it and Koshien's ratings will stay high.

The final score is 7–2. The Chuo players do their oblig-atory home plate bow, stand at attention as the PL School song is played, then rush down the line to thank their respective cheering sections. Then they race back to their dugout area, where they produce plastic bags and begin filling them with Koshien's sacred dirt, a memento of their one shining day in the summer sun. It is a ritual that has been repeated thousands of times in this park.

When the youths finally leave, they turn and bow toward center field, as they would at any park, really, but at Koshien, their bow is more reverential, because this stadium is a very special repository of the spirit—like a cathedral. One should pay it utmost respect.

In the interview area underneath the infield seats, the press crowds around the victors and the losers alike. It is said there are more reporters covering the Koshien tournament then there were for the last Tokyo Summit. The NHK cameras focus on the PL pitching ace, his head slyly bowed as he answers questions, his arm going un-iced. Then it is PL manager Nakamura's turn.

Nakamura is one of the better-paid managers in high school ball. His income is estimated to be near six figures, which is not unusual in big-time high school baseball. (Another highly paid manager, Tatsunori Hara's father, Mitsugu, was wooed from Kyūshū to Tokai High School for a reported 10 million yen a year. He now drives a Mercedes.) For years Nakamura was an assistant coach and before that he worked at Mitsubishi Caterpillar. These days all he does is manage the team . . . and win.

One day he will write a best-selling book on how to educate and motivate young people, as all other top high school managers have done. Perhaps he will draw the title from the motto of PL's baseball club, "The Way of Baseball is the Way of a Human Being."

Many players on the Chuo team are still sobbing openly, uncontrollably, their big chance at everlasting fame over.

"Suishu Tobita would be proud," exclaims one elderly magazine writer, eyeing the scene.

"Tobita who?" asks a young newspaper reporter, taking a sip from a plastic cup of Kirin beer.

The older man looks disgusted. "Get serious," he snaps. "You shouldn't be drinking beer at an event like this."

No one seems especially happy that PL has won, except those from PL, of course. The games at Koshien have been called daily morality plays, with their emphasis on fighting spirit and manners. But the lesson of today's play was, as usual, Might is Right. The Lions always eat the Christians. And certain types of schools finish last.

"Rooting for PL," says one fan, contemptuously, "is like rooting for a professional team against amateurs. PL should be forced to play in the Central League."

According to High School Baseball Federation officials, the ultimate purpose of this great national preoccupation is to produce good citizens through baseball. Yet many dispassionate critics wonder if that is what is really happening.

They bemoan the increasing commercialization of high school ball and the glitzy show biz atmosphere that has invaded the games. "Koshien is not an athletic meet," said one writer, "it is a social event." Said another writer, after witnessing the unnerving sight of a losing team sobbing en masse before equally distraught supporters, "This isn't sportsmanship. It's group hysteria."

Japanese high school baseball stars are perhaps the best players in the world for their age group and usually have little difficulty downing their American counterparts (who practice far less but perhaps enjoy the game more). Japanese critics, however, worry the Koshien mentality is producing a continuous line of passive robots, a charge that is frequently made in regard to the Japanese system of education as a whole, with its emphasis on rote learning, corporal punishment, and blind obedience to dogmatic rules.

The story is told of a young pitcher who entered Waseda University from a high school where he had undergone extremely rigorous training. In practice one day, he complained to fellow players of abdominal pains. The manager overheard him and asked, "Tell me, where exactly does it hurt?"

The youth stood up straight and barked, *"Hai!"* (Yes; Yes, sir), but said nothing more. The manager asked again. Once more the boy shouted *"Hai!"* and stood at rigid, silent attention.

Several times more the manager tried, but all he could get was the same robotlike response. Finally, he gave up and sent the boy to the school doctor. He found out later that the youth had been taught in high school to respond as he had whenever the manager spoke. That had been his "education."

A system which stymies creativity and independent thinking is, some analysts say, one reason why Japanese baseball players fall behind their American counterparts in later years. Said columnist Kazuo Chujo, "Rigid training can produce results, but the results don't last because the players are merely following orders and not developing their own styles. No amount of coaching or teaching can make a passive athlete rise to great heights. But too many Japanese fail to realize this simple fact. The Japanese must liberate baseball from the realm of education and elevate it to that of fun and games."

Author Tomomi Muramatsu is among those who see something *more* sinister in the Koshien phenomenon. Wrote Muramatsu (in the *Asahi Shimbun,* no less), upon watching rows of unsmiling youths file stiff-backed into the stadium for the opening ceremony—column after column of pumping legs and swinging arms, in endless, military-perfect duplication, "They remind me of Hitler's Brownshirts at a gathering of Nazis."

The steely discipline and references to divine attributes also disturb some foreigners, looking for signs of resurgent Japanese militarism. Americans were particularly alarmed when surveys taken at the height of U.S.-Japan trade friction revealed that a majority of Japanese high school students believed the United States would be their most likely opponent in the event of a war.

Referring to the apparent xenophobic implications of the survey, Shoichi Suzuki, a twenty-five-year-old reporter for the weekly *Gendai*, said, "I don't think there's much to worry about. . . . Older people in their thirties and forties might find the Koshien spirit admirable, but among young Japanese, opinion is divided. Lots of young people think the whole thing is really stupid. They don't think about the past or draw any significance from it. Koshien is just there."

Atsushi Imamura, a thirty-two-year-old editor for the weekly *Bunshun,* was even more emphatic: "They're just skinheads—out of step with the times. They don't represent modern Japan at all."

Perhaps, but Koshien has left a powerful influence which is felt in many areas of Japanese society. As the parents of an eleven-year-old boy from Chiba named Jiro can attest.

Little Jiro liked to play softball. And on a very hot day in July of 1986, he showed up for a game with the rest of his school's team in Funabashi, Chiba, near Tokyo.

The boys' pregame workout alone would have exhausted most adults. It consisted of twenty 160-yard dashes, a 2-mile run, a Japanese running drill in which players run back and forth in front of a coach at full speed for several minutes trying to catch a ball tossed up in the air, and a fielding session of one hundred ground balls. Jiro and the other boys were not allowed to drink water during practice.

This was, according to the weekly *Asahi Journal,* which wrote an article about the event, a standard pregame workout for any young boys' ball team.

Jiro's team lost the game, so the manager ordered a postgame workout. This one consisted of ten 30-yard dashes, ten 60-yard dashes, ten laps around the field (310 yards), ten sprints up and down the stadium stairs, and, finally, three 60-yard dashes to wrap it all up.

It was, said the *Asahi Journal* again, not an unusual postgame workout for a young boys' ball team.

It was estimated that the boys ran a total of ten miles all told and when it was all over, little Jiro, who had apparently been in good health, keeled over and died of heart failure.

Jiro's school eventually paid 40 million yen in consolation money to Jiro's parents, who filed a lawsuit anyway. They didn't think much of the coach or the school's philosophy.

⚾ ⚾ ⚾

Masayuki Tamaki thinks his countrymen are attracted to baseball because they perceive it as the ultimate macho sport. He became convinced of that after he wrote a magazine article in which he made practical suggestions for turning the Koshien tournament into a less brutal experience for those involved.

He suggested holding the tourney in October when it is not so hot, or moving the locale to Hokkaido where summers are cool, as a way of avoiding the sauna bath heat of Osaka in August. He also proposed scheduling games every other day so that ace pitchers would not have to go through the arm-wrenching ordeal of pitching nine-inning games several days in a row.

His piece was met with overwhelming silence.

From this, Tamaki concluded that the Japanese, no matter what they might say to the contrary, were hopelessly addicted to the tournament the way it was. To change it would mean that Koshien would no longer be the modern manhood rite—in which fighting spirit is pitted against adversity—that had attracted people in the first place.

"Koshien is a big festival," said Tamaki. "It's like *gion*, or *obon*. Only it's dedicated to spirit and guts."

12

Foreign Devils

We're mercenaries, pure and simple. Our job is to do well and let the Japanese players have the glory and take the blame when things go bad.

Leon Lee

It really seemed to me that the Japanese didn't want us around. And that's about the way it was. We were there for one thing, to make a contribution to the club. As far as I was concerned, my job was to play baseball, make my money, and go home.

Gail Hopkins
ex-Hiroshima Carp

Japan is like a big club. It's like Club Med, if you can imagine that. Membership is based on one's Japaneseness, and gaijin *can only be guest members.*

Yoshiki Nishiyama
magazine editor

The old isolationist thinking is still prevalent here. Gaijin *are useful as scapegoats whenever things go wrong. But they are not really welcomed by the baseball establishment.*

Takenori Emoto
author

The Japanese either kiss your feet or sit on your face.

Kennichi Takemura
critic

You're an outcast no matter what you do. You go 5-for-5 and you're ignored. You go 0-for-5 and it's, "Fuck you. Yankee go home."

Warren Cromartie

October 1987. He sat there in the cramped and crowded dining room at Kawasaki Stadium, surrounded by buckwheat noodle–slurping teammates, his six-foot-one-inch, 200-pound frame dwarfing all but two or three of them. He had always marveled at how they would go out and run themselves silly for two hours, then come in and gorge themselves with *soba* just before a game. It was one of the many things he still didn't understand about Japan.

For eleven years now, American Leron Lee had been coming to this decrepit park redolent of linament and soy sauce and other stronger odors. (The Kawasaki team toilet had only recently been used as a set in a prison movie. Its squalor, said one screen-writer, was magnificent.) He had endured the park, its perpetually empty stands, and the haze of industrial smog that constantly engulfed it, to become one of the best baseball players in the history of the Japanese game—as well as one of its least-recognized stars.

Since joining the Lotte Orions in 1977, Lee, a left-handed outfielder–designated hitter, had won every major batting title there was to win. He had the highest career batting average of any player to play the game in

Japan: .320. He had hit .300 for ten consecutive seasons. He also had more hits (1,579), more home runs (283), and more RBIs (912) than any other foreigner.

Warren Cromartie once called him the Godfather of the *Gaijin*—the one everyone turned to for advice. Now, at age thirty-nine, he had had his first bad year. There had been injuries, his average had dropped to .272, his home runs to 9. Lotte's grim-faced rookie manager, Michiyo Aritoh, had made it clear there was no room for Lee in his future plans.

Tonight would be his last game. Everyone knew it. But there would be no farewell ceremony, no Leron Lee Day, no one from the front office to come down before the game to say thanks for all the memories. The announcement of his release would not be made until later, when, hopefully, Lee would be out of the country and an unpleasant confrontation would be avoided.

It was typical, he thought, of the way he had been treated throughout his entire stay. In his first season, he had won the home run and RBI titles, with 34 and 109, respectively, barely missing out in the batting average category. A Lotte executive had said the team might have won the pennant if only Lee had won the Triple Crown.

Lee won a batting title in 1980, to become at the time only the fifth American in the history of the Japanese game to do so. But that too had been a distasteful experience. "Only five people in the Lotte organization congratulated me," he said. "One was my brother Leon, who also played on the team; another was my interpreter. The following spring when they gave me my silver bat for being the batting champion, they did it in the clubhouse. No presentation at home plate in front of the fans. They just handed it to me. They seemed ashamed."

Over the years, team posters for Lotte games frequently omitted Lee's name in order to stress the Japaneseness of the team. There were autograph parties for the Japanese Orion stars on the team, but never for Lee. "I guess I'm what you'd call a necessary evil," he said.

Perhaps the biggest blow came when a Tokyo advertising executive told Lee flatly that Japanese did not want black role models. Blonds, maybe. But no blacks, unless you were Carl Lewis or Mike Tyson. In all his years in Japan, Lee had no commercial endorsements. Unlike other players of his stature, he had no equipment contracts either. He even had to buy his own bats.

Not that he didn't have his moments. When the Orions won a first-half pennant in 1980 (the Pacific League employed a split-season format from 1973 to 1981), stadium police had to rescue him from a delirious mob that stormed the field. At the end of that year, Kawasaki fans chose him "Mr. Orion" in a season-end poll and he and his brother Leon (who had joined the team in 1978) recorded a song, "Baseball Boogie." The tune reached number 12 on the Japanese charts.

That was the year the great Kawakami had come out to the ballpark to meet Lee, the great American hitter. They stood there in front of the dugout, with all the reporters looking on, and the avuncular Kawakami told Lee that as a player, standing in the batter's box, he had been able to see the heart of the ball as it came hurtling toward him at eighty-five miles per hour. Lee replied that that was interesting, because he could too. Kawakami liked that. Then Kawakami said that the ball used to stop for him also, just before he swung his bat. And Lee asked why he thought that was so.

Kawakami smiled . . . shrugged . . . and walked away. A star like Lee already knew the answer.

Far too often, however, Lee felt like the outsider that he was. There was the time he had struck out to end a ninth-inning rally and an irate, very inebriated fan somehow worked his way through to the row of flimsy wire mesh cubbyholes that served as the Orion locker room.

"Ree *bakayaro!*" (Lee, you stupid SOB!) he yelled several times. He stood there and kept yelling—and Lee's teammates did nothing. They all stared awkwardly, embarrassed by the behavior of a fellow Japanese, until finally, Lee himself escorted the man out. To Lee, the incident seemed to symbolize his career.

He knew Japan was not a bed of lotus blossoms. An unassuming, rather taciturn man, Lee was deeply proud of what he had done there. On good days, he rated Lotte the equal of a major league second-division team. On bad days, only Triple A. But with the different pitching and strike zones and inconsistent umpires, to succeed a man had to change his swing, his way of thinking, and his whole style of play to succeed. Hell, there was no guarantee that even Pete Rose could have made it in Japan.

Lee had always considered himself as good as many major league name players, but felt that he had never been given a decent opportunity to demonstrate his ability. "In every stretch I played regularly in the majors," he said, "I hit .300. I did it at St. Louis and at Cleveland, but I was always filling in for a starter and eventually I'd wind up back on the bench pinch-hitting and my average would fall. At San Diego I had an argument with Don Zimmer in my capacity as player representative and wound up getting traded. It seemed I was always in the wrong place at the wrong time."

Jim Lefebvre, who had scouted Lee for Lotte, said, "Both Lee and his brother had the potential to be major league stars. But sometimes you don't get the chance to show what you can do. Sometimes, that's the way it goes in baseball."

Lee liked Japan. He had married a Japanese woman, a translator he had met in Tokyo, and he had two daughters by her. He wasn't crazy about the idea of putting his girls through the Japanese school system, given the exam hells and the custom of requiring young children to wear short pants to school even in the dead of winter as a means of strengthening their spirit. Nor did he care for the patronizing Japanese attitude toward those with mixed blood, especially black mixed blood. But, all in all, there were fewer hassles. People traveled through life at a slower speed. The society was well organized. It was safe and relatively drug-free. The taxis and subways were immaculate. More important, he had worked his salary up to $600,000 a year and had put $2 million in the bank.

The Japanese liked Lee well enough, too. They thought he and his brother comported themselves with dignity and restraint. But they did not treat him like a star and that bothered him the most. He wanted the perks that were supposed to accrue from having the highest lifetime batting average in the Japanese game. He wanted the press to solicit his opinions as they did all the other big Japanese stars. He wanted to be asked to manage or coach when he retired, or at least have his own newspaper column like Kawakami and Koji Yamamoto. But Japan was not disposed to provide any of that for him.

"I can't believe this," he said, his voice dripping bitterness. "You don't hit .320 for ten years and then get shoved aside. You don't treat a guy that way."

Aahhh, but they did. His brother Leon, a first baseman from the Cardinal chain, had hit an impressive .308 with 268 home runs over ten years in Japan, including a season in 1980 when he hit 41 homers and batted .340. He was strong as a sumo wrestler and could hit the ball five hundred feet. But Lotte had shipped him to the Taiyo Whales in 1983 when a young player named Ochiai began to show his stuff. Leon went on to have three good years with Taiyo; he set a new Central League record for RBIs in one game (10) and hit a ball completely out of Yokohama Stadium. But after batting .303 with 31 homers and 110 RBIs in 1985, he was released. Whales manager Sadaaki Kondo said Leon didn't hit when the team really needed him to.

Leon and Leron, however, thought they knew the real reason. The Whales had finished low in the standings and someone had to take the blame. It was always easier in harmony-conscious Japan to point the finger at the *gaijin*. That way no one would be upset. No one that counted, that is.

Next, Leon signed on with the Yakult Swallows. In 1986, he hit 34 homers and batted .319 and the year after that, playing alongside Horner, he hit .300 with 22 homers. Again he was released. The Swallows signed Doug DeCinces and Terry Harper, and then Bob Gibson, who joined the team when Harper did not pan out.

Lee hated the way the Japanese fawned over any American player with a reputation in the big leagues and ignored people like him and his brother who consistently compiled better stats than almost anyone. It was disgusting, he thought, the way the Swallows had rolled out the red carpet for Bob Horner. When Horner's parents visited Japan in the summer of 1987, the front office had supplied them with an interpreter and had paid the air freight back to Dallas for all the souvenirs, gifts, and other things they wound up buying. No one had ever done anything like that for the Lee, and his debut in Japan had been even more striking than Horner's: 20 home runs in his first forty games.

Lee's position on Lotte had begun to deteriorate when Lotte's longtime first baseman and captain Michiyo Aritoh was appointed manager. Aritoh ran a tightly disciplined ship. He put an end to the special treatment Lee had received over the years from other managers which included first-class hotels on the road and carte blanche in practice. Lee would henceforth be compelled to act like everyone else, he declared. At an early spring workout, Lee took his BP, did his running, and when he was finished, he picked up his gear and started to go home, as he had always done.

"You can't leave now," snapped one of Aritoh's new

coaches, "You'll disturb the team's harmony." So with nothing else to do, Lee spent the rest of the afternoon sitting on the bench watching the reserves sweat and groan.

A hip injury kept Lee out of action for several weeks during the middle of the season. The team sank in the standings and when he came back, Aritoh used him sparingly. In the middle of one game, Aritoh took him out for a pinch hitter. Lee, insulted, had a rare attack of temper and threw his bat in anger at the bench. For this, Aritoh fined him a million yen and forced him to apologize in front of the entire team for upsetting its *wa*.

Lee felt that perhaps a heart-to-heart talk could have helped matters, but this was Japan and managers did not usually have heart-to-heart talks with their players. Especially a manager like Aritoh.

"He hasn't talked to me my entire career," said Lee, "I've been on the same team with this man for eleven years. I've traveled with him. I batted next to him in the lineup, but I've never spent a social evening with him. After all these years, I don't even know who he is."

The front office had been no help. The Lotte Orions were run by people from Lotte Gum, the parent company, who did not know much about baseball. Once Lee was introduced to a newly appointed club executive and the man said, "Oh, I know you. I've seen you on TV once or twice." Another team official once asked Lee what a batting average of .300 meant.

In 1986, he was hitting .321 with ten games left and the general manager told him that the remainder of the season would be a "test" for Lee to see if he could still play baseball. If he did well, then they would bring him back another year. Lee hit 6 homers and drove in 18 runs in those ten games to finish with .331, 31 homers, and 94 RBIs. He won a new contract, but sometimes he wondered about his employers. He really did.

"Playing in Japan," he said, "is a real test of what you

have inside. You learn the meaning of the Japanese word *gaman* (forbearance) when you live here."

Lee spent his last evening in a Japanese uniform thinking about *gaman* and sitting on the bench. The stadium was a chilly fifty-five degrees. The sparse crowd watched halfheartedly as the Lotte cheerleaders, four men wearing brightly colored coats bearing the Orions crest, rhythmically waved banners and chanted "Gooooo—goooo—gooooo." Every now and then a diminutive miniskirted girl scurried out to hand the plate umpire some new balls. Occasionally, someone yelled Lee's name.

He sat there shivering, staring at the neon-lit Sapporo Beer sign winking atop the left field stands in the October night. He thought he might be asked to pinch-hit, at least. But Aritoh never looked his way. Not even with the score tied 3–3 in the tenth inning. The Orions scored a *sayonara* run without Lee's help amidst a din of pounding *taiko* drums, shrieking whistles, and tooting horns. And thus did one of the most sparkling careers in Japanese baseball come to an end.

In the locker room, Lee's teammates packed their gear for autumn camp. A couple of them stopped by his cubicle to say goodbye. A few days later Lotte officially informed the baseball world of Lee's release.

Sometime that winter, the team announced the signing of Bill Madlock, the thirty-seven-year-old four-time batting champion, to a million-dollar contract and set about building him a thirty-thousand-dollar private dressing room. They also made arrangements to put Madlock up at the plushest hotels available when the Orions went on the road. Said Aritoh of his new *gaijin*, "Madlock is a big leaguer." (Madlock finished the 1988 season with a .263 average, 19 home runs, and 61 RBIs.)

   ♗ ♗ ♗

Some history: In 1639, the Japanese Tokugawa shogunate, fearing further Christian incursion into Japan, banned visits by Europeans. This was the so-called *sakoku* or "closed country" policy which greatly limited contact with foreigners—or foreign devils as they were also known—and contributed to Japan's self-image of purity and homogeneity in the ensuing years.

According to the eminent sociologist Chie Nakane, this act of exclusionism was strengthened in the nineteenth century by a sharp increase in population and a rise in land prices. There was also a perspective, she wrote, that "one's share would be lessened if outsiders became members of the community. . . . The close social and structural bonds of a community were like finely woven cloth. Relations among groups and communities were similarly fixed, leaving no room for newcomers."

Sakoku helped keep the Tokugawa shogunate in power and the Japanese isolated from the rest of the world until 1853, when American Commodore William Perry and his Black Ships forced Japan to open its ports and join the world's community of nations.

Since then, Japanese have lived with foreigners in their midst, but not always with the greatest enthusiasm. A survey conducted by the Japanese government in 1981 revealed that 64 percent of the Japanese did not wish to associate with foreigners. That figure dropped to 53 percent in 1988 amidst a government campaign to internationalize the country.

But Japanese ambivalence toward outsiders could still be seen in many ways. Many Tokyo real estate agents still refused to deal with apartment-hunting foreigners, and more than one Tokyo night club had a "Japanese only" policy.

For most Japanese, the word *gaijin* referred to North American and European Caucasians (blacks were usually described by the term *kokujin* "black person"), but not other Asians whom they have historically viewed with somewhat less respect than fair-skinned people. In 1988, the 675,000 or so Korean residents of Japan who were born and raised in Japan were still being fingerprinted, forced to carry special alien registration cards, and were otherwise discriminated against.

In Japanese baseball, many of the great stars have been indigenous Koreans who have taken Japanese names. One is Isao Harimoto, born and raised in Hiroshima, the only man in the Japanese game with 3,000 hits. Another is 400-game winner Masaichi Kaneda.

But nobody dwells much on this because Harimoto and the others can be conveniently lumped under the general rubric of products Made in Japan. It is the presence of the big, physically different *gaijin* that causes problems.

Americans have played in Japan ever since the prewar era when Harris McGalliard, a catcher from the Sacramento Solons of the Pacific Coast League, won a Fall MVP award in 1937 (the old prewar Nihon League as it was called played spring and fall seasons). In the postwar Americanization of Japan, a number of minor leaguers from the U.S. played there successfully (including many *nisei*) while retread major leaguers like Don Newcombe and Larry Doby started the *Dai-reega* (big-leaguer) era in the early 1960s.

Over the years, however, protectionism has frequently reared its ugly head. In 1963, the allowance of three *gaijin* per team was reduced to two and league officials were urging teams to win without relying on foreign imports (the rule was later amended to allow a third foreigner on the farm team). Although no such rule has ever existed in the U.S. where Latin-American players have been a significant force, Japanese officials have contended such restrictions were necessary to foster development of local talent.

In the fall of 1982, at a time of escalating trade friction between the U.S. and Japan (and when even Prime Minister Yasuhiro Nakasone was urging his fellow citizens to buy, buy American), Japanese baseball commissioner Takezo Shimoda was flatly telling reporters that foreigners just didn't belong in the game. "The *gaijin* are overpaid, underproductive, and generally annoying," he said, adding that their higher salaries "demoralized" the Japanese player.

The success ratio of the *gaijin* was, in fact, about 50 percent. It indeed took a certain type of person to make it in Japan, to cope with the different style of play as well as the cultural, environmental, and other psychological differences.

That there were people like Leron Lee who performed well, who were not outrageously overpaid, and who behaved like civilized human beings did not seem to matter to Shimoda. Nor did it matter that approximately a quarter of all players who had hit over .300 with 30 home runs in a single season up until then had been Americans, or the fact that Americans had made significant contributions to nearly every pennant-winning team since the end of the pure-blooded Giants era.

It was an emotional argument but all the leading figures in the game seemed to agree with a writer for the *Sankei Shimbun,* a major daily, who wrote a baseball series entitled "Time of Peril." The series called for a total ban on foreign players—"What the Japanese fans really want to see is a big home run by a Japanese star, not a *gaijin.*"

Commissioner Shimoda, a former ambassador to the United States who had a curious penchant for being undiplomatic, made the rounds of all the camps in February 1983, exhorting players to stop depending on their foreign teammates in games. This startled Reggie Smith, who was in the audience for Shimoda's speech at the Giants training facility in Kyushu.

"After all," said Shimoda, getting down to the heart of the matter, "it is only natural that Japanese baseball be played by Japanese alone as the gap between the respective levels of the Japan and the American games narrows. Besides, Japanese baseball will never be considered first rate as long as there are former major leaguers no longer wanted in their own countries in key spots in the Japanese lineup."

Americans in Japan at the time drew parallels with Japan's foreign trade policy. Added Reggie Smith, "I can't imagine any major league team rejecting a potential star because of where he comes from. Look at Fernando Valenzuela. He's a big idol in the States, but he's Mexican. To ban foreigners is discrimination pure and simple."

An *Asahi Shimbun* reporter huffily responded to these charges by saying, "The problem is that Americans, being a multiethnic, diverse group of people, can't appreciate the feelings of a homogenous people with special common characteristics like the Japanese."

Smith wondered if that was why he and other Americans could not understand the rule limiting *gaijin* participation in the mid-season All-Star games to two foreigners per side. In 1980, Tony Solaita, who would hit 44 home runs that year, was the overwhelming choice of the fans for starting first baseman in All-Star fan balloting. But he couldn't play because two other Americans had also been voted in. In mid-1985, the leading hitter in the Pacific League, Dick Davis, watched the All-Star game at home on TV simply because he was a foreigner and there was no room for him.[1]

In 1986, the *Asahi Shimbun* published the results of a survey that asked the question, Are foreigners necessary? Of those polled, 56 percent of the fans said yes. But only 10 percent of the players, four of the twelve club owners,

---

1. The rule was revised to the effect that any number of foreigners could be voted in, but that only three could be in the lineup at any given time. If none were voted in, only two could be chosen as reserves.

and none of the managers agreed. The big complaint was not that foreigners cost too much money or deprived younger players of a spot on a team, or even that they caused too much trouble. It was simply a delphic, "Japanese-only teams are ideal."

In 1987, the new commissioner of Japanese baseball, Juhei Takeuchi, a doddering seventy-eight, added his two-yen worth about the signing of Bob Horner in a newspaper interview: "If Japanese baseball keeps trying to acquire high-priced free agents, we will be thrown into chaos. There isn't much we can learn from foreigners anymore and it's time we stopped trying. Is there any foreign player who has ever taught the Japanese anything of value?

"Besides, there are too many troublemakers among foreigners. In the future, pure-blooded baseball is ideal. We have to have a real World Series in the future between the U.S. and Japan. We can't do that with foreign players here."

Ⓦ ⓌⓌ ⓌⓌ

The centuries-old inbred exclusion mentality of the Japanese could take many forms, as a player named Charlie Manuel would attest. Manuel had come up through the Minnesota Twins farm chain and was the kind of player, Whitey Herzog once said, who was capable of hitting .300 with 15 to 20 home runs if he played regularly in the major leagues. But a broken ankle robbed Manuel of a shot at a starting outfielder's job and he bounced around until, in 1976, at age thirty-two, he found himself in Japan with the Yakult Swallows.

Manuel was an American original—a fun-loving free spirit who could drink all night and still play hard the next day. An American professional wrestler named Richard Bayer who billed himself as "The Destroyer" recalled drinking with Manuel in Roppongi once until eight o'clock in the morning. The Destroyer then went home to sleep while Manuel went to have another beer and report for a day game at Korakuen, where he hit two home runs and fell asleep on the bench between at-bats.

With this kind of background, no player could have been more ill-suited to the Swallows in 1977 when Tatsuro Hiroka, the hard and haughty Iron Shogun, took over as manager. The two clashed immediately. Hiroka complained that Manuel did not shine his baseball shoes before every game, that he took too much time getting into the batter's box, and that Manuel's habit of walking around in a little circle at his right field position and gazing up at the stands between pitches "did not look good."

Hiroka even complained about Manuel's diet of hamburgers, steak, and pizza. Once he gave him a thermos of turtle soup and ordered him to drink it for his health. "I'm thirty-four years old," Manuel grumbled, "and I figure I'm old enough to decide what to eat and whether or not I should shine my shoes for a baseball game."

Manuel and Hiroka nearly came to blows one evening when Hiroka removed him from a game for making an error. Manuel was particularly enraged not only because fifty thousand fans and a nationwide TV audience had been watching, but also because Hiroka made what seemed to be a disparaging remark to him upon his return to the bench. Dropping his glove, Manuel grabbed his interpreter, Luigi Nakajima, by the lapels and growled, "Tell me what he said or I'll punch your lights out." Fortunately, for Nakajima, and perhaps Hiroka, coaches intervened and prevented a fistfight.

Manuel combined the ridiculous and the sublime all in one player. His fielding bordered on the atrocious, but he was a fearsome hitter. He had gained weight in Japan, and at six feet three inches and 200 pounds, he could drive the ball farther than ever before. After an injury-filled year in 1976 in which he managed only 11 home runs, he hit .316

in 1977, with 42 home runs and 97 RBIs (in just 100 games). The following year he hit .312 with 39 homers and 97 RBIs, as the Swallows won the pennant and the Japan Series. He could conceivably have been chosen the 1978 CL MVP. But Manuel, in a "quality control" move, was traded to the Kintetsu Buffaloes in the other league instead.

Manuel found the Buffaloes a breath of fresh air. Since the Pacific League used the designated hitter rule, he was relieved of the pressures of playing defense. More important, his manager, silver-haired Yukio Nishimoto, liked him and left him alone. As a result, Manuel went absolutely berserk at the plate. He clobbered 24 home runs in the first eight weeks of the 1979 season, leading the Buffaloes, who had never won a pennant, into first place.

The press began calling him *Akaoni* (the Red Devil), as much for the fear he put into the hearts of opposing pitchers as for the swatch of red hair on his head.

Then the opposition found a way to stop him. One afternoon in early June, Manuel stood in the batter's box at Fudidera Stadium as shadows gripped the field and took a fastball to the face that dropped him to his knees and sent blood spurting from his mouth. Chuck was rushed to the hospital where it was found that his jaw was broken clean through in six separate places.

Doctors performed an operation lasting several hours to repair his mangled face. Because Manuel wore an upper bridge (playing Class A ball in Albuquerque in 1967, pitcher Jerry Reuss had hit him in the mouth with a fastball that fractured his upper jaw, broke his nose, cut his mouth, and knocked ten teeth out) there was nothing to wire together. To keep his jaw in one piece, doctors put three steel plates in his head, removing the nerves from the affected area.

The man who had thrown the beanball, pitcher Soroku Yagisawa of the Lotte Orions, swore it was an accident. Lotte manager Kazuhiro Yamauchi said that Manuel probably was not concentrating. Another coach remarked that Manuel's technique at getting out of the way was poor.

Manuel, however, was certain it had been intentional and said as much to anyone who would listen.

I stand way away from the plate. I'm tall and I stand erect in the batter's box. The ball didn't slip. Yagisawa is a veteran pitcher and his control is too good. When he hit me in the jaw, he didn't come off the mound. I couldn't breathe and he just turned away and started playing catch with one of the infielders like it was no big thing. When I left the field, I turned and pointed at him and said, "I'll get you." He just grinned at me and tipped his cap.

Besides, the day before in pregame practice Haku, the left fielder of Lotte, came over and said, "Watch out, we're going to 'deadball' you." He laughed. I laughed. I thought he was joking.

Then in the game that day, Murata threw a ball behind my head. When I talked to him the next day, he didn't say he was sorry. He didn't say it was an accident. All he said was, "You are a home run king. You hit a big home run off me in Kawasaki."

The Japanese don't throw at each other that much. But they watch U.S. baseball on TV and they see beanballs and they think it's the American way, that it's okay for them to throw at a *gaijin*. What they don't understand is that it is part of our code of behavior for the batter to retaliate.

The beaning did not draw a great deal of attention in the Japanese press, nor did Manuel receive a great deal of sympathy. Most sports papers carried the story of his "unfortunate accident" on the second or third pages of their editions, making the activities of the Giants, as usual, the top story.

One party, however, took Manuel's side: A columnist

named Morse Saito, who wrote a scathing piece in the English-language *Mainichi Daily News*. It is excerpted below:

BUSH LEAGUE

Japanese baseball has proven itself bush. It is by no means major league. . . .

Charles Manuel was hit in the face by one of Japan's leading control pitchers. The brushback pitch is part of a pitcher's livelihood. But to the head? Manuel was rushed to the hospital and underwent a five-hour major operation. This was major league treatment.

The NHK sportscaster spread much light when he excused the pitcher Soroku Yagisawa by almost partly blaming Manuel because he had once been hit in the teeth in America by a pitched ball. Furthermore, the NHK sportscaster never mentioned the Japanese pitcher. After all, the local product must be protected from foreigners.

Earlier, Manuel was about to break Japanese baseball history by hitting 16 homers in one month. Since it would be a disgrace for a foreigner to hold this record, Manuel was constantly walked. That is baseball. However, such walks are part of the game only if it is to prevent your side from losing. In Manuel's case, they walked him partly because he was a foreigner. That is bush.

No pitcher would dare throw at a top Japanese batter's head. Try it on Oh or Kakefu and half the stands would soon be on the mound, pounding the pitcher. Foreigners? They are different. They are tough.

Japanese baseball limits each club to two foreign players. This quota will forever assure that the local product will never be major league. It is typical of protectionist thinking: keep out the imports and nurture the locals. The goal is not to present the best baseball possible. It is, first of all, to protect the weaker and inferior Japanese. Personally, I know many Japanese ballplayers who could make it anywhere in the world. The protectionists suffer from an inferiority complex.

This complex is what leads to the racist attempts to justify throwing at Charles Manuel's face. The psychologically more mature Japanese are shocked and regret that pitch. There is no justification for it.

The pitch at Manuel was a bush thing. It almost ranks with the ugliness of honorary white status given Japanese businessmen in South Africa.

Manuel was discharged from the hospital in six weeks and said he wanted to play again immediately. Family and friends urged him not to. It was too soon, they said. He would still be paid his full salary by Kintetsu, even if he packed up and left. And no one would blame him. Besides, what if he got injured again? Doctors had told him that if he got hit in the face a third time, he could forget about eating normally for the rest of his life.

But Manuel insisted. His team needed him and he had too much going for him to give up. So he returned to action in early August wearing, while at bat, a custom-made football-style helmet with a special face guard. His teammate Chris Arnold was suitably impressed. "It was the most courageous thing I've ever seen a ballplayer do," he said. "He really shouldn't have come back so soon. He had no feeling in his mouth because he had no nerves. He'd eat, food would fall out, he'd drool, and not even know it. Anybody else who got hurt like that would never start playing again that quickly. Everybody was amazed and simply in awe of what he did."

After a few games back in the lineup, Manuel discarded the helmet because it obscured his vision. He went on to win the home run title with 37, carry the Buffaloes to a pennant, and become that rarity of rarities in Japan—an American hero, at least in Osaka. For a *gaijin* he had showed heart and fighting spirit and also magnanimity by not following through on his threat to commit homicide on Yagisawa (although he refused to shake Yagisawa's hand in a much publicized pregame meeting one day in August).

Manuel's galvanizing comeback generated more goodwill between Americans and Japanese than anyone since Joe DiMaggio brought Marilyn Monroe to Tokyo. He was an overwhelming choice for league MVP—the first foreigner so honored since Joe Stanka, an American who had won twenty-six games for the Nankai Hawks back in 1964.

Manuel could not have been more pleased, aside from the condition of his jaw (he faced a second operation to remove the steel plates). "Back in 1978, when Yakult won the pennant," he said, "there was a reception to celebrate. They called the top Japanese players up on the stage, but not me, even though I'd hit 39 home runs. I was standing there in the crowd with my son. It was embarrassing. When Kintetsu won the pennant, they rode me around the ballpark. They treated me great. I couldn't believe it. Nishimoto actually wanted me to be the leader."

The love affair with Manuel lasted until the following June when he left his team for a week to attend his son's high school graduation in Virginia. He had had a clause inserted in his contract the previous winter which allowed him to leave. Team executives had agreed, thinking perhaps that he would change his mind if the pennant race was really close. Well, with three weeks left in the first half of the season and the Buffaloes two games out of first place, Manuel left as promised. The fans, the press, and the Kintetsu front office never really forgave him for it.

Manuel returned to lead the Buffaloes to a second-half title and another pennant victory in the league playoffs. He hit .324 with 48 home runs and 129 RBIs. It was the best season an American had ever had in Japan up to that point. Yet the baseball writers voted the MVP to a rookie Nippon Ham pitcher who had won twenty-two games. They also voted the first- and second-half MVPs to someone other than Manuel and passed over him in every Player of the Month and Player of the Week award.

That winter when Manuel asked for a 15 percent raise in salary to $210,000, as well as a two-year contract, Kintetsu absolutely refused. Other Americans might demand and receive such deals, but by Buddha, no one on the Kintetsu Buffaloes was going to do it, especially someone who had deserted his team in midyear. The Buffaloes offered their *gaijin* ingrate a one-year $215,000 deal and told him take it or leave it. "Sign or we're going to release you," said the general manager.

When Manuel indignantly refused, Kintetsu—as promised—gave him his release. An incredulous Manuel went back to the Yakult Swallows, who now had a new manager and were willing to give him what he wanted. That settled, he suddenly began to show his age and after hitting .242 with 15 homers, he retired.

Ⓢ   Ⓢ   Ⓢ

Beanings aside, foreign players in Japan have long spoken of barriers, both visible and invisible, that effectively kept them from winning titles, breaking records, or otherwise gaining recognition. The most frequent targets of their complaints have been the umpires. As Leron Lee once said, "It's almost a natural law for a *gaijin* that the higher your batting average goes, the wider your strike zone becomes. The umpires will see to it because you're not supposed to outshine the Japanese."

The umpires have angrily denied favoritism one way or the other, but the estimable former catching star Katusya Nomura once confessed to a journalist that there was some truth to claims such as Lee made. "There are some umpires who haven't forgotten the war," he said. "Others don't like *gaijin* because they argue too much. Those umpires don't mind making life unpleasant for the foreign player."

Lee said his worst experience with the umpires came the year after he won the batting title in 1980.

> After my first month, I was hitting about .158 or something like that. Everything that even came close to the strike zone was a strike. So I rode back from Sendai on the train one day with the league PR director, Pancho Ito, and I complained to him. I said, "Look, if that's the way you're going to treat us, then why not just send us back? Because this is really bad."
>
> So Pancho got off at Tokyo and I went on to Osaka. And that very next game, I was at bat and the pitcher threw three straight pitches—all called balls, which was strange. And the umpire bent over and swept off home plate, which was even stranger, because they never do that with a *gaijin* player. There can be so much dirt on the plate that you can't even see it, but the umpires won't make a move. So anyway, the umpire bent over and as he's cleaning the plate, he says to me, "Don't swing." And the pitcher threw the next pitch down the middle of the strike zone and it was a ball. I couldn't believe it. I guess Pancho must have done some talking.
>
> But after a while, things went back to normal.

In addition to questionable arbiters, the *gaijin* have pointed to devious machinations by opposing pitchers and managers to keep the foreign barbarians in their place. In 1965, Daryl Spencer threatened to become the first American ever to win a home run title in Japan and opposing pitchers around the league took to walking him. In one meaningless series against the Orions, Spencer was passed eight straight times, once with the bases loaded. He was also walked while holding his bat upside down.

Spencer's chief rival, Nomura of the Hawks, eventually won a Triple Crown.

In 1982, Tony Solaita of the Nippon Ham Fighters was tied with Ochiai for the home run lead late in the season, when opposing pitchers began walking him to give him fewer opportunities to hit. When Solaita's manager offered to have Ham pitchers walk Ochiai in retaliation, Solaita refused. "No, I don't want to win a title that way," he said. In the last game of the season, one home run behind the leader, Solaita saw nothing but balls. In the seventh inning, he removed himself from the lineup in protest, deliberately surrendering his chance at the title.

Walking the opposition to protect a teammate's title or a team record is a common, if unsavory, practice in Japanese baseball. In the final game of the 1984 season, the Tigers and the Dragons faced each other with their leading cleanup hitters, Kakefu and Uno, tied for the home run lead. Both men were put in the leadoff spot to give them more chances to hit. Both men were walked intentionally every time up and wound up sharing the title.

In 1982, the Taiyo Whales and the Dragons met in the final game of the season with the Whales batter, Keiji Nagasaki, a fraction of a point ahead of the Dragons leading batter, Yasushi Tao, in a battle for the Central League batting title. To most baseball fans, the more significant thing about the game was that it would decide the pennant. If the Dragons won they would clinch the CL flag with a winning percentage of .577. If they lost, then the Yomiuri Giants, who had already completed their schedule, would be the league champions, because they had played to fewer ties. The standings that morning stood as follows:

	W	L	T	
Yomiuri	66	50	14	.569
Chunichi	63	47	19	.567

The Whales ignored their kingmaker role, however, and they walked leadoff batter Tao five times while Nagasaki rode the bench. The walks helped the Dragons win the game but Nagasaki got the title, which was all the Whales seemed to care about.

When a foreign player is involved in a title or a record quest, however, there is clearly more at work than mere team loyalty, as Solaita would no doubt attest. In 1980, his first season in Japan, he broke the Nippon Ham season home run record with 44 homers, yet nobody in the organization told him about it, much less congratulated him on it.

In 1981, he hit .284 and led the Pacific League in home runs (44), RBIs (108), and game-winning hits (17), helping his team to a pennant. But when the sportswriter voted for MVP, Solaita, a designated hitter, finished a distant third behind the winner, Ham relief ace Yutaka Enatsu. He also garnered only half as many votes as Ham first baseman Junichi Kashiwabara, whose statistics read: .310, 16, 81.

When the MVP results were announced a Nippon Ham front-office official said, quite candidly, "If Solaita had been Japanese, he would have won it easily."

What bridled Solaita and many other Americans was the Japanese term exclusively reserved for foreign ball-players: *suketto*, which means "supporting player." Solaita thought the catch-all phrase *gaijin* was pejorative enough: In Japan he was not an American or a Samoan to his hosts, he was just an outsider. But *suketto* was beyond his comprehension. "How the hell can I be a *suketto* when I'm the best player on the team?" he asked querulously. "If that's the Japanese attitude, then the only reason for a foreigner to come here and play really is for the money. That's all."

Solaita, a former major league platoon hitter who played with several clubs, was six feet and 215 pounds of rock-hard muscle and was perhaps the strongest person ever to play baseball in Japan. He hit four home runs in a row—twice.

Solaita had an unhurried, friendly manner. He always had a smile and kind word for everyone. But he also had a violent temper and his outbursts could be frightening. Once, absolutely choleric at an umpire who had called him out on strikes in an early season game, he smashed an iron heater in the dugout with his fist. "Watch out," cautioned his manager, "you'll hurt yourself."

Solaita snorted in derision. "You worry about the heater," he replied.

In Solaita's final year in Japan, his average dipped and his strikeouts increased, although he still managed to hit 36 home runs. When he was benched late in the season and knew he was going to be released, he was so distraught that he threw the team message board—a six-foot-by-three-foot affair—out of a hotel window and scattered his teammates.

In Spencer's day, many Japanese had considered it a big loss of face for a foreigner to win the home run title. Yet, after Kintetsu's Clarence Jones broke that particular barrier in 1974 when he hit 38, it became commonplace, at least in the Pacific League, to have an American lead the league in home runs. Jones, who won the title again in 1976 with 36, was followed by Leron Lee in 1977 (34), Bobby Mitchell in 1978 (36), Chuck Manuel in 1979 and 1980 (37 and 48), and Solaita in 1981 (44). No one seemed to mind a *gaijin* home run king that much as long as he didn't try to move in next door or marry into the family.

In 1984, Gregory ("Boomer") Wells performed what was then the unthinkable for a non-Japanese by winning a Triple Crown. Wells, at six feet five inches and 250 pounds, was built like a redwood tree. A one-time pro football prospect, he was a powerful right-handed hitter who in 1988 would hit the longest home run in Japanese baseball history, 532 feet.

Wells had started out in the Minnesota Twins chain. In 1982, at age twenty-eight, he hit .335 with 29 home runs for the Twins Triple A affiliate in Denver, winning the American Association batting title. Minnesota, however, sold his contract to the Hankyu Braves. Baseball executives said he had "holes" in his swing and thus did not hold much promise for the big leagues. Wells, however, a benign and blithe giant, had a different explanation.

Calvin Griffith had a team of good young players that year, and he had his quota of blacks on the squad, so he sold me to Japan—to make money.

I asked to be traded to another big league club, but he wouldn't do it. He wanted the money from Hankyu. If he let me go in the draft, another major league team would only have to pay $25,000, whereas from Japan he gets $100,000. It was economics pure and simple. My agent warned me that if I didn't agree to come to Japan, Griffith would put me on the forty-man roster and keep me in Triple A.

I didn't want to play another season in Triple A. So that's why I came to Japan. If I had not come to Japan, I'd be stuck in the Twins minor league system. I'd have been dead meat. I had no choice.

Whatever the reason he was there, Japanese fans had not seen anything like him since Frank Howard played briefly in Japan. "Boomah," as he was known in the box scores, hit .304 with 17 home runs and 62 RBIs his first year. Then he changed his form and won the Triple Crown, hitting .355 with 37 homers and 130 RBIs. Wells credited some of his teammates for giving him support and encouragement. Veteran Yutaka Fukumoto, the man who had stolen 1,000 career bases, gave him advice on how to hit certain pitchers. But Boomer had his doubts about certain others on the team and said as much in an interview for *Number* magazine:

The only one who had a chance to catch me in the second half of the season was Ochiai of Lotte and that was in home runs. But during the last couple of months of the season, he was getting nice, easy fastballs down the middle of the strike zone. Even here, at home in Nishinomiya, whenever we played the Orions, there was a pitcher on our team named Imai who would give Ochiai nice easy fastballs down the middle of the strike zone. It was obvious that our guy was trying to help Ochiai win. I thought it was strange.

I remember a situation in one game with Lotte during the second half of the season. There was a runner on second, with first base open, Ochiai at bat and a guy named Yamamoto hitting fifth. My man Imai was pitching.

At that time we were still fighting for the pennant with Lotte. I had hit a two-run homer in the first inning and the score was 2–0. The thing to do in that situation was to walk Ochiai or pitch around him to get to Yamamoto because we had been getting him out easily all year. But no, the first pitch was a nothing fastball down the middle and Ochiai hit it for a home run. Why, I wondered, did Imai do that?

When we'd clinched the pennant near the end of the season, some of the writers were telling me that the only way I could win the MVP was to win the Triple Crown. They said that was because Imai had wrapped up two pitching crowns, with the ERA title and most wins with twenty-one, so he would get the MVP. If I had only two titles, I couldn't get it. I'd tell them I won twenty-one games, too, because I had twenty-one game-winning hits. I carried the team all year. While some of our key players were out, I had played every game. How could they not give the MVP to me? How could they give it to a pitcher?

But I think a lot of people didn't want a *gaijin* to accomplish what I did.

Seibu, Kintetsu, and Nippon Ham were fair to me, but the Hawks wouldn't pitch to me. They'd give me fastballs about four feet outside and walk me. Ochiai's team Lotte, of course, was the worst.

Upon reading of Wells's comments, Hankyu began demanding prepublication approval of all *Number* interviews with their players.

Wells followed his big year with seasons equally memorable: .327, 34 homers, and 122 RBIs in 1985; .350, 42 homers, and 103 RBIs in 1986; and .331, 40 homers, and 119 RBIs in 1987. Yet he never received the recognition one might have expected. He had one TV commercial, which featured a clip of him angrily charging a pitcher who had just plunked him in the leg. An *Asahi Shimbun* poll taken in 1985 to name the best player in the land placed Wells a distant eighth place with only 4 percent of the vote, far behind Hara, Koji Yamamoto, Ochiai, and other homegrown heroes. Neither Leron Lee nor any other *gaijin* was mentioned in the survey.

As one Japanese fan, a business executive in his mid-forties, put it, "Boomer won the Triple Crown, yet I'd say that only 5 percent of the fans are happy about that. The rest have no interest in him at all. If Oh or some other Japanese star walked down the street, people would make a big fuss, but not Boomer. People just don't care."

⑪ ⑪ ⑪

Snobbery thrives in every society and Japan is no exception, despite the fact that everyone in Japan believes he belongs to the middle class. One's status is derived primarily from what organization one belongs to. Todai beats Keio and Waseda as far as universities go, for example. The foreign ministry outranks Mitsubishi in job prestige. And the Central League is considered superior to the Pacific League in baseball.

Although the PL dominated the first thirty years of All-Star competition, the CL won 60 percent of the Japan Series in that time span. It is the league of the Giants and thus it has long been regarded to have more class. When Shigeo Nagashima became eligible for the Hall of Fame in 1987, he was voted in over former Hawk catcher Katsuya Nomura, even though he had fewer career homers (444 to 657) and fewer RBIs (1,422 to 1,988). Nagashima, the spiritual leader of the "all-Japanese" Giants, had been able to see the "heart" of the ball. Nomura had only been able to hit it.

In the public's perception, CL title winners have always ranked higher than those of the PL. What added to the Central League's overall snob appeal was the fact that although Americans Wally Yonamine and Felix Millan had won CL batting titles, no *gaijin* had been able to win a home run title in that league in a quarter century of play. Since the CL home run crown was the most coveted of all titles in Japanese ball, the fans could take some measure of comfort in knowing that there was at least one important area of their game that was still "pure."

In fact, American players in Japan had long considered it an impossibility for any one of them to capture that particular prize. They believed the league's pitchers, and the umpires, would simply never allow this gem to fall into foreign hands.

That is, until an American named Randy Bass came along.

Bass was a blond-haired, bearded first baseman who came to the Hanshin Tigers at age twenty-eight in 1983. At six feet one inch and an adiposal 210 pounds, Bass was a lefthanded power hitter who had hit many home runs in the minor leagues, but only 9 in the majors where he warmed the bench for several teams. "I don't want to be like those other guys and complain that I never got my chance," he said on coming to Japan. "I got called up six times. A lot of guys never get called up once. I just didn't do it."

In Japan, Bass shortened his big American-style stroke to adjust to the slower, breaking-ball style of pitching and also learned to poke the ball into the opposite-field stands. In 1983, he hit .288 with 35 homers and 83 RBIs, and in 1984, he hit .326 with 27 homers and 73 RBIs, despite missing several weeks of the season due to his father's death. Said Warren Cromartie, with whom Bass played briefly on the Expos, "In America, Bass was a good hitter who never got much of a chance to show what he could do. But he improved a hell of a lot in Japan. In my opinion, right now he could be the starting first baseman for any number of major league teams."

Bass really burst forth in 1985. By the All-Star break of that year, he had 30 home runs and his Tigers were in first place for the first time in nearly a decade. Because of their perennial bridesmaid status, some people compared Hanshin to the Chicago Cubs, but now that they were winning, much of the country was struck with Tiger fever. Moreover, Bass was several games ahead of the pace set by Oh when he established the Japan single-season home run mark of 55 in 1964—a state of affairs which caused more than a little alarm among Japanese baseball purists.

One day in July, over lunch at Tokyo's Trader Vic's in the Hotel New Otani, Cromartie turned to Bass and said, "You know, Randy, the Japanese will hate you if you break Oh's record."

Bass nodded and stared out the window at the stone lanterns in the Otani garden. "But they'll never let me do it," he said finally. "I'll get to 54 and they'll start walking me. You'll see. They'll never let a *gaijin* break a record like that."

In the second half of the season, Bass continued hitting home runs, helping the Tigers stay atop the league. By September 15, he had 46. Although he hit only one more in the next two weeks, he was still ahead of Oh's pace because there were still many rained-out games to be made up.

Thus it was that when Bass hit home run number forty-nine in Hiroshima on October 12, there were still eight games left on the schedule. He hit four more home runs in the next five days as the Tigers clinched the pennant and after hitting number 53, Bass confided to a friend that he was getting a little scared. "As a foreigner," he said, "I don't know if this is the proper thing to do."

On October 20, Bass hit number 54, putting him one behind Oh with two games left—which as fate would have it were against the Giants, now managed by Oh. In the penultimate game on October 22 before 58,000 spectators at Koshien, he singled in his first at-bat, walked his second time up, and popped out his third. Giant starter Suguru Egawa tipped his cap to show Bass the walk was not intentional, but a Giants reliever was less accomodating, delivering four straight balls that were nearly out of the catcher's reach.

The stage was set for the final game on October 24 at Korakuen Stadium. On a clear, crisp autumn afternoon Bass stepped up to bat in the first inning and thirty thousand people leaned forward in anticipation. High atop the center field scoreboard, the Giants flag snapped and fluttered in the wind. Sunlight glinted off the bust of Oh in the right field stands.

Bass took four straight balls on pitches so far outside the strike zone they were unhittable. Tigers fans in the outfield cheering section screamed their disapproval and angrily brandished their yellow megaphones. Oh watched expressionless from the bench.

Bass's next at bat in the third inning was a repeat of the first. So was the one after that in the sixth inning. After looking at three consecutive balls in that particular trip to the batter's box, Bass lunged in frustration at an outside curve which a Giants reliever had accidentally thrown too close to the plate and poked a fluke single to center. It was the only time he reached base. In his final two appearances, even a boat oar would not have helped him hit the ball. After Bass's final walk, angry Tigers fans pelted the field with beer cans, bottles, and other missiles, but no one else in the park seemed to be very upset. Giants supporters, wearing their orange-and-black cheering uniforms, giggled their approval in the right field cheering section.

All of the newspapers the next morning ran factual accounts of Bass's failure to break the record, along with Oh's denial that he had ordered his pitchers to walk Bass. They did not carry any outraged editorials on fairness in sport or any suggestion that Bass's 54 home runs in a 130-game season be regarded as special because Oh had hit his 55 when the league played a 140-game schedule.

Also missing was any mention of something Keith Comstock, an American pitching for the Giants that year, had told Bass. Prior to the final game, said Comstock, a certain Giants coach had taken his pitchers aside and threatened them with a hefty thousand-dollar fine for every strike they threw to Bass. "I lost respect for Oh when I heard that," said Bass, bitterly dejected. "Perhaps he himself didn't directly order his pitchers to walk me. But then again, I'm sure that in the back of his mind he didn't want his record broken."

Bass won more titles in that year than the Roppongi Baskin-Robbins has ice cream flavors. He led in average (.350), home runs (54), RBIs (134), hits (176), doubles (54), game-winning hits (22), also a new Japan record, slugging percentage (.718), on-base percentage (.428), and total bases (357). He also led in postgame celebratory beers consumed.

Bass was voted the Central League MVP and after hitting three homers in six games to lead the Tigers over the Seibu Lions in the Japan Series, he won the Japan Series MVP as well. He was feted at a number of off-season awards ceremonies, which were more lucrative than he had ever dreamed. "Every time I turned around someone was trying to give me money," said Bass. "One man took me into a back room and said, 'Randy, I'll give you ten thousand dollars in cash, right now, if you'll stay here one more day.' He counted it out right in front of me."

Bass's batting exploits even won him recognition in the U.S. He was a guest on "Nightline" and on the David Letterman show, where he deadpanned, "It's just as well they walked me. If I had broken Oh's record, they probably would have taken away my visa."

In the wake of the Tigers' Cinderella year and his own profligacy, Bass became more popular than anyone ever imagined an American ballplayer in Japan could become. The following year Bass T-Shirts debuted on the market, along with a Bass candy bar. There was even a "Bass Kit" for kids which contained a glove, a bat, a uniform with Bass's number 44 on the back, and a fake blond beard.

Bass also appeared in a number of commercials, including the one for Gillette in which he shaved off his famous beard and another one for a life insurance company in which he waltzed with his wife in formal ballroom attire.

Many of the younger generation sympathized with him for the cavalier way in which the Giants had denied him his chance at the home run mark. A leading talk show host openly condemned Shoriki's Giants. "If Bass has the ability to break the record," he said, "then give him the opportunity." Added writer Masayuki Tamaki, then thirty-three, "People like me grew up watching foreigners. We're not prejudiced like our fathers were. It's time to accept *gaijin* as equals." Said one young secretary, summing up the general attitude of the New Breed, "Oh's a wimp."

The fans took to Bass for his quiet, unassuming manner, his lack of condescension, and the way he always gave credit to his teammates. "Shucks," he would say in his Oklahoma drawl, "if it hadn't been for a great leadoff hitter like Mayumi always on base when I came up and home run hitters like Kakefu and Okada behind me, I never would have gotten so many good pitches to hit and I wouldn't have won all those titles."

Teammate Kozo Kawato had great admiration for Bass. "We call him Sky because he's so big and sunny," he told an *Asahi Shimbun* reporter. "When he asked me to teach him to play *shogi* (Japanese chess), I told him he'd have to treat me like a teacher then and give me a proper bow. He did. He understands Japanese feelings."

Such praise was touching. Bass, however, was not about to apply for permanent residency. He made it clear, in his open, honest way, that baseball, Japanese or otherwise, was not the top priority in his life. He did not like the travel and the frequent separations from his family. It was not a pleasant life, he said, and if it weren't for the enormous sums of money that ballplayers were paid he did not see how anyone would want to play baseball for a living.

In Japan it was even worse, he would say. The games were longer, the season dragged on, and the press was always there. One photographer broke into his new house atop Mount Rokko to get photos for a magazine. Another flew all the way to his home in Lawton, Oklahoma, in the dead of winter and camped outside his front door waiting for "photo opportunities." It wore on his nerves.

"I like and respect the Japanese people," Bass said. "But frankly, back home I can't impress anyone with what I have done because no one knows anything about the Japanese game. They think the only thing is the major leagues. I can't even talk to them about Japan because they just wouldn't understand. Hell, they wouldn't believe me if I told them half the things that happened here."

One of the things they would not comprehend was the way Bass had been criticized for leaving the team in midyear to be at his father's deathbed in 1981. He was called irresponsible and self-centered when he returned to

Japan, to which an incredulous Bass replied, "How the hell can you put a game ahead of someone you love?"

Bass's wife Linda was even more dubious about life in Japan.

Before coming, I had expected that everything would be pretty and green because when you read about Japan in magazines back in the U.S., you see pictures of tea gardens and nice trees. But what we saw were cement buildings, the color gray, and pollution. The day we arrived, they put us up in a hotel. The room was real small and the bed so short Randy's legs stuck out. We kept telling ourselves it was better than Mexico.

Randy was never home. I only saw him a couple of hours a day when the Tigers were on a homestand. The worst day I can remember was the time I got sick. I had a fever of 103 degrees. I was in bed. I couldn't get up. And I had a nine-month-old baby and a two-year-old boy to take care of. There was nobody to help me. That particular day there was no game, but there was a practice session. I asked Randy if he could take the day off. But the team refused. They wouldn't let him come home. I thought that was too much.

I thought I would meet more of the wives of the Tigers players than I did, but none of them go to the games.

The club didn't really want me to come anyway. The first year I was here, I asked about getting tickets to the games, and a Hanshin official told me not to come. He said that in Japan, it's not the custom for the wife to go to the ballpark.

When I finally did go to the stadium, they gave me a seat far away from the infield by myself back up behind some post where it was hard to see.

I got to like it better, though, the more I stayed. The Japanese people are nice people and everything, but the longer we stayed the more lost we felt. All in all, Oklahoma is better.

The rapidity with which Bass went from hero to scape-goat in 1986 amazed even veteran observers who were used to seeing violent oscillations in the fortunes of for-eign imports. When Bass asked for a three-year contract worth over a million dollars a year, along with permission to arrive in camp two weeks late, team officials reluctantly acquiesced but did not hide their dismay at his "extrava-gant" demands. In training, when he half-heartedly shuf-fled through workouts because it was "too cold," then headed for the golf course, coaches accused him of getting a big head. His arrival seventeen minutes late for one morning practice was headline news in Osaka sports dai-lies.

When the Tigers faltered at the starting gate, it was Bass, hitting in the low .200s, who was singled out by his manager Yoshio Yoshida for blame. Although others on the team were not performing well either, Yoshida told reporters, "It's all up to *Basu*. When he starts hitting, we'll start winning."

TV commentators made frequent reference to Bass's new salary, wondering out loud what incentive he could possibly have now that he was wealthy beyond anyone's wildest dreams. When word got out that Bass owned an Apple IIC, which he would toy with each night after the game, one writer said, "This shows Bass is not really seri-ous about baseball. Serious ballplayers are supposed to come home at night, watch the baseball news, then go directly to sleep, their minds strictly on the game."

It was almost as if the previous summer had never hap-pened.

Because of a mix-up in communications in one early-season game, Bass, who had been nursing a bad leg, thought he had been taken out for defense in the final inning. As he began picking up his gear, Yoshida yelled at him, "Where do you think you're going?"

The next day, a sports daily played up Bass's great escape attempt on page one. *"Wagamama* (Selfish) *Basu!"* the headlines howled. "Yoshida Furious!" No reporter had bothered to ask Bass his side of the story, nor had Yoshida felt obliged to take Bass's part.

All of this set the stage for Bass to counterattack in a highly controversial magazine interview later that season. In it, Bass took exception to Yoshida for benching many of the veteran players who helped the Tigers win their pennant the previous year and for bunting so much. Said Bass, "If there's a runner on first and I'm in the on-deck circle, Yoshida sacrifice bunts him to second and that automatically ensures that I get walked. It's stupid. I've never seen a manager make so many mistakes. He doesn't seem to care whether we win or lose."

For this, Bass was fined several thousand dollars and once more bombarded by righteous newspaper editors. "Verbal Pollution!" ran a headline in the *Daily Sports.* According to teammate Rich Gale, however, when Bass walked into the clubhouse the day after the interview appeared, many of his Japanese teammates broke out into grateful applause.

Some publications contrived ways of getting at Bass. *Focus* magazine ran a mock ad of a new product, "*Basu*-Clean." (Bass and Bath are homonyms in the Japanese language.) It featured a photo pasteup of Bass sitting in a western-style bath, pouring "*Basu*-Clean" liquid soap into the water. Underneath ran the following copy.

> Had a hard day hitting home runs in tiny stadiums and then being walked by gutless pitchers? That's the time to put "Basu-Clean" in your bath and sit back and think about those days in the major leagues when you sat on the bench.
>
> When you do that, you realize that Japan is not such a bad place after all. In press interviews, all you have to do is say you're thinking only of the team, even if you

really aren't. Then you can take your money back to the U.S. and start a new business. For making money, you'll find there's no better place than Japan.

Bass recovered from his April slump (although his teammates did not). He hit the .400 mark in June and stayed there for the next three months. Now he threatened the Japan single-season mark of .383 held by Isao Harimoto. A flurry of magazine articles appeared on how to get him out, replete with computerized graphs and statistical studies. (One story, written by retired star pitcher Yutaka Enatsu, was entitled, "If Bass Hits .400, It Will Be the Shame of the Central League.")

Bass was nonplussed: "How come all anyone talks about is how to stop me?" he asked acerbically. "If the Japanese Self-Defense Force worked as hard as everyone in the media has been working to find my batting weaknesses, then Japan would have the strongest military force in the world."

As it turned out, Bass had learned something from his experience of the previous year. When his batting average fell below .400 in the final days of the season, he made a private vow to remove himself from the lineup if and when he dipped to .384. As Bass put it, "I knew that once I fell below Harimoto's mark, the pitchers wouldn't pitch to me and I'd never get back up. So I had decided to bench myself for the rest of the year to protect the record. You might say I learned the Japanese style."

Bass's last stand proved unnecessary, however, as he finished with a new mark of .389. He also led the league with 47 homers and 109 RBIs to win his second straight Triple Crown. The Japanese press tried hard not to pay attention. Bass's new mark was perhaps the least-covered record-breaking achievement in the history of Japanese sports journalism. When Bass left the Tigers two years later, the *Nikkan Sports* summed up his career in a page-one story. The paper listed his statistics and major achievements. But nowhere was there any mention of his league record of .389. As one fan put it, "I think lots of Japanese are blocking it out. They still think Harimoto holds the record."

Moreover, the writers voted the 1986 MVP to pitcher Manabu Kitabeppu of the pennant-winning Carp, who had a record of 18–4, with an ERA of 2.43. The Matsutaro Shoriki award, inaugurated in 1977 for "most outstanding baseball figure" of the year, went to Masaaki Mori, rookie manager of the Japan Champion Seibu Lions. As one spokesman for the award committee reportedly put it, "There were no splendid players this year. That's why we chose Mori."

Harimoto, now reduced to former record holder status, suggested closing the barn door. "Let's have Asian baseball for the Asians only," he said in a postseason TV interview. "The *gaijin* are going to take all of our records and that won't be very much fun."

Bass's trials and tribulations continued. Like a character in some tragicomic opera, controversy swirled around him. In March 1988, three days after his teammate Kakefu, a popular player who had once hit 48 home runs in a season, was arrested for drunk driving, Bass was stopped by a Kobe traffic cop for driving eleven miles over the speed limit in a twenty-five-mile-per-hour zone and taken in for questioning. The news of his "apprehension" was flashed on TV in special bulletins along with his picture as if he had been on the Ten Most Wanted list. Said Bass, "By the time I arrived at the police station there was a crowd of reporters waiting for me. It seemed to me that the whole thing had been staged to take the heat off Kakefu."

Bass played much of 1987 with a bad back, hitting .320 with 37 homers. The Tigers fell to last place, thirty-seven-and-a-half games out of first, and Yoshida was forced to resign. New manager Minoru Murayama took over with a plan to revive the Tigers into a "bright team with hot blood." That meant no more special privileges for Bass and his teammate Matt Keough, who had joined Hanshin in 1987.

"Bass and Keough are just *gaijin suketto*," said Murayama. "That's all I'm viewing them as. It's only natural that they should do well since they are being paid more than Japanese players ever dream of. However, the real leaders of the team are Kakefu [who batted .227 with 12 home runs hitting in the cleanup spot all of the previous year] and Okada [who batted .255 with 14 home runs]. It's strange in general to rely on *gaijin*."

Murayama agreed with the newspaper columnist, a former Tigers star, who wrote, "A *gaijin* can never be the real leader of a Japanese team because his main interest is only money."

In May of that year, Bass's eight-year-old son Zachary was discovered to have a brain tumor and Bass took him to San Francisco for surgery on a "compassionate leave" without pay granted by the Tigers. When Bass postponed his scheduled return, a month later the Tigers abruptly released him and announced the signing of a new American, Ruppert Jones. A Tigers spokesman was quoted as saying: "There's no way Bass could be physically or mentally ready to play after so long away from the game. Even if he came back right now, he wouldn't be able to help the team."

Americans wondered how the Tigers management could do something like that. At the very least, they thought Bass could have been kept on the inactive list in anticipation of his return the following year. Indeed, it would have been utterly inconceivable for a Japanese player of Bass's stature to be dropped in such circumstances. But then again, as many, many commentators were quick to point out, no Japanese player would ever have left his team for such a reason. In the corporate nation that is Japan, the company always comes first, even before a family crisis.

While many individual Japanese seemed deeply moved by Bass's plight—cards and gifts from well-wishers flowed into his residence, and one person sent a thousand hand-folded paper cranes—it was difficult for many diehard Tigers fans to accept the fact that while their beloved Tigers were floundering in the second division their big American gun was several thousand miles away. No matter that Bass's son's life was in danger and that a drainage pipe had been inserted into his skull. Regardless of the reality, it looked like, once again, the *gaijin* was taking the Japanese lightly. As a result, several fan groups put pressure on the Tigers management to do something.

Hiring another big American home run hitter with Bass still officially on the team would, it was felt, only make an awkward situation even more uncomfortable. So letting Bass go was deemed the best option—although the idea of telling him was apparently so daunting that a team executive chose to call him at 4:00 A.M. California time, to give him the news.

As the story unfolded further, however it turned out that Hanshin had other reasons for releasing Bass. One, it appeared, was a reluctance to pay the Bass family medical expenses which the team had contractually obligated itself to do. Tiger officials had originally made the agreement thinking, perhaps, that all they would be accountable for were cold pills and the like. But Bass's son had begun undergoing regular radiation treatments which were enormously expensive and no one in the Hanshin organization had bothered to take out medical insurance.

Bass claimed he had been unfairly let go, that the team was legally bound to pay off his salary in full including the one-year extension for 1989 he signed calling for nearly a million and a half dollars as well as the medical costs.

The Tigers retorted that Bass had violated a written agreement he had signed prior to his departure that he would return to Japan by mid-June. Bass replied that a Tigers vice president had told him by phone that he could stay in the U.S. until his son's condition stabilized. When the Tigers denied this, Bass produced a tape recording he had made of the phone conversation. Soon, Bass was talking through his lawyer.

Upon Bass's departure, some Japanese confessed respect and admiration for his decision to stick by his family at the risk of his job. In the wake of recent surveys which showed that most Japanese children prized their personal computers more than they did their fathers, prominent writers and commentators wondered if it wasn't time for Japanese to start rethinking their own values. Said one TV reporter, "Basu-*san* has taught us that there are things more important than work."

The response of the powers-that-be in Japanese baseball was less enlightened. There was much talk among upper management and certain newspaper columnists of "reconsidering" attitudes toward foreign ballplayers, which of course, was the standard kneejerk reaction in such cases. Sighed one team general manager, "There's always problems like this with the gaijin. It's tiring. We should spend our money developing young Japanese." Added Harimoto, "Foreign players are just not a good example for young people. As a side attraction, they might be okay, but they are too big and muscular for kids to try to emulate."

      ✇   ✇   ✇

But Bass's tale was not quite over. Not just yet.

At about 2:00 A.M. on the morning of July 19, as rain fell on Tokyo for the seventh consecutive day, Shingo Furuya, the 56-year-old managing director of the Hanshin Tigers, walked out onto an eighth-floor emergency exit balcony of the Hotel New Otani and jumped into the rock garden below, ending his life.

Furuya, it was said, had been suffering from severe stress from dealing with the Bass matter as well as a sudden announcement a week earlier by Kakefu that he wanted to retire.

None of those problems had been created by Furuya, a middle-level executive from the Hanshin Railways who had been appointed to his post. Bass's contract had been negotiated by a previous managing director and Bass's release was mandated by a new Tiger president, also a railroad man, who was acting on the instructions of the board of Hanshin Railways. Kakefu's desire to quit was due to recurring injuries, his declining ability to hit, and the painful realization that after seasons of .252 with 9 homers in 1986, .227 and 12 homers in 1987, and .253 and 5 homers in the first half of 1988, that it was impossible for even the most understanding manager to keep him in the cleanup spot.

Yet, the new, managing director had been ordered to somehow straighten things out and he had been constantly besieged by the press who wanted to know how he was going to solve his seemingly insoluble problems. (It was also said that in private he was deeply embarrassed by the ill-advised attempt of his superiors to invalidate Bass's contract.)

Bass, in San Francisco, expressed his sympathy for Furuya's family and said, "I hope there was some other reason besides baseball for what he did." Some people blamed Bass for what had happened. "No Japanese ever had a contract like his," wrote one magazine editor, "which provided for all family medical expenses. That's what is causing all the trouble. . . . All this wouldn't have happened if Bass had been more cooperative."

The Tigers lawyer expressed regret that Bass had not been more understanding of Furuya's position. Only days before, Furuya had flown to San Francisco with Hanshin's attorney for a meeting with Bass and his lawyer. Furuya had hoped that Bass might act like a good Japanese would in a situation like this and work with him toward a harmonious resolution of a difficult problem, thereby relieving some of the enormous pressure Furuya was under. He had suggested a settlement estimated to be in the neighborhood of $1.3 million, in lieu of fulfilling the terms of Bass's contract to the letter.

The Central League commissioner interpreted events in a Japanese way. "I wish Bass had been more appreciative of Japanese thinking and accepted a settlement instead of demanding his full two years' pay. Bass could easily get a job with another team in Japan for 1989."

But to Bass, the American, a contract was a contract and in his opinion, the Tigers were obligated, legally and morally, to pay it in full. No rational-minded Westerner would have thought any differently in his situation.

Above all, Furuya's death pointed out a fundamental difference between the American business world and that of Japan's, where the remnants of feudal thinking are still in evidence.

As one commentator put it, "It's a typical problem of middle management in Japan. If the boss orders you to do something, then you have to do it, no matter how impossible it might be or how unqualified you are for the task."

Friends and co-workers of Furuya told the *Asahi Shimbun* that Furuya was a "very serious, uncomplaining man who felt a strong sense of responsibility to his work," and was "not the type to admit weakness." It was a description that would fit most Japanese managers.

When he found the stresses and ramifications of his job too much to handle, he took his life rather than quit, admit failure, or blame the originator of his problem. That would have been too big a loss of face.

After spending five years in Japan, Warren Cromartie would say, "I think foreigners are accepted more than they used to be but we're still regarded as less worthy than the Japanese."

Few Americans played better than Cromartie did in Japan, yet he was a victim of unrealistic expectations as were so many before him. He was frequently criticized for his inability to personally deliver a Japan Championship as Bass had done for Hanshin. When Cromartie failed to hit in one key September series with the Tigers in 1985, Giants coach Toshimitsu Suetsugu publicly pronounced his performance a "first-degree crime." He hit .363 with 37 homers in 1986 and a commentator lamented on TV, "It's too bad he doesn't hit like Bass."

After five years in Japan, 160 home runs and an aggregate .313 batting average, Cromartie's photograph was not even displayed in the Giants Gallery of Stars outside the team's home park nor was it on the schedule along with the other top players. One endorsement aimed at Little Leaguers was all he had to show for his success, in addition, of course, to a bank account with several million dollars in it.

"If I'd been Japanese," he said, "my photo would be all over the place. And I'd have lots of endorsements."

There was, of course, no lack of exclusionary thinking on the American side. There were lots of foreigners who looked down on the Japanese and for every denigrating remark about *gaijin* that Japanese came up with, there was a counter-remark on the American side. More than one foreign player incorporated denigrating slang like *Jap, Nipper, slant-eyed bastard,* even *gook* into his daily speech.

Even those who liked Japan spent much of their time commiserating over the Japanese game. Many Americans openly ridiculed the way their hosts played ball. One former major leaguer, when asked by a writer what he thought of his fellow outfielders on the team, replied, "They look like dogs chasing cars."

During the mid- to late-1980s, Japan-bashing reached its height in the U.S., mostly over trade disputes but for other reasons too. When a Toshiba company was discovered to have sold equipment to the Soviet Union which enabled them to build quieter submarines, a group of congressmen called a press conference on the lawn of the Capitol and smashed a Toshiba stereo with a sledgehammer. Months later, Japanese farmers returned the compliment by burning the American flag and smashing an American car.

As the decade of the 1980s came to an end and Americans poured into Tokyo, the new finance capital of the world, many had come to the ineluctable conclusion that the Japanese talent for organization and efficiency was better than theirs.

Many big-league ballplayers, however, did not appear to share that view. When Bill Madlock was asked in an interview what he thought Japanese baseball had to offer, he laughed out loud and said, "Are you kidding me?"

⚾   ⚾   ⚾

The success of a number of Taiwanese players in the 1988 season presented for team owners in Japan a pleasant alternative to their traditional dependence on imports from North America: Seibu's fireball starter Ku Tai-yuan (Taigen Kaku) won his first ten games of the season; Lotte's Chuang Sheng-hsiung (Katsuo-Soh) won his first eight; Chunichi relief ace Kuo Yuan-tsu (Genji Kaku) led the league in saves; while Yomiuri's incandescent rookie, Lu Ming-tsu (Meishi Ro) hit 11 home runs in his first month of play to become an overnight hero.

Giants owner Shoriki, among others, argued that Taiwanese should be placed in the same category as Japanese because they were fellow Asians. And Seibu's Kuo agreed. Said Kuo in a *Weekly Baseball* article, "Chinese have the same skin color and size as Japanese. I myself don't want to be called a foreigner."

With Taiwanese there was also less trouble. Unlike Americans, they always did their training, they always obeyed their coaches, they learned the language, and best of all, they would take whatever the team wanted to pay. Moreover, they would also come under the heading of "Japanese baseball" so Japanese coaches could take credit for their achievements in a way they couldn't with Americans.

As Shigeo Nagashima said of Lu (or Ro as the Japanese pronounced his name, much to the annoyance of Taiwanese residents of Japan), "Ro really has the sense of Bushido . . . the attitude of 'leave everything to me.' "

Japan had introduced baseball to Taiwan on a high school and college level when Taiwan was part of the imperial Japanese empire. The motto of a top Taiwanese college team which had a Japanese manager was *"Shinu made yaru"* ("Practice until you die").

After the war, however, things Japanese fell into disfavor in Taiwan and baseball fell from popularity. When it was played, terms like *sutoraikku* and *bōru,* were banned. To the Taiwanese, those words were not English.

In time, interest started up again on a Little League level. Dragons relief ace Kuo led a Taiwanese team to a Little League World Series title in 1969, becoming a national hero in Taiwan. Thus followed the Taiwanese hegemony as their teams won the Little League World Series again in 1972, 1973, and 1974.

The ironic thing about postwar Taiwanese baseball, for Japan at least, was that it was influenced by the American military presence in Taiwan and was played American style. In Taiwan, high schoolers practiced until it got dark—not until they were dead—then went home. Lu had a ferocious swing and he looked more like Reggie

Smith at bat than he did the contact-oriented Japanese batters who liked to punch the ball to all fields. Japanese coaches were quick to remark on this and also on the fact that he "concentrated less" in practice than he did in the game (a curious phenomenon found for the most part only among American players.)

Still, Lu was self-effacing and telegenic and would say things like, "I want to be the type of player who is loved by the Japanese fans." After being called up to the first team in June, he was such a big hit that Japanese officials at the urging of Shoriki temporarily revised the number of foreigners who could be selected by the All-Star team manager from two to three, just so Lu could play. As one spokesman put it, "The fans want to see him play. That's why we did it."

It was something they had never done for an American player. Not even for Jim Paciorek of the Taiyo Whales who was second in the League in batting that year with a .332 average.

And they probably never would.

Epilogue

There was an awful lot of misunderstanding between Japanese and Americans about how you should play baseball. Stan Musial came over with the Cardinals and someone asked him, "How do you hit the forkball?" And he said, "Between the seams."

And then someone asked him, "How do you hit a spitball?" And he replied, "On the dry side."

Musial was joking. But some people thought he was serious. They thought he was talking Zen.

Then there was the time the Giants trained in Vero Beach with the Dodgers back in the early 1960s. That was the year the Dodgers had Sandy Koufax and Don Drysdale but very little hitting power. Al Campanis was teaching the Dodger batters to swing down at a pitched ball to create high-hopping grounders for infield hits.

Giants manager Kawakami looked at this and said, "So this is how the major leaguers hit . . . hmmmmm." After that, the down swing became one of the main batting theories in Japan.

M. Tamaki
Author

You can have all the Japanese spirit there is, but it still won't help you hit a good curveball.

Don Blasingame

To say, like Oh and the others are saying, that Japanese baseball should be played by Japanese or Asians alone and that a real World Series between Japan and the U.S. would be impossible as long as there are American players in Japan, seems to me to be just racist.

In Oh's case, it's hypocritical. He considers himself Japanese, yet he was a subject of discrimination as a boy because he was Chinese. (Oh was once barred from playing in a national tourney because he was not a Japanese citizen.)

The world is getting more international anyway and the Japanese should be thinking "team versus team" or "league versus league." Instead it seems that Japan is still vicariously fighting World War II. It's like the South in the U.S., still trying to hang on to slavery and segregation.

Reggie Smith

The Japanese and American games are running on parallel tracks. And they'll never, ever cross.

Leron Lee

The Japanese are stubborn. They want to do it their way. It isn't enough just to beat the Americans, they want to prove that their way is better, come hell or high water."

Warren Cromartie

The Japanese had long hoped that despite a decided lack in natural resources, the same dynamics of hard work and group cooperation that made their country an economic power would also eventually help make it a world baseball power as well.

If they could manufacture a product of superior quality and uniformity through teamwork and tireless effort, their reasoning went, why shouldn't they be able to create a world-class baseball team with the same formula?

Reality has not worked out that way, however. Although Japan has done well in international amateur competition—it handily won the 1984 Olympic gold medal in baseball—beating the American pros has been something else again.

In a 1949 tour of Japan, the minor league San Francisco Seals won all their games against Japanese professional teams with ease, and in subsequent post-season visits major league teams handed the Japanese many disheartening defeats.

Perhaps the most painful setback occurred in 1971, when the American League champion Baltimore Orioles with Brooks and Frank Robinson swept eight straight games from the Yomiuri Giants of Sadaharu Oh and Shigeo Nagashima fame, a team that is still regarded as the greatest Japanese squad ever assembled (and which many thought might be the equal of the Orioles). The Orioles overall record was 12–2–4.

But the Japanese, being nothing if not persistent, kept at it and in 1981, held the Kansas City Royals to a 9–7–1 record on the Royals' goodwill tour of Japan.

The Royals were only 50–53 in that strike-torn season, seventeenth best in the major leagues, but critics in Japan were sure that the gap between Japanese and American baseball had narrowed. As columnist Orichi Terauchi wrote, "The image we have had for a long time of the big leaguer as a superstar has changed. Except for a few players like George Brett, the Royals are just average. Perhaps this is because the number of teams has increased, but the level of American baseball has indeed dropped compared to the past."

Interpreter Toyo Kunimitsu, who accompanied the

Royals throughout their travels in Japan as team translator, agreed:

> I think some of those American players are overpaid.
> Dennis Leonard, their star pitcher, he makes over half
> a million dollars a year, but I think Egawa is much
> better.
>
> I think the Royals were surprised the Japanese were
> so good. The mood on their bench was terrible. Nobody
> was talking very much. They would really get mad
> when Egawa or some other Japanese pitcher threw a
> breaking pitch on 3–2 or 2–2, which is very unusual in
> America. They would strike out and come back to the
> bench yelling at the pitcher, "Why don't you challenge
> me, damn it?"
>
> Of course, Royals manager Howser had excuses. He
> said the team hadn't practiced for three weeks, and that
> they were playing many games versus pickup teams
> which used the best players from two or more teams.
> He said that if America had sent such a team that the
> results would have been much different.
>
> But in the end, I think he was very relieved that the
> Royals managed a winning record of 9–7–1. He didn't
> want the Royals to be the first U.S. team to have a losing
> record in Japan.

In 1984, the Baltimore Orioles, who had finished fifth in
their division with an 85–77 record, fumbled their way to
eight wins, five losses, and a tie against various Japanese
teams and combined squads. No one denied that the U.S.
major leaguers were still superior, but many fans agreed
with Yukio Nishimoto, the former Buffaloes manager,
who thought the Orioles had looked even worse than the
Royals. Said Nishimoto, "It might be just a vacation for the
Americans, but they still have nothing left to offer us. As
far as baseball technique goes, there's no difference between us. They're just bigger, that's all."
Thus it was with considerable anticipation that Japa-

nese fans watched their heroes take on a group of visiting major league All-Stars in the autumn of 1986, under the aegis of Fuji Film. The Americans included Dale Murphy, Jesse Barfield, Ryne Sandberg, Cal Ripken, Jr., Jack Morris, Mike Scott, and other luminaries. The Japanese side featured Egawa, Ochiai, and others, but not Bass or Cromartie or Boomer Wells or the Lee brothers. As the Japanese All-Star pilot Sadaaki Kondo had said when selecting his squad, "The fans want to see Japanese play the big leaguers." When Leron Lee asked if he could participate he was told, "No. Japanese only. Sorry."

The results caused considerable chagrin in Japan. Murphy, Barfield, and company did more than win six of seven games from their Japanese counterparts—they virtually annihilated them. They outscored them 59–21. They out-homered them 19–1. And they outdistanced them in many other aspects of the game. Catcher Tony Peña of the Pittsburgh Pirates picked a runner off second base from a sitting position behind home plate. The Japanese had never seen anything like it.

The Japan All-Stars committed several ghastly errors and did not hit a home run until the sixth game, a match they lost 15–3. Their lone victory, achieved in the fifth game, 6–4, on a barrage of singles and an admirable relief performance by Hankyu Braves ace pitcher Yoshinori Sato, gave little cause for celebration. By then most fans had stopped watching and the sportswriters had begun to look elsewhere for headline stories. Three-time Triple Crown winner Hiromitsu Ochiai, who had hit but .261 with no home runs in the series, was disconsolate. "It's a mistake to think we can ever challenge the Americans," he said flatly. "We're like a team of Little Leaguers playing adults. . . . Their pitchers are just too fast."

Perhaps what separated this series of games from those of the past was the all-out brio with which the Americans played. Few touring teams, with the possible exception of the 1971 Orioles squad, were as intense on the field—and off. Most ballclubs emulated the New York Yankees of 1955 who coasted to a 15–0–1 record amidst a constant round of parties. In his autobiography, *The Mick*, Mickey Mantle wrote of his teammates running through a Japanese hotel corridor at 3:00 A.M., yelling and singing, some wearing nothing but jockstraps. One Yankee player also told of Mantle, Whitey Ford, and Billy Martin arriving for pregame practice one morning having spent the entire night in revelry. That afternoon, Japan's great pitcher, 400-game winner Masaichi Kaneda, struck out Mantle four times, and dueled Ford to a 1–1 tie. It was one of the great moments of Japanese sports.

The 1981 Royals had similarly spent their evenings in Japan being wined and dined by their Japanese hosts. They proved, if anything, how easy it is to lose with a hangover. Newspaper reporters noted that the Royals played some of their games in Japan with a supply of beer visible in the dugout. (One member of the 1984 Orioles squad later claimed his team's Japanese hosts were intentionally trying to get the Baltimore players as drunk as possible every night.)

The rousing performance of the 1986 American contingent was augured by the selection of Davey Johnson as manager. Johnson, the man who had just guided the New York Mets to a World Series triumph, was still bitter from his own experience playing in Japan. He remembered all too well the names the sports press had called him, how humiliating it had all been.

"It was the only time I had ever failed at anything," he said, "and it drove me crazy." Johnson had handpicked his stars as much for their aggressiveness as for their ability, and, it was said, urged them in private to play extra hard. "I especially wanted to do well in Japan because of what happened before," Johnson confessed. "You might say I had something to prove."

It was sweet revenge. The series was, he said, "a true indication of the difference between our two games."

Then he added, more graciously, that there were some major league level players in Japan, like Ochiai and a sharp singles-hitting second baseman for Yomiuri named Toshio Shinozuka. "I think that if their All-Star team entered one of our major league divisions," he continued, "they might win half their games. Their batters may not have much power, but they always make contact with the ball. There's just not enough pitching depth."

Two years later, Bill Madlock, ending his first season, would say "They play good ball. There are a number of guys like Ochiai, Yoshimura, Akiyama, Kiyohara, and all the Seibu starting pitchers who could play in the big leagues. . . . But there's no way you can compare Oh's 868 home runs with what the big guys are doing in the States."

By the end of the decade, it seemed as if the Japanese and American games were going in opposite directions.

※　　　　※　　　　※

The one-sided defeats called for another reexamination of the Japanese basic approach to baseball, which in its emphasis on endless practice, iron-handed discipline, and the belief that good players are made, not born, is so different from that of the Americans.

Loyalists argued that giving away an average of four inches and twenty pounds per player was simply too much of a handicap to overcome. Without constant practice, special tactics, or adroitness—breaking-ball pitchers nipping the edges with pinpoint control, the unexpected squeeze—there was no way the smaller Japanese could compete.

Others said that size was not that big a factor. Baseball was a game of quickness and timing, and besides, home run power was something that even smaller players could develop with specialized weight-training programs— something many Japanese coaches had a long-running superstitious aversion to. As Reggie Smith told a Japanese magazine after his retirement from the Yomiuri Giants:

There are a lot of players in the major leagues—stars—who were not particularly physically big or particularly strong. But they used weights to make themselves stronger. Joe Morgan. Steve Garvey. Ron Cey. Every major league team today has a weight-training facility . . . at home and on the road.

The Japanese coaches have that old fear that lifting weights will tighten a player's muscles up. But with the new Nautilus machines it's possible to develop strength and maintain flexibility at the same time. I think if Hara followed Garvey's example and started a weight-training program, his home run production would increase dramatically. To start with, he's bigger physically than Garvey and lots of others were.

It has also been proven with U.S. players that weight training will prolong a player's career and his longevity in terms of performance and excellence. That's why you see so many older players in the major leagues these days.

Sports training techniques have developed greatly over the years in the States. In one big-league clubhouse, there is a box filled with water in which the player lies in the dark, listening to soothing music and watching videos of himself at bat. Lots of players also use hypnosis.

Japanese coaches, however, are reluctant to pick up such new ideas. As one Japanese writer put it, "That's because if they do, it's tantamount to admitting they didn't know what they were doing in the first place."

Critics of the Japanese system also argue that the nation's philosophy of unremitting hard work, so useful in industry, is counterproductive when applied to baseball—that too many players are constitutionally incapable of understanding the word *rest* or answering the question, How much is enough? As a result they burn themselves out in their quest for athletic excellence.

The Japanese coaches and players, for example, seem to believe that three days off in the middle of the year from a routine of constant practice will erase all the gains made till then. "They practice so hard they are worn out before the game, said Madlock. "Their thinking is that the way to improve a .230 hitter is to run him to death in pregame practice. Well, the only result that produces is an in-shape .230 hitter. They have the same hard pregame practice schedule all year. It doesn't change from April to August."

"There's such a thing as too much work," said Leron Lee. "In Japan, pregame practice is like running a marathon before a twelve-round boxing match. They are exhausted by the middle of the season, especially the pitchers. The players would be a lot better, if the coaches wouldn't wear them out on the practice field. But in Japan, the coach doesn't understand what he is getting his players in shape for. He runs the players until their tongues are hanging out. Only then do the players do quickness drills and stuff. In the major leagues, the players run sprints, sprints, sprints, because baseball is a game of quickness. Maybe a little bit of jogging is needed to warm up, but that's all."

"Americans who succeed in Japan," added Cromartie, "are those who stick to their own routines. They come on strong in the second half, Ochiai too. But that doesn't seem to make any impression on the Japanese coaches at all—or the players. They are more interested in showing how much guts and fight they have in pregame workouts than in getting ready to play a baseball game."

Although Japanese coaches have moved to a set, American-style pitching rotation of one start every four to five days, they have yet to abandon the custom of making pitchers throw on the sidelines every day. This is in direct conflict with what modern sports physicians preach and is perhaps the main reason why many Japanese pitchers usually wear out their arms by the age of thirty and people like Murata develop arm trouble.

"The pitchers look very sharp in the spring," said Bob

Horner, "but they are dragging in September, because they practice so much."

Ironically, it appears that the cookie-cutter approach and fabled "team spirit" philosophy that helped make Japan a flawless manufacturing, money-making machine may not really suit baseball.

Japanese-style quality control means that everyone has to do everything the same way. No one is allowed to think for himself. Nothing is left to chance, or individual need. Managers and coaches demand blind obedience to traditional methods, and the players who don't go along are weeded off the assembly line.

The result is a passive approach to playing baseball, or as Reggie Smith once said, "They play as if they are punching a clock." Smith added these comments:

> Major leaguers are self-assertive and aggressive, perhaps too aggressive for the Japanese, yet they develop their own individual styles and find something that works for them and stick with it.
>
> The attitude the Japanese coaches (especially the Giants coaches) take toward their younger players is, "You're dumb. You don't know anything about baseball. Don't think I'll tell you everything you need to know." The philosophy here is that they have to work hard, to struggle, the same way the past generation did; take the one-thousand ground ball drill, for example. They're not allowed to use their creative imagination.
>
> There is very little anticipation on the part of the players during games. They just wait to be told what to do. They don't predict what the pitcher will throw or what direction the ball will be hit. They don't run bases on their own, so their reaction time is slower in taking the extra base. They are always looking at the coaches.
>
> Another big problem in Japan and with the Giants, especially, is that they don't give the younger players enough of a chance. With the Giants, seniority rules and

the senior players are locked into their positions. It often seems they won't let a young player play simply because he is too young. How can you find out what someone can do?

It's just a general passive state of mind. The coaches try to take too much responsibility, at times, for winning and losing. But, ultimately, it is up to the players.

Japanese efforts to organize a baseball game reached their peak with the development of a special numbered code sheet called *ransu-hyo*. Don Money described it thusly:

It was this chart we had to wear on our wrists. On it were the numbers 1 to 5 across and 1 to 5 down, relating to the type of pitch. The coach would flash a sign such as 1-5, or 1-3, and you would have to look down at your wrist chart to see what the pitch was going to be. Now you can imagine getting the sign and having to look down and decode it with a runner on base.

They said that the opposition had a camera in center field, stealing our signs. That's why the chart was necessary. Bullshit. All you needed, I said, was two sets of simple signs and you could change or alternate them.

How can you look at your wrist with a runner on base? The runner at first is going to steal second while the infielders are examining their wrist charts.

The commissioner of Japanese baseball eventually outlawed the *ransu-hyo* because they slowed the already turtlelike pace of the game.

Finally, perhaps the biggest problem with the Japanese pro game is its fundamentally truncated structure, which is radically different than in the U.S. American major league clubs are business franchises. They are highly profit oriented and dependent on the cultivation of strong regional loyalties for their continuing success. Each team has its own multitiered farm system for player development and most athletes who make the parent club have progressed through lengthy seasons at several levels of the minor leagues.

In Japan, however, since nearly all teams exist as public relations vehicles for large business enterprises, they are, in many cases, administered by men who know nothing about running a baseball team. Prohibitive budgets allow each club only one farm team, which plays a short eighty-game schedule each year, greatly limiting opportunities for young players and aspiring coaches to learn and polish their skills.

Tatsuro Hiroka summed things up in a national TV interview when he said, "Our biggest weakness is in the area of player development. We've come this far but we can't further narrow the gap without a structure comparable to that of the U.S. farm systems to nurture our young players. Unless we do that, I don't think we'll ever catch the Americans, no matter how hard we train."

Hiroka and others have made the point that American big leaguers learned to play when they're sick or hurt because there are 150 players in a franchised farm team system waiting to step in and take their jobs away. In Japan, there is no depth, no one waiting. "If a veteran player gets sick," said Madlock, "he is pampered like hell. He is sent to the farm team to recover. He gets to pick his pitcher. There's really no mental pressure. They just don't have that killer instinct here.... They're satisfied with ties. ... It's a much more mental thing involved in the US."

⚾   ⚾   ⚾

Of course, the Japanese game is not without its lessons to teach. And Davey Johnson learned a number of them.

> As a manager I adopted the Japanese concept of special practice. They would take a different player out and just work on his weaknesses in a special practice session.

And of course, the Japanese are very good in batting, contact batting, so I picked up some things in that area as well. We have a tendency to lurch here in the U.S., while in Japan, they don't do that.

The Japanese have detected that there are three major flaws in a batting swing: overstriding, opening the hips too early, and uppercutting. They have developed drills that overemphasize exactly the opposite of a flaw—exaggerating, opening up the hips and dragging the barrel of the bat, swinging up, and so forth. Or they pick up that front foot and plant it, as opposed to shifting it, closing the hip and swinging over it. They hope that when they do stride, the hips will stay square and they will hit the ball squarely.

Oh used to have a drill he did all the time where he picked his foot up and swung over it and hit down. What he was doing in that drill, instead of trying to approach the ball level he was hitting downwards and hoping that would automatically result in a level swing when he was at bat in a real game.

So I incorporated that into my teaching of hitting and it has worked pretty well, that aspect of it.

I also believe in conditioning. Hard conditioning. Not to the extent that the Japanese do, but more than the Americans do. Not enough ballplayers in the States take their training seriously. And I also believe in the old "All for one and one for all" approach, on sacrificing for the team. In the U.S., there's too much emphasis on individualism.

Columnist Kunikazu Ogawa, who has played professional baseball in Mexico and in the U.S. minor leagues, said, "What Americans can learn from the Japanese is the value of cooperation. No other people work a rice field more effectively than the Japanese. The Americans spend too much time arguing and bickering and too many of them are reluctant to sacrifice themselves at bat to help the team. They're not as efficient as they could be. If more Americans tried the Japanese system, I think they could realize more of their full potential. Americans simply don't get the best out of their talent."

Brad ("The Animal") Lesley added, "One thing about Japan is that there is definitely more of a family feeling on a Japanese team. In the States everyone is into his own thing, especially with the big bucks the players are making. There's not that sense of belonging to a group you see in Japan."

Even Bob Horner, in his Japanese autobiography declared, "There are lots of things that Japan has to teach. Things like organization in workouts, the attitude of the coaches and the players toward practice, teamwork."

Japanese workouts might be long, but they are also models of efficiency. One seldom sees players standing around talking, unless they are foreigners. There are two batting cages, a toss batting area, and all is arranged to get maximum use of time and space.

"Japanese camp is better than in the U.S.," said Reggie Smith, "as long as you don't have to report in January. You get in shape a lot quicker. It's more intense and more serious. It's longer, but the good thing about it is you're always busy. You don't realize or notice the amount of time you spend on the field. In the U.S., it's shorter, but there is a lot of 'dead time'—standing around, waiting. So Japan's is very well organized; in my opinion, it's better."

Yet, when all is said and done, most American players and coaches do not get overly excited about the educational benefits of Japanese baseball. "In the end," Johnson said, "the question should really be what they need to learn from us. I think the Japanese need to have more American coaching and training methods incorporated into their routine." He added:

> The Japanese are certainly getting bigger. They have guys who are six feet four inches. The diet is getting better. To me, they will be able to compete with the Americans if they change their coaching technique and

thinking a little bit toward training. For the Japanese to compete on a level with the ballclubs in the U.S., they have to get something out of every player on the team. They have to get the maximum amount of all their resources, which they don't. They wear their players out in training. A guy pitches until his arm falls off.

But the culture is such a strong part of their being, in the way they look at games or life. There is no way that they could change their approach. It wouldn't be accepted by the fans.

If you don't practice twice as hard in the August sun, then you have no fight. No guts.

If a player booted a ball, made an error, and I left him out there as manager, the fans would say, "Change him. Get somebody else. Even if he is a Diamond Glove shortstop." The fans expect that.

The Japanese player is human, and maybe he is used to being abused, criticized, and browbeaten. They all accept that as part of the system, but I know they would rather not go through with it.

The coaches, however, don't know how to leave the ballplayers alone to play the game by themselves. They don't know how to stop messing with the players. That's the nature of the animal in Japan.

⚾   ⚾   ⚾

Competition is probably the biggest single factor that would boost the Japanese game. The more competition, the sharper the stimulus, the better the product, or so the free-market theory goes. The major leagues are strong, one can argue, because they are open to all ethnic groups. Japan's game, on the other hand, has grown stagnant because it limits outside participation. "The more players you have, the more open the game," said Blasingame.

When Reggie Smith heard in 1986 that another plan was afoot in Japan to ban foreigners, he was quick to reply, "If Japan does lock its doors, then the game over there is as good as it will ever get. I can understand their argument about money, that they are paying Americans too much and that the money could be better spent developing good Japanese players. But why not just put a spending ceiling on *gaijin* contracts, instead of unilaterally shutting out foreign players."

However, opening the doors further to more Americans, or other *gaijin,* would mean further changes in the Japanese game and that is something Japan does seem unwilling to accept. If Americanizing the game is the price of progress, then it appears to be too high. Thus far, that is.

The Japanese have not minded importing certain aspects of the American game—the *shooto* ball (screwball), the downswing, the double steal, as well as the fist-raised *gattsu pozu* and the "high five" player salutes. But technique and cosmetics are one thing, basic philosophy is another.

Many teams have taken spring training in the U.S., but upon their return to Japan their coaches would usually caution their players to forget what they learned. Teams would employ American coaches in the sincere hope of learning something, but then usually shunt them aside when the *gaijin* teachers actually tried to effect a change in the system—such as training less in the middle of August. Former Oakland shortstop Bert Campaneris quit midway through his second year, 1988, as a Seibu coach because he felt badly treated. A previous imported Seibu coach, Vern Law, also left before his contract was up. (Said Bill Suzukawa, a reporter for the *Daily Sports,* "If they were good coaches, they were often viewed as a threat to Japanese authority by some people. But that wasn't all. Vern Law insisted every year that Seibu pitchers learn the change-up. But they resisted. Because they already had to practice the fastball, the curve, the *shooto,* the slider, and the fork. It was just too much.")

Jim Marshall, the former big leaguer and manager of

the Cincinnati Reds and Oakland Athletics, served as a head coach with the Chunichi Dragons for three years. He started out sitting next to the manager on the bench during every game. By the end of his third year, however, he was sitting at the far end of the dugout. When the Dragons won the pennant in 1982, there was a restriction on the number of coaches who could suit up for the Japan Series. Marshall thus suffered the indignity of being dropped from the team and having to watch Series games from the Nagoya Stadium first-aid booth.

Defenders of the Japanese way maintain it is not the system that is imperfect, but the human beings in it. After all, the system had produced Sadaharu Oh who, many Japanese believed, ranked with Aaron and Ruth. It also produced Sachio Kinugasa, who broke Lou Gehrig's consecutive-games played record, and Koji Yamamoto, who hit 536 home runs. Yamamoto was one of the two men to get a home run off major league All-Star pitching in the Fuji Film series, hitting .364. In their prime Oh, Kinugasa, and Yamamoto were all recognized as major league star material by the Americans. And all those three believed devoutly in the Japanese method.

In the fall of 1987, Koji Yamamoto gave a speech at Waseda University during which he told an assembled crowd of several thousand students paying rapt attention, "The key to my success was *doryoku* (effort), and the one-thousand-fungo drill."

Moreover, the Seibu Lions won their Japan Championships in 1986 and 1987 with almost no help from the Americans on the team. Their young outfielder, a man named Ty Van Burkleo, who burst forth in 1988 with 38 home runs and a batting average of .263, was bred in the Seibu system, signing with the Lions in 1987 after five years in the lower levels of the minor leagues. No team trained harder than the Seibu Lions.

So it is not the system, apologists for Japan will tell you, it is the players who haven't been up to it. If they couldn't beat the big leaguers, the only way to rectify that is to train even harder until they do.

If the average player runs out of gas in midseason, it isn't that he is overworked, but that he isn't tough enough, isn't in good enough shape. Kinugasa and Yamamoto and Oh never had problems like that.

Sooner or later, the belief seems to be, if the Japanese keep at it, evolution will produce an athlete capable of practicing all his waking hours and never, ever tiring—a kind of baseball superman.

Some forward-looking Japanese have argued for more flexibility. Said Kunikazu Ogawa, the former Giant, "The Giants ought to make room in their organization for people like Johnson and Smith. Sure they are critical, maybe too critical for Japanese ears. . . . but they also have got something to offer."

But people like Ogawa are definitely in the minority.

"Sure, there are changes we can make," said Oh. "But most Japanese players won't train on their own as Americans do. They need to be told what to do and therefore it is necessary for us to have a disciplined system. And as for working too much, well, we're smaller so we have to practice harder. How else can we improve?"

American Jim Lyttle, who played for the Hiroshima Carp for several years, said that a coach once told him he realized the Japanese way of playing ball needed fixing. But he also said that if he became a manager and adopted the American way and didn't win the pennant, he would be heavily criticized by everyone for being too soft and, undoubtedly, be fired.

In that sense, the rigorous spring training and pregame workouts have their own special uses. If the team does not do well, it can at least offer the excuse that it really practiced hard. In Japan, that counts for a lot. Adopting the American way would mean teaching players to be individualistic, an idea which goes against the very fabric of

Japanese society—harmony, *wa*. If you allowed a player to start thinking for himself and doing things his own way, sooner or later discipline would unravel. It would set a bad example for the rest of Japan. It would also mean the Japanese would no longer be "pure" Japanese—descendants of the heroic, selfless samurai.

All in all, it would be too big a risk to take.

⚾   ⚾   ⚾

In the fall of 1988, a team of major-leaguers managed by Sparky Anderson and featuring Kirby Puckett, Paul Molitor, Andres Galarraga, and World Series hero Orel Hershisher traveled to Japan for a seven-game series against a team of Japanese All-Stars. They finished with a record of 3–2–2, and no one on either side suggested the time had finally come to play a Real World Series.

Hershisher, who had a 7.71 ERA in two appearances on the tour, cited a number of Japanese players who could play in the major leagues but, at the same time, confessed, "I didn't have my Game Face on. There wasn't the intensity of the NL Playoffs or the World Series. It was like in sandlot baseball. I was just having fun."

Added Sparky Anderson, "The Japanese have improved a lot. I think people ought to stop comparing them with us."

Appendix

Visits to Japan by U.S. Professional Teams

Year	Team	Record
1908	Reach All-Americans	17–0
1913	New York Giants and Chicago White Sox	1–0
1920	Herb Hunter All-Americans	20–0
1922	Herb Hunter All-Americans	15–1
1927	Royal Giants (Negro League)	23–0
1931	Major-League All-Stars	17–0
1932	Royal Giants	23–1
1934	Major League All-Stars	17–0
1949	San Francisco Seals	7–0
1951	Major League All-Stars (with Joe DiMaggio)	13–1–2

1953	Eddie Lopat All-Stars	11–1
1953	New York Giants	12–1–1
1955	New York Yankees	15–0–1
1956	Brooklyn Dodgers	14–4–1
1958	St. Louis Cardinals	14–2
1960	San Francisco Giants	11–4–1
1962	Detroit Tigers	12–4–2
1966	Los Angeles Dodgers	9–8–1
1968	St. Louis Cardinals	13–5
1970*	San Francisco Giants	3–6
1971	Baltimore Orioles	12–2–4
1974	New York Mets	9–7–2
1978	Cincinnati Reds	14–2–1
1979**	Major League All-Stars	1–1
1981	Kansas City Royals	9–7–1
1984	Baltimore Orioles	8–5–1
1986	Major League All-Stars	6–1
1988	Major League All-Stars	3–2–2

*Spring tour.
**National and American league All-Star teams also played seven games against each other in Japan, finishing with a record of 4–2–1, favor of the National League.

APPENDIX

Data according to the *Official Baseball Guide* (authored by Office of the Commissioner of Japanese Professional Baseball) and the Japanese Baseball Hall of Fame and Museum.

Bibliography

Chapter 1. "Chikyu no uragawa ni chigau yakyu ga atta" *(Eureka! Different Baseball Across the Globe)*, Bob Horner. Hinode Publishers, Ltd., Tokyo, 1988. Bob Horner Interviews: *Shukan Gendai,* March 30, 1987; *Sports Graphic Number,* June 20, 1987; *Gekan Gendai,* February 1988; *Gekan Playboy,* New Year issue, 1988.

Chapter 2. "Hakkyu taiehiyo wo wataru," (White Ball over the Pacific), Masaru Ikei. Chuko Shinsho, Tokyo, 1976. "Nihon yakyu shi—Meiji hen," Kyushi Yamato. Baseball Magazine Sha., Tokyo, 1977. "Nihon yakyu shi—Taisho hen," Kyushi Yamato. Baseball Magazine Sha., Tokyo 1977. "Nihon yakyu shi—Showa hen," Kyushi Yamato. Baseball Magazine Sha., Tokyo, 1977. "Nihon sports bunka shi," Ki Kimura. Baseball Magazine Sha., Tokyo, 1978. "Spotsu no gijutsu shi," Y. Kishino, T. Tawa. Taishukan Shoten, Tokyo, 1971. "Tokyo Roku Daigaku yakyu gaishi," Masaru Ikei. Baseball Magazine Sha., Tokyo, 1977. "Tobita Suishu senshu" (6 volumes), Suishu Tobita. Baseball Magazine Sha., Tokyo, 1960. "1945–1985 Gekido no supotsu 40 nenshi," Tetsuji Kawakami, Kazuto Tsuruoka Kanshu. 1986. Baseball Magazine Sha., Tokyo, 1986. *Outdoor Games,* F. W. Strange. Tokyo University, Tokyo, 1883. "Saikin yakyu jutsu," Makoto Hashido, Hakko Jo no Haku Bunkan. Tokyo, 1905. "Roku Daigaku yakyubu monogatari." Kobunsha, Tokyo, 1975. *The Homecoming,* compiled by R.W. Lardner and Edward G. Heeman. John J. Gleason, Chicago, 1914. *The Babe Ruth Story,* Babe Ruth and Bob Considine. E.P. Dutton & Co. Inc., New York. 1948. *Babe Ruth and I,* Mrs. Babe Ruth with Bill Slocum. Prentice Hall, Inc., Englewood Cliffs, New Jersey, 1959. *Baseball As I Have Known It,* Frederick G. Lieb. Coward, McCann

335

and Geoghegan, Inc. New York, 1977. *My 66 Years in the Big Leagues,* Cornelius McGillicuddy. John C. Winston Company, Philadelphia, 1950. *My Luke and I,* Eleanor Gehrig and Joseph Durso. Thomas Y. Crowell, New York, 1976. *Articles:* "The Giants," *Sports Graphic Number,* Special Issue, Bungei Shunju, March, 1984. "Dai ichi koto gakko bushi," Imuburi Jiken, *Undokai,* Vol. 3, April 10, 1899. "Boku no nayami," Eiji Sawamura, *Shinseinen,* January 1936.

Chapter 3. "Ashita arite," Yoshiko Murata. Kirihara Shoten, Tokyo, 1985. "Zoku ashita arite: yomigaetta otoko," Yoshiko Murata. Kirihara Shoten, Tokyo, 1985. "Jubun to do to tatakae tsuzukeru ka," Sachio Kinugasa. PHP, Tokyo, 1985. "Hara Tatsundri: oyaji to musuko no ni–ju san nen," Sadanori Gunzi, Bungei Shunju, Tokyo, 1981. "Aku no kanri gaku," Tetsuharu Kawakami. Kobunsha, Tokyo, 1980. "Watashi no kaigun shiki yakyu," Tatsuro Hiroka. Sankei Shuppan, Tokyo, 1979. "Ishiki kakumei no susume," Tatsuro Hiroka. Kodansha, Tokyo, 1983. *Articles:* "Tetsuharu Kawakami," *President Magazine,* "Za Man" series, October 1987. "Dame ningen wo ikikaeraseru ho," Tatsuro Hiroka, *Gekan Gendai,* November 1979.

Chapter 4. Lee Brothers interview: *Sports Graphic Number,* December 5, 1980. Leon Lee interview: Tokyo *Journal,* October 1984. Don Money interview: *Sports Graphic Number,* September 20, 1984. Jim Tracy interview: *Sports Graphic Number,* October 5, 1984. Dick Davis interview: Tokyo *Journal,* August 1986. *Article:* "You Gotta Have Wa," R. Whiting, *Sports Illustrated,* September 24, 1979.

Chapter 5. "Tokyo Roku Daigaku monogatari," Kobunsha, Tokyo, 1975. *Articles:* "Kurutta no Tora no Fan . . . ," *Shukan Gendai,* July 20, 1985. "The Bully Boys in Black," Charles Fleming, Tokyo *Journal,* August 1985. "The Japanese (Baseball) Fan," R. Whiting, *Winds,* June 1986.

Chapter 6. "Nippon yakyu eikyu ni fumetsu," R. Whiting. Chikuma Shobo, Tokyo, 1985. "Dare mo kakanakatta pro yakyu kyudan tsuyaku monogatari," R. Whiting, *Chuo Koron,* December 1981.

Chapter 7. "Blazer to Okada . . . ," *Shukan Shincho,* May 8, 1980. "Hanshin Ozu shacho no hara no naka." *Shukan Shincho,* May 29, 1980. "Wadai I," *Shukan Besuboru,* December 14, 1981. Don Blasingame Inteview: *Shukan Sankei,* May 15, 1980.

Chapter 8. "Fumetsu nari! Shigeo Nagashima," Bungei Bunko, Tokyo, 1984. "Kaiso," Sadaharu Oh. Keibunsha, Tokyo 1981. *A Zen Way of Baseball,* Sadaharu Oh and David Falkner. Times Books, New York, 1984. Dave Johnson Interviews: *Sports Graphic Number,* August 20, 1984; *Tokyo Weekender,* October 26, 1984. Clyde Wright Interviews: *Shukan Bunshun,* November 16, 23, 1978. Reggie Smith Interviews: *Sports Graphic Number,* April 5, 1983 and December 5, 1984; *Shukan Post,* September 2, 1983; June–July Series, 1984; August 25, 1984. *Articles:* "The Education of Reggie Smith," David Halberstam, *Playboy,* October 1984. "SOS! Shigeo Nagashima e rabu koru wo!" *Sports Graphic Number,* Special Issue, September 5, 1980. "Sadaharu Oh," *Shincho 45,* R. Whiting, April 1986. "Kuno no tosho Oh kantoku ni tsukimatoru katei nai no shinkoku jitai," *Shukan Gendai,* October 18, 1986. Warren Cromartie Interviews: *Gekan Playboy,* New Year issue, 1987. *Shukan Gendai,* July 4, 1987. *Penthouse,* November 1987, *Gekan Playboy,* December 1988.

Chapter 9. Hiromitsu Ochiai Interview: *Esquire Japan,* Spring 1987. "Yutaka Enatsu–Hiromitsu Ochiai No Honne buchimake taidan," *Penthouse Japan,* December 1986. Ochiai Interview: *Penthouse Japan,* September 1987. *Sports Graphic Number,* Tokushu: "Randy Bass to Hiromitsu Ochai," September 5, 1986. "Sayonara Egawa," *Sports Graphic Number,* Tokushu, November 1987. "Ochiai–Oh Taidan. San-kan Oh ni wa dai Kanshu ga Yoku Niau," *Sports Graphic Number,* New Year issue, 1987.

Chapter 10. "Mikado no shozo," Naoki Inose. Shogakkan, Tokyo, 1986. "Tsutsumi Yoshiaki ga kataru," Yoshiaki Tsutsumi and Toshiaki Kaminoga. Kodansha, Tokyo, 1984. Yoshiaki Tsutsumi Interviews: *Shukan Shincho,* July 31, 1965. *Zaikai,* June 15, 1977; August 1, 1978; October 15, 1978. *Shukan Gendai,* November 2, 1978. *Sunday Mainichi,* October 15, 1978. *Gekan*

Shokun, December 1978. *Keizaikai,* January 9, 1979. *Gekan Playboy,* February 1979. *Zaikai,* Shinnen Tokudaigo, October 30, 1979; April 8, 1980. *Chuo Koron,* November 1980. *Zaikai,* Shintokudaigo, 1982. *Zaikai,* November 30, 1982. *Will,* February 1984. *Shukan Gendai,* January 5, 1982. *Gekan Gendai,* January 1983. *Shukan Hoseki,* January 7, 21, 28, 1983. *Bungei Shunju,* February 1984. *Shukan Shincho,* July 23, 1987. Articles on Yoshikai Tsutsumi: "Seibu guntai no ikikata, *Keizaikai,* August 1, 1974. "Family Fortunes: Rising Sons," *Newsweek,* August 23, 1976. "Yoshiaki Tsutsmi wa 43 sai no kabe yaburi, Kooki eigawa," *Gekan Gendai,* April 1978. "Waga ichizoku Chi No himitsu," Kunio Kamibayashi, *Bungei Shunju,* August 1987. "Tsutsumi Seibu vs. Shoriki Yomirui," *Shukan Gendai,* New Year issue, 1982.

Chapter 11. "Koko yakyu no jiten," Junji Kanda. Sanseido, Tokyo, 1986. "Koko yakyu yusho monogatari," Hirose Kenzo and Kazuyuki Matsui. Baseball Magazine Sha., Tokyo, 1988. "Koko yakyu, 1945–1985, kando no supotsu 40 nenshi." Baseball Magazine Sha., Tokyo, 1985. *A Japanese Mirror,* Ian Buruma. Jonathan Cape, London, 1984. *Articles:* "The Frenzy Over High School Baseball," Mitsuyoshi Okazaki, *Look Japan,* August 1984. "The Schoolboys of Summer," R. Whiting, *Winds,* July 1987. "A Celebration of Spirit," R. Whiting, *Winds,* August 1986. *Sports Graphic Number* magazine "Koshien Specials," 33, 57, 105, 153, 201, *Bungei Shunju.* "Sensei No Iu Torori Ni Yatte," Kazuhiko Ogasawara, *Asahi Journal,* July 24, 1987. "On Japan's Mt. Olympus," Clyde Haberman, *International Herald Tribune,* August 22, 1986.

Chapter 12. *"Ah! Taiwan,"* Akira Suzuki. Kodansha, Tokyo, 1985. Charlie Manuel Interviews: *Shukan Bunshun,* July 12, 19, 1979. Gregory Wells Interview: *Sports Graphic Number,* September 20, 1985. *Articles:* "Hired Bats," PHP, March 1984. "Striking Out the Foreign Devils," R. Whiting, *Winds,* April 1985. Randy Bass Interviews: *Sports Graphic Number,* July 5, 1985; September 5, 1986; *Gekan Playboy,* March 1986; September 1988, *Shukan Pureiboi,* September 16, 1986; *Penthouse Japan,* September 1988. "Japan's Game," Ron Fimrite, *Sports*

Illustrated, September, 1985. "The Hottest American Import," Craig Neff, *Sports Illustrated,* March 24, 1987. "Basu ni 4-Wari Utaretara Hajiyade," Yutaka Enatsu, *Shukan Post,* July 18, 1986. "An Oklahoma Batter Makes Good," Shibahashi hachiro, *Japan Quarterly,* April–June 1987. Rich Gale Interview: *Shukan Post,* October 21, 1986. "Japan's Passionate Affair with Baseball," R. Whiting, *Asia,* October 1982.

General. "Pro yakyu no tomo," Masayuki Tamaki. Shincho Sha., Tokyo, 1988. "Pro yakyu dai dai dai jiten," Masayuki Tamaki. Toto Shobo, Tokyo, 1986. "Pro yakyu wo ju-bai Tanoshiku miru hoho," Takenori Emoto. KK Best–Sellers, Tokyo, 1982. "Rookie! mo hitotsu no Kiyohara Kazuhiro monogatari," Junji Yamagiwa. Mainichi Shimbun Sha, Tokyo, 1987. "Taka ga Egawa saredo Egawa," Suguru Egawa. Shinchosha, 1988. "Yakyu wa dandyism," Sadao Kondo. Asahi Shimbun Sha., Tokyo, 1988. "Pro yakyu kai so roku," Kai so Roku, Takezo Shimoda. Baseball Magazine Sha., Tokyo, 1988. " 'Bungei Shunju' ni miru spotsu Showa shi," *Bungei Shunju,* 1988.

Statistical data. Various Japanese sports dailies. The record book, *Nippon pro yakyu kiroku shi* (5 volumes), Isao Chiba, Baseball Magazine Sha. The annual, *Nihon pro yakyu kiroku nenkan,* Baseball Magazine Sha. The annual, *Official Baseball Guide,* Office of the Commissioner of Japanese Professional Baseball, Kyodo Tsushin. The annual handbooks: *Suponichi proyakyu techo,* Sports Nippon; *Nikkan Supotsu gurafu proyakyu zukan,* Nikkan Sports; and the *Japan Pro Baseball Fan Handbook,* compiled by Wayne Graczyk, Fan Te–cho Co., Ltd.